THE ETHOS OF
THE SONG OF ROLAND

THE ETHOS
OF THE
SONG OF
ROLAND

BY

GEORGE FENWICK JONES

JOHNS HOPKINS PRESS
BALTIMORE 1963

© 1963 BY THE JOHNS HOPKINS PRESS,
BALTIMORE 18, MARYLAND
PRINTED IN THE UNITED STATES OF AMERICA BY VAIL-BALLOU PRESS
DISTRIBUTED IN GREAT BRITAIN BY OXFORD UNIVERSITY PRESS, LONDON
LIBRARY OF CONGRESS CATALOG CARD NUMBER 63-11891

THIS BOOK HAS BEEN BROUGHT TO PUBLICATION WITH THE
ASSISTANCE OF A GRANT FROM THE FORD FOUNDATION.

Foreword

As an intruder in the field of Old French literature, I am indebted to the many Romance scholars who have aided and encouraged this study of the *Chanson de Roland,* especially to those who, while disagreeing with many of my conclusions, have urged me to publish them. I am particularly grateful to the members of the Société Rencesvals in session at the Venice Congress of 1961 for giving a fair hearing to my most dissident views; and I am also obliged to the readers and editors of *Modern Language Quarterly, Romanic Review,* and *Studio Neophilologica* for accepting and publishing four preliminary studies which have subsequently been incorporated into this volume. Above all I wish to express my thanks for the generous suggestions, comments, and corrections of the following experts: Alfred Foulet, Robert A. Hall, Jr., Helmut Hatzfeld, Pierre Le Gentil, Hans F. Norbert, Thomas Thornton, and William S. Woods. Although all their advice was good and all of it was appreciated, not all of it was taken. Therefore, in viewing their names on the list, the reader of this book should remember that: "Cil ki la sunt n'en deivent aveir blasme!"

University of Maryland
College Park, Maryland
1962

Contents

INTRODUCTION

ACCORDING TO Alfred North Whitehead, "it is in literature that the concrete outlook of humanity receives its expression. Accordingly, it is to literature that we must look, particularly in its more concrete forms, namely in poetry and drama, if we hope to discover the inward thoughts of a generation."[1] To ascertain the "inward thoughts" of twelfth-century humanity, one could choose no better work than the *Song of Roland,* an epic generally accepted as the most significant and most representative literary creation of its time and place. To be sure, popular epics like the SR may not have impressed scholarly individuals like Abélard or Thomas à Becket, yet they definitely appealed to a large part of the population. Being delivered orally and in the vernacular, they enjoyed far wider reception than did any monastic writing; and consequently they give us a better picture of the ideals and aspirations of the people in general, or at least of the fighting and ruling classes.

Like other *chansons de geste,* or popular epics, the SR owes much of its value as a cultural document to the very fact that it is an epic. As Maurice McNamee (p. x) has observed, "since the epic is structured precisely to elicit our admiration for the hero, for the great man of the society out of which it comes, it should be an excellent place in which to discover concretely what a nation's or a culture's concept of human progress actually was. Its very spaciousness and diversity of episode should engender a confidence that it reveals rather fully what the culture it pictures considered particularly admirable and honorable in human achievement. . . ." In 1944 Ernst Robert Curtius wrote that the *chansons de geste* should not be scorned as sources of cultural history and

[1] Whitehead, p. 110. Authors and works cited in the text or notes are identified in bibliography, pp. 197–203.

1

that they had scarcely been investigated in this sense.[2] Now that eighteen more years have produced no significant cultural-historical investigations of these songs, this study will make a start by attempting to delineate the ethos of the *SR*, which is universally recognized as their best representative. According to Edmond Faral, the *SR* "is perhaps the most impressive depiction we possess of the moral physiognomy of the century in which it appeared. It draws its strength from the great currents that traverse it." [3]

Scholars once believed that the *SR* represented a culture anterior to the date at which it was written down, but this obviously reflected their romantic view that the completed epic was but a fortuitous compilation of fossilized folk ballads still steeped in the attitudes and customs of a much earlier period.[4] Today most scholars would agree with Faral in believing that the song's "moral physiognomy" belongs to the century in which the song appeared.[5] Joseph Bédier maintains that the twelfth-century French romances belonged to twelfth-century France rather than to the remote Germanic past. "One should treat them as one treats any other epic. One should study them in their relations with the social, religious,

[2] Die *chansons de Geste* sind eine unverächtliche kulturhistorische Quelle und sind in diesem Sinne noch kaum untersucht worden (Curtius, p. 320).

[3] La *Chanson de Roland* est peut-être la peinture la plus expressive que nous possédions de la physionomie morale du siècle où elle a paru; elle tire sa force des grands souffles que la traversent. . . . (Faral, p. 275).

[4] William A. Stowell (p. 416) says that the presence of "compagnonage of the higher degree" in the Arthurian Cycle and in the *SR* "is due to the . . . fact that these works reflect the cultural conditions of a period much earlier than the date of their composition." For a discussion of recent views on the origin of the *chansons de geste,* see Holmes, pp. 72–81.

[5] According to Maurice Wilmotte (p. 145), "En somme, c'est le monde féodal, plutôt que les contemporains de Charles et de ses successeurs, que les textes conservés de l'épopée nous décrivent." Prosper Boissonnade (p. 237) agrees: "Ce n'est pas la lointaine expédition de 778, dont on ne savait presque rien; ce ne sont pas des chants ou des légendes populaires, dont on n'a pas retrouvé trace; ce n'est pas un effort de reconstitution archaïque, qui ont inspiré le trouvère. C'est le spectacle de l'effort héroïque et continu accompli par le monde chrétien et surtout par la France, pour la défense de Dieu et pour le triomphe de la foi." Philip August Becker (p. 1) is of the same opinion: "Und doch ist auch diese Dichtung, genial und unpersönlich wie sie dem Beschauer erscheint, aus ihrer eignen Gegenwart hervorgewachsen und spricht zu uns als lebendiger Zeuge ihrer Entstehungszeit . . .".

moral, and imaginative conditions of the epoch which produced
them: and that epoch begins in the eleventh century." [6] In discussing the themes of the *chansons de geste*, Italo Siciliano states
that "the spirit in which these themes are conceived, the emotional
conflicts, the human dramas, the conceptions of fatherland and
duty and honor—the true essence of the *chanson*—belong to the
poet or to his times and are born of him and with him." [7] Siciliano
further denies that medieval poets wrote for their public and maintains that they wrote what they wanted to write or what they had
to write, and that their works later found a suitable public. This
principle holds "for the Chrétiens de Troyes and Prousts of all
time." [8]

One might well reject Siciliano's dogmatic view and argue that
first-rate medieval poets, unlike first-rate modern ones, often wrote
to please their public or patron. This would seem to hold true of
Chrétien himself, who wrote what his patrons requested; [9] and it
would surely hold true of his German imitator, Hartmann of Aue,
who frankly admitted that he wrote what people wanted to hear.[10]
Yet, whether or not a medieval author really wished to write what
he wrote, he could win popularity only by presenting values acceptable to a majority of his potential public. Because modern
fiction is read privately and can therefore reach a scattered reading public, an author can write an individualistic, eccentric, or
deviationist work with every expectation of finding a quorum of

[6] . . . il fallait les traiter comme on traite ceux d'une autre époque quel-
conque, les étudier en leurs relations avec les conditions sociales, religieuses,
morales, imaginatives, de l'époque qui les a produits: et cette époque com-
mence au xi⁰ siècle (Bédier, *Commentaires*, p. 9). Today most scholars try
to reconcile individualism and traditionalism. The author remains an inspired individual who used traditional material. See Dougherty, pp. 289–99.

[7] Mais l'esprit dans lequel ces thèmes sont conçus, les pathétiques con-
flits, les drames humains, la conception de la patrie, du devoir, de l'honneur
—la véritable essence de la chanson—appartiennent au poète ou à son
temps, naissent de lui et avec lui (Siciliano, p. 223).

[8] Et le même principe vaut, dans un autre domaine, pour les Chrétien de
Troyes et les Proust de tous les temps (Siciliano, p. 214).

[9] Crestïens, qui entent et paine Par le comandement le conte A rimoier le
meillor conte Qui soit contez a cort roial: Ce est li Contes del Graal, Dont
li quens li bailla le livre (*Perceval*, vv. 62–67).

[10] In his introduction to *Iwein* (vv. 26–27), Hartmann says that he writes
what people wish to hear: daz man gerne hœren mac, dâ kêrt er sînen
vlîz an.

open-minded readers distributed among a far greater number of conformists. This did not hold in the Middle Ages, especially in the case of social literature like the *chansons de geste*, which were presented orally and therefore required a fairly homogeneous audience. Unless its values satisfied a majority of each audience, a work would have suffered ridicule and quick oblivion.

The *SR*'s immediate and widespread popularity proves that it expressed the sentiments of the dominant social element of twelfth-century France; and its numerous translations and adaptations into other languages show that it appealed to other European nations as well. Many of the words and expressions discussed below also appear, often in similar contexts, in the many *chansons de geste* written during the century following the *SR*. In some cases the similarities in usage may result from direct imitation, but even then they probably express the verbal habits and attitudes of their authors and of the public for whom they were written.

The translations and adaptations of the *SR* not only attest its popularity but also help illuminate some of its terms by showing how they were understood by early translators. The oldest of these is the *Rolandslied*, a Middle High German adaptation written by a certain Priest Conrad (Pfaffe Kuonrat).[11] This work follows the *SR* fairly closely but has become much more clerical in tone. Also of interest is a section of the Old Norse compilation, *Karlamagnús saga*, which was written near the end of the thirteenth century. The episode about Roland follows its Old French source quite closely and generally retains its ethos. Of somewhat less value are the *Roelantslied*, a Middle Netherlandish version that survives in several fragments of varying quality, and the Middle English *Song of Roland*, an inferior redaction that survives in a single fragment of 1049 verses.[12] Of minimal value is the thirteenth-century Middle High German epic, *Karl der Grosse* by Stricker.[12a] Because this work was based on Conrad's *Rolandslied*, it throws but little new light on the original French song.

[11] In *Das Alexanderlied des Pfaffen Lamprecht, Das Rolandslied des Pfaffen Konrad*, ed. Friedrich Maurer, Leipzig, 1940.
[12] *Karlamagnús saga*, ed. B. Vilhjálmsson, III, Reykjavik, 1950, pp. 771–851, German translation by E. Koschwitz, "*Der altnordische Roland*", in *Romanische Studien*, ed. E. Boehmer, Strassburg, III, 1878, pp. 295–349; van Mierlo, R.P.: "Het Roelantslied", *Kon. Vlaamsche Academie voor*

Of very mediocre quality, but valuable for our study, are the *Carmen de Prodicione Guenonis* and the *Pseudo-Turpin,* two Latin works written in France sometime after the *SR*.[13] It was long believed that the former of these was based on an older and therefore more genuine version of the Roland story than that found in the Oxford manuscript, but Curtius has recently produced convincing evidence that the *Carmen* was only a rhetorical exercise based on the *SR*.[14] This crabbed poem, which prefers word-play to sword-play, is a most uninspired production; yet it does help us ascertain the precise meaning of several ambiguous or obscure passages in its vernacular source. Although the *Pseudo-Turpin* strays far from its source, it too helps clarify some ideas expressed by the original poet. For want of a better name, we will call the original poet Turold, which is the name of the poet, chronicler, or scribe mentioned in the last and most controversial verse of the Oxford manuscript.[15] And, as Pierre Le Gentil states, only the Oxford manuscript deserves the name of *Song of Roland*.[16]

To ascertain the ethos of the *SR* we will first examine Turold's ethical terminology in order to deduce the meaning of controversial terms from their context. While observing the etyma of many of his words, we will remain wary of their subsequent semantic development. Perhaps the greatest barrier to understanding medieval works is the fact that their ethical terminology has subse-

---

Taal-en Letterkunde, verslagen end Mededeelingen, 1935, pp. 31–166; *The English Charlemagne Romances,* ed. S. J. Herrtage, II, London, 1880, pp. 107–36.

[12a] ed. Karl Bartsch, Quedlinburg & Leipzig, 1857.

[13] *Carmen de prodicione guenonis,* ed. Gaston Paris, *Romania,* XI, 1882, pp. 465–518; *The Pseudo-Turpin,* ed. H. M. Smyser, Cambridge, 1937.

[14] "Das Carmen de prodicione Guenonis," *Zeitschrift für romanische Philologie,* 62, 1942, pp. 492–509.

[15] Ci falt la geste que Turoldus declinet (v. 4002, all citations from ed. Bédier). For theories concerning its meaning, see Boissonnade, pp. 454–56; Bédier, *Commentaires,* pp. 31–36; Junker, pp. 113–14. W. A. Nitze argues that the Latin form of the name Turoldus indicates that he was the author of a Latin source ("Turoldus, Author of the Roland?," *Modern Language Notes,* 69, 1954, pp. 88–92).

[16] Lui seul a le droit d'être intitulé la Chanson de Roland (Le Gentil, p. 15). Cf. Jede Untersuchung über das Rolandslied muss . . . von der Oxforder Fassung ausgehen (Becker, p. 3).

quently changed so much more in meaning than in form.[16a] If a medieval poet tells us that a *bon chevaler* should be *gentil, de bon aire,* and *vertuus* and that he should cherish *honor,* hate *honte,* and love his *ami,* we agree with him wholeheartedly because he seems to be speaking the same language we speak. We fail to reflect that he may only mean that an effective cavalryman should be physically strong and aided by powerful kinsmen and that he should seek glory, shun public disgrace, and keep peace with his allies. In other words, it is like a conversation between two deaf men who talk right past each other and agree heartily with everything the other has not said.

Provided they could have understood his pronunciation, the twelfth-century barons would have accepted a seventeenth-century divine's assertion: "Heureux les débonnaires; car ils hériteront de la terre." For them it would mean that the wellborn shall inherit the earth, a fact they saw illustrated every day. Words associated in a given culture often remain associated even after that culture has decisively changed. As Christian and Stoic values gradually displaced the military and aristocratic values of the medieval gentry, they inherited the latter's terminology. The epithet "virtuous" now suits a man of moral stamina even though he be physically weak.

In investigating a primitive society, anthropologists must deduce the meaning of its vocabulary directly from the contexts in which they hear it, and thus they are free of any preconceived opinions about its meaning. On the other hand, scholars who try to construe the thoughts of their own cultural ancestors are often misled by conceptual or emotive values now attached to their language but unintended by the speakers of the language in its earlier stage. As George Bernard Shaw once said of the English and Americans, they are separated by a common language. Having been conceived in English, this study should benefit from greater linguistic perspective than is possible for studies conceived in French. Moreover, the meaning of ambiguous Old French words must be definitely determined before being translated into a nonderivative

---

[16a] This problem is discussed in my paper: "The *Chanson de Roland* and Semantic Change," which was read to the Medieval French Group of MLA at its 1960 meeting in Philadelphia and was later published in *Modern Language Quarterly* (Vol. 23, 1962, pp. 46–52).

language, whereas this is not the case when they are merely orthographically rehabilitated in Modern French translations.

All recent translations of the SR corrupt or confuse its ethos, and therefore its motivation as well, by failing to make sufficient allowance for semantic change. This study will criticize particularly Joseph Bédier's translation, which is perhaps still the best after nearly forty years and has influenced all subsequent translations, especially in their rendition of difficult value-words. As late as 1955 Le Gentil saw fit to quote it unaltered in his excellent account of the song in the series *Connaissance des Lettres*. Several of its inadequately translated words were noted and correctly explained in Lucien Foulet's glossary to Bédier's commentary in 1927, yet these corrections have escaped general notice and were not even incorporated into Bédier's definitive edition of 1937.

As Vera Vollmer has shown, the meaning of many words can be ascertained only through an exact familiarity with the culture of their age.[17] Therefore, after deriving the meaning of Turold's value-words as far as possible from their context and origins, we will next study Turold's cultural environment to see if the meanings ascribed to his words conform to it. Thus we will double-check the meanings previously deduced. Finally, we will see whether an investigation of Turold's ethical outlook might illuminate the question of his song's literary unity.

The reader will please remember that this study concerns Turold's ethical outlook rather than his literary artistry. Bédier, Becker, Pauphilet, Faral, Curtius, Le Gentil, and other scholars have rightly called attention to his vivid scenes, his emotional intensity, his dramatic power, and his structural skill; and nothing in this study gainsays their aesthetic evaluations. Yet Turold's artistry, which still appeals to us so directly today, should not blind us to the culture gap separating the values he champions and those we profess today. In attempting to understand his heroes, we must not attribute to their actions the motives we now admire. Instead we must deduce their sanctions and incentives directly from the language of our text and avoid being misled by subsequent semantic developments. By so doing, we will learn to appreciate them on

[17] Es bricht ja überhaupt die Erkenntnis immer mehr Bahn, dass sich der Bedeutungsinhalt vieler Wörter nur bei genauer Kenntnis der Kultur der betreffenden Periode feststellen lässt (Vollmer, p. 1).

their own terms. In a review of Albert Junker's *Roland* bibliography, F. Whitehead concludes that "the most important problem—that of the relation between the *Roland* and its cultural and ideological background—is receiving the least attention." [17a] This study is largely devoted to that very problem; and it is hoped that its semantic approach will help clarify the cultural and ideological background of the song.

[17a] In *French Studies*, 12, 1958, p. 362.

CHAPTER I

SEMANTIC ANALYSIS
Part One

To DETERMINE THE VALUES held by Turold and his public, we will first investigate a vocabulary dealing with the concepts of right and wrong, good and bad, virtue and sin, honor and disgrace, etc. Important among these terms are *dreit, tort, bon, malvais, prod, prodhome, ber, fel, vertut, honur, honte, leal, fier, orgoill, amis, doel, estultie, feid*. In studying these words we will try to note all cases in which their context clarifies their meaning. In addition, we will observe their consociations, that is to say, the words most often appearing with them. This method is particularly effective in the *SR* because the poet usually groups epithets that reinforce rather than oppose each other.

Ethics being the science of right and wrong, an investigation of Turold's ethos might well begin with a study of his use of the words *dreit* and *tort*. The word *dreit* (modern *droit*) was related both etymologically and conceptually to the Old High German word *recht*, which was cognate with modern German *Recht* and English *right*.[1] It is safe to assume that, upon adopting the Ro-

---

[1] *dreit* was derived from *directu* and related to *rego*, which in turn was related to *Gmc. rehta. The OHG spelling of this word was *reht*, but this

mance vernacular, the Frankish invaders used the word *dreit* to render their traditional concept of *recht;* for it is an accepted fact that the Germanic invaders retained much from their native codes of customary law for centuries after occupying their new territories in the old Roman world.[1a]

It is difficult to ascertain just what the ancient Germans meant by the term *recht;* but it seems to have referred to that which should be, to that which is fitting or proper. Having a "tradition-directed" society, they believed that what is is right. It was right for a man to enjoy the wealth that he had or was to inherit, provided of course that no stronger man could take it from him and thus prove his own greater right to it.[2] It was also right for a free man to be free and for a slave to be a slave; and it was wrong for either to try to change his condition. (Paradoxically enough, if a man did succeed in changing his condition, his success was pragmatic proof that he had been in the right! As in the fairy tale, the beggar's son who marries the princess turns out to have been of royal birth.) Since all traditional customs were right, the word *recht* could mean either right or law.

In pagan days it was right (*recht*) for a vassal to obey the law (*recht*) of his leader. Therefore, after the conversions, it was proper for the converts to accept the *recht* of their new Heavenly Liege Lord, as best they could understand it. The pagan Germans had a strong sense of right and wrong. When told that the Chris-

---

study will use the more phonetic spelling *recht* to render the older pre-literary form of the word.

[1a] This is attested by the retention of vernacular legal terms in Latin codifications of Frankish, Lombardic, and other law codes. Heinrich Mitteis (p. 19) states: "Den Germanen . . . war das Recht nicht eine unter mehreren sozialen Ordnungen, sondern die Ordnung des sozialen Kosmos schlechthin. Die germanische Welt ist eine Welt des Rechts. Diese Auffassung beherrscht noch das Mittelalter."

[2] When Julius Caesar obstructed his invasion of Gaul, Ariovistus explained that it was the "law of war" (*jus belli*) "that the victors command the vanquished in whatever way they wish" (*Gallic War*, I, 36). Since war was the normal relationship between strangers in Germania, might was right.

tian god was a god of *recht*,[3] they naturally attributed to him many of their own ideas of what is right, such as respect for inherited wealth and privilege, keeping of oaths, and vengeance of insults.[4] God and right (*Dieu et Droit*) have been associated in the occidental mind ever since the conversions, and it is not surprising that the Franks called God a *droiturier*, like any other feudal lord.[5] In keeping with our modern egalitarian ethos, we assume that men have certain "inalienable rights" by virtue of being human beings. Any such idea was utterly foreign to the twelfth century, when, according to the principle of "gradualism", an individual's rights and duties were commensurate with his divinely ordained condition.[5a] The original meaning of *droit* is therefore better preserved in the royal motto of Great Britain: "Dieu et *Mon* Droit".

As the Lord's anointed, Charlemagne is a *dreiz emperere* (308, 766, 2441). After Clovis made his pact with God, the Franks were obliged to increase God's territory on earth at the expense of the infidels; and therefore Charlemagne can assure his troops that he has *dreit* in Spain (3413), even though he has no historical claims on their territory. Whereas the SR only implies this reasoning, the

[3] The thirteenth-century Low Saxon jurist, Eike of Repgau, expressed this thought as: Got is selve recht, dar umme is em recht lef (*Sachsenspiegel, Prologus,* v. 9). Cf. Deus fidelis et absque ulla iniquitate iustus et rectus (*Deut.* 32:4).

[4] The SR stresses particularly God's love of oath-keeping and vengeance: ki unkes ne mentit (1865), ki unkes ne mentis (2384); Cf. por Dieu qui ne menti! (*Raoul*, vs. 981). The belief that fealty was commanded by God is suggested in the *Chançun de Willame* (vv. 308–9) when some knights pledge their faith to Vivien "by that law that God gave to the world" (En cele lei que Deus en terre mist). For God's aid in vengeance, see notes II, 136, 139, 141.

[5] *Girart de Viënne* uses the word *droiturier* of God (4158, 4849, 5118, 6324) and also of feudal lords (*seignor droiturier*, 4176, 5154). Chrétien de Troyes expresses the idea as follows in *Yvain* (4444–4445): Des se retient devers le droit, Et Des et droiz a un se tienent.

[5a] This principle is clearly expressed in the *Rolandslied* when Conrad says that Ganelon has great *recht* because of his high rank (Sîn recht wære vil grôz, er wære aller fursten genôz, *RL* 8737–8738).

Pseudo-Turpin expounds it very clearly. Aigolandus, the king of the Saracens, asks Charlemagne why he is taking away their land even though he and his father and his ancestors had no hereditary right to it, and Charlemagne answers that the Lord Jesus Christ, maker of heaven and earth, has chosen the Christian nation above all nations and set it to rule all nations of the world and to convert the Saracen nation to the Christian Law.[6] Because Charlemagne has *dreit* (3359, 3367), his troops are free to ask God for aid. On the other hand, the heathen king Marsilie claims that his suzerain, the Emir, has *dreit* in Spain (2747); and the Emir vows that he will take Charlemagne's head because he has no *dreit* (3290).

Roland accuses Marsilie of killing the Christians wrongfully (*a si grant tort,* 1899), and later he says that it is not *dreiz* for the pagans to get possession of his sword (2349). Ganelon states that it is not *dreiz* (228) for Roland to give such haughty advice, and Marsilie's son says it is not *dreiz* (497) for Ganelon to live any longer after his insolence. Marsilie and Ganelon discuss their treacherous conspiracy against Roland "without right" (*seinz dreit,* 511). Only once does a Frank seem to set himself above "right". When Roland falls unconscious shortly before his death, an Arab tries to take his sword. Waking up, Roland smites him dead with his horn with the boast that people would consider the Arab a fool for having dared to touch him, be he right or wrong.[7]

In the *Carmen* the equivalent of *dreit* is *jus.* Rollandus states that Marsilius is holding everything *injuste* (26) and nothing *jure* (26). Here too the concepts of right-wrong and lawful-unlawful depend not upon natural law or international treaty or even upon equity or justice, but solely upon the right conferred by God. A

[6] Quia dominus noster Ihesus Christus, creator celi et terre, gentem scilicet nostram christianam pre omnibus gentibus elegit et super omnes gentes totius mundi dominari instituit; tuam gentem sarracenicam legi nostre, in quantum potui, converti (*Pseudo-Turpin,* XV, vv. 20–24).

[7] Culvert paien, cum fus unkes si os que me saisis, ne a dreit ne a tort? Ne l'orrat hume ne t'en tienget por fol (2292–2293).

similar explanation of right and wrong appears in Einhard's biography of Charlemagne, which was probably an important source of the Roland story. In speaking of the great treasures that Charlemagne captured from the Huns, Einhard states that he took from the Huns rightfully (*juste*) what they had previously taken wrongfully (*iniuste*) from other nations.[8] As the *Roland* poet so succinctly states: "Pagans are wrong and Christians are right." [9]

Whether a man had *dreit* or *tort* could be verified through trial by combat or *judicium dei* (judgment of God), of which God alone knew the outcome.[10] After Roland has been betrayed, Charlemagne dreams that thirty bears tell him that it is not *dreiz* for him to hold the traitor Ganelon captive (2561); and, upon returning home from Spain, he calls a council to decide the *dreit* in the matter (3751). Because the defendant's formidable kinsman, Pinabel, threatens to prove his *dreit* through combat, the judges hesitate and decide to acquit him; but Thierry accepts the challenge, defeats Pinabel, and thereby proves that Ganelon is in the wrong. The culprit is then quartered by four horses, and his thirty kinsmen who have stood his bail are hanged (3958). The poet first refers to this punishment as revenge, yet in the opening verse of the next strophe he echoes this passage with a slight variation: "When the Emperor had thus done his justice and his great anger was appeased." [11] In this way we see that the poet drew little distinction between justice and revenge, and it will be noted that the defendant had already been beaten and humiliated before his trial. The vicarious punishment of Ganelon's kinsmen

[8] Merito credi possit, hoc Francos Hunis iuste eripuisse, quod Huni prius aliis gentibus iniuste eripuerunt (*Vita Karoli*, #13).

[9] Paien unt tort et chrestiens unt dreit (1015); nos avum dreit, mais cist glutun unt tort (1212).

[10] Deus set asez cument la fins en ert (*SR*, 3872). God's function as source of justice is suggested in His epithet *li verai justissier,* which is found in *Renaus de Montalban* (p. 20, v. 17).

[11] Quant li empereres ad faite sa venjance (3975); Quant l'empere ad faite sa justice e esclargiez est la sue grant ire (3988).

suggests Old Testament rather than Germanic practices, although Germanic custom did allow revenge on any or all of a malefactor's kinsmen.[12] Vicarious revenge was clearly the rule in most *chansons de geste*. In *Girart de Viënne* Renart de Pevier enunciates the principle in telling the emperor that, if he cannot kill their father, he will make Garin's sons pay for their father's crime.[13]

Ganelon's trial is not the only *judicium dei* in the poem, for most of the victories in Spain are looked upon as divine judgments. Rabel and Guineman open the final battle by attacking two Saracens in individual combats. When Rabel kills his opponent, the Franks cry: "God aid us. Charlemagne is in the right! We must not fail him!" When Guineman kills his opponent, they cry: "Strike barons! Do not delay! Charles is in the right against the heathens. God has sent us to render a true verdict."[14] The second strophe is not a true *laisse similaire*, since it presents a different person and action, yet structurally it is a repetition of its predecessor. Because the second strophe clearly asserts that God is directing the Franks, one might logically expect a statement rather than a wish in the previous strophe when the Franks shout: *Damnedeus nos aït*. In fact it is tempting to think that the subjunctive mood was used for the sake of the assonance. By slaying his pagan opponent, Rabel

[12] For Old Testament example of vicarious punishment, see story of Achan (Joshua, 7:24–25). Since the extended family or clan was the basic unit in Germanic society, vengeance for an offense could be taken on any or all of the offender's family, as it so often is in the Icelandic sagas. Gregory of Tours relates that the Frankish king Chlothar punished his rebellious son Chramnus by burning him together with his wife and daughters, and that Chlodomer put Sigismund to death along with his whole family (*Historiarum Libri Decem*, IV, 20; III, 6). Vicarious punishment was necessary when an offender was incapable of giving satisfaction.

[13] Qant ne me puis de lor pere venchier, Li fil por li le comparront molt chier (*Girart de Viënne*, vv. 791–92).

[14] Damnesdeus nos aït! Carles ad dreit, ne li devom faillir (3358–3359); Ferez, baron, ne vos targez mie! Carles ad dreit vers la gent . . . Deus nus ad mis al plus verai juïse (3366–3368). Because of these preliminary victories, Charlemagne can tell his barons that they know he is in the right (Ja savez vos cuntre paiens ai dreit, 3413), and they can readily agree that he is telling the truth (Sire, vos dites veir, 3414).

has proved that God is aiding the Christians and that Charlemagne is in the right; and for this reason the Franks know they will be victorious. It will be noted that the first engagement at Roncevaux had also been recognized as proof of right, even if it had not been expressly labeled a *judicium dei*. Upon killing the first enemy champion, Roland urges his men forward with the promise: "We are right, and those wretches are wrong!" The second engagement, on the other hand, is clearly attributed to God; for upon killing the second Saracen champion, Archbishop Turpin declares: "This first blow is ours, thank God!" [15]

The Christians are not alone in accepting victory and defeat as proof of right and wrong. Upon seeing how few Franks are left, the pagans say that Charlemagne is wrong.[16] Later the Emir maintains that Charlemagne is wrongfully claiming his kingdom, even though he had previously begun to see that he was wrong and Charlemagne was right.[17] The poet remarks that the battle would never have ended until one recognized that he was wrong.[18] Priest Conrad leaves no doubt that the duel between Charlemagne and the Emir is a *judicium dei;* for, when Charlemagne is about to succumb, a voice from heaven tells him that judgment has been rendered in his favor.[19] Although Turold considers might only a divine proof of right, might actually *was* right. After taking Saragossa, Charlemagne spends the night there *par poestet* (3653). Bédier is probably correct in rendering this as *par droit de conquête,* rather than as "in full force", as T. A. Jenkins does.[20]

[15] Nos avum dreit, mais cist glutun unt tort (1212); Cist premer colp est nostre, Deu mercit! (1259).

[16] L'empereor ad tort (1942).

[17] A mult grant tort mun païs me calenges (3592). Que il ad tort e Carlemagnes dreit (3554).

[18] Josque li uns sun tort i reconuisset (3588).

[19] Wes sparstu den man? Diu urtaile ist uber in getân: verfluchet ist al sin tail. Got gît dir daz hail (*RL,* 8545–8548).

[20] Bédier, p. 303; Jenkins, p. 355. In disagreeing with traditional interpretations, this study will regularly cite Bédier's translation. Henceforth no

The *SR* does not stress "fair play" with regard to method of fighting, type of weapons, or ratio of combatants. Medieval poets generally considered it blameworthy to strike a man from behind or to fight him with superior weapons or for two to fight against one.[21] These scruples were not a matter of "fair play". To take advantage of the enemy was to acknowledge fear or inferiority and thus to defeat the purpose of the struggle; since the chief aim of fighting, at least in heroic literature, was to win renown.[22] The pagans being always wrong, the Christians in the *SR* feel few scruples when fighting them. It is quite permissible for Gerin and Gerier to join together against Timozel (1379), even though they violate the honor code of both Germanic warrior and medieval knight by fighting two against one.[23]

On the other hand, only the pagan Marganice strikes an opponent in the back; and only the Saracens throw darts and javelins.[24] Twelfth-century knights scorned the use of missiles

---

page numbers will be given for his translation, since it is found opposite the verse under discussion.

[21] See notes I, 22–27.

[22] In Old Norse literature the approved incentives for fighting were fee and fame: *fé ok frami*. (See *Germanische Altertumskunde*, p. 205.) In Middle High German literature they were *guot und êre* (See George F. Jones, *Honor in German Literature*, Chapel Hill, 1959).

[23] Saxo Grammaticus tells of two youths, Ket and Wig, who won more shame than honor by attacking and killing Athisl of Sweden in concert (*Gesta Danorum*, pp. 111–113). In the *Waltharius*, when Trogus pierces Walter's shield with a harpoon and his friends help him pull on the rope, the poet calls it a "shameful rope" (*funis nefandus*, 1021) and calls the struggle a "shameful battle" (*bellum nefandum*, 1145). In *Alpharts Tod* (# 15) two warriors are censured for fighting together against one: Zwêne bestuonden einen: daz was hie vor niht site. Witege und Heime swachten ir êre sêr dâmite, daz sî ûf einer warte vrumten grozen schaden an den jungen Alpharten. des wurdens lasters überladen.

[24] derere en mi le dos (1945). When Siegfried is mortally wounded from behind, he calls his attackers "craven cowards" (*boese zagen, NL*, 989, 1). Il lor lancent e lances e espiez e wigres e darz e museras e agiez e gieser (2074). Knightly scorn against javelins is expressed in Chrétien's *Perceval* (v. 1113) when the young and still boorish hero kills the Vermillion Knight with a *gavelot*.

partly because they assumed that people threw them only when afraid to close in, and Turold himself says that the Saracens were afraid to approach.[25] Similar contempt for bows and arrows is expressed in the *Waltharius* when Werinhard shoots at Walter from a safe distance.[26] In contrast, when Hadawart attacks with a sword, Walter praises him for using equal weapons.[27] Marsilie almost throws a javelin (*algier,* 439) at Ganelon, much as Saul threw one at David. The *Karlamagnús saga* and the *Rolandslied* omit this incident and only let Marsilie grasp his staff.[28] The scorn against javelins was partially social, since they had long been an infantry weapon.[29] The same was true of bows and arrows, for these were a favorite weapon of the yeomen, who could not afford the horses and armor required of the knights. The upper classes resented the ability of the illborn archers to kill their social betters in battle; and, as a result of their antipathy, the Church declared it a sin to use bows and arrows against Christians.[30]

This fact seems to have been overlooked by Prosper Boissonnade (p. 271), who states that the heroes of the *SR* used bows. He bases his argument solely upon verse 767, in which Roland

[25] Men escientre nes osent aproismer (2073). This view is expressed in *Girart de Viënne:* .c. daaz et qui archier fu premier! Il fu coart, si n'osa aprochier (vv. 226–27). This was the attitude of the Japanese in World War II, who reproached the Americans for trembling behind their artillery instead of mixing white steel.

[26] The poet says that Werinhard is fighting with "unequal weapons" (*haud aequo Marte*) when he uses his bow but with "equal odds" (*iusto pondere*) when he uses his sword (*Waltharius,* vv. 731, 743).

[27] laudatque virum, qui praebuit aequam pugnandi sortem (*Waltharius,* v. 788).

[28] *staf* (*KS,* #9); *stab* (*RL,* 2060).

[29] Tacitus relates that Germanic horsemen had preferred the spear and had left javelins to the foot-soldiers: et eques quidem scuto frameaque contentus est, pedites et missilia spargunt, pluraque singuli . . . (*Germania,* #6).

[30] In 1139 the Church prohibited the use of bows and arrows against Christians: Artem autem illam mortiferam et Deo odibilem balistariorum et sagittariorum adversus christianos et catholicos exerceri de caetero sub anathemate prohibemus (cited by Fawtier, p. 204).

asks Charlemagne to give him his *arc* when he is about to set out
on his rear-guard mission. Philip August Becker (p. 151) suggests
that Charlemagne's bow may have served in hunting, but this
would not explain its symbolic meaning. It is unlikely that the
word *arc* is a scribal error, for it appears twice (767, 780). The
Karlamagnús saga renders *arc* as *boga* (*KS*, #15), but in the
Rolandslied Roland asks the emperor for a banner (*van*, v. 3207)
rather than for a bow. The *SR* and its German and Norwegian
imitations agree in having Charlemagne give Ganelon a glove and
a staff,[31] which were appropriate for a diplomatic mission, as can
be seen when Baligant gives a glove and a staff to his emissaries
to Charlemagne.[32]

In the absence of any accounts or pictures of Charlemagne
carrying or presenting a bow, it is possible that the word *arc* had
some meaning unknown to us and to the Norwegian poet. Perhaps
it is an ambiguous word like *ewe*, which usually appears in the
SR in its meaning of water (from *aqua*) but appears in verse
3968 in its meaning of mare (from *equa*) rather than of water, as
most scholars have believed.[33] Possibly Priest Conrad was correct
in interpreting *arc* as a banner, since Roland is taking command

---

[31] guant, bastun (*SR*, 247, 268, 320); stap, hantscuch (*RL*, 1434, 1435);
staf og glófa (*KS*, #6). That there has been some confusion in this episode
is suggested when Roland states that Ganelon dropped his *bastun* (765),
whereas in reality he dropped his *guant* (331).

[32] guant, bastun (2687, 2727). The glove served for either diplomatic or
military missions (*SR*, 2687, 873).

[33] The image of four horses proceeding to a stream of water is certainly
less vivid than that of four excited stallions chasing and fighting for a rutting
mare running loose in the field. Nevertheless, the former interpretation is
accepted by Bédier and many others, including Ruggieri (p. 18), who has
devoted the longest study to the trial of Ganelon. Giulio Bertoni (p. 409)
renders *ewe* as *torrente,* explaining: "L'interpretazione di *ewe* per 'cavala'
(equa) è, no v'ha dubbio, seducente e si capisce che da alcuni sia preferita
alla nostra; ma è più probabile che qui si tratti di una corrente d'acqua nel
prato di Aix." As evidence he cites a poem by Ermoldus Nigellus showing
that there is a stream by Aachen. In his commentary Bédier acknowledges
that his translation of vv. 3967–68 was erroneous, but he does not correct
the item in the glossary, nor does he give a better translation (Bédier, *Commentaires,* p. 388).

of a military expedition rather than of a diplomatic mission.[34] It
is to be remembered that Roland carries an ensign and a white
banner while commanding the rear guard (*enseign*, 708; *gun-
fanun tut blanc*, 1157).

Just as Turold had no idea of "fair play", he also had no inkling
of "good sportsmanship" in the sense of chivalrous treatment of
the vanquished. After Roland has sliced Chernuble through his
face and body and hurled him and his horse down dead, he taunts
his dead victim by calling him a cowardly churl (*culvert*) and by
telling him that Mohammed will not help him and that no battles
are ever won by such craven wretches as he (1335–1337). Although contrary to modern ideas of gentlemanly behavior, such
conduct seems to have been admired in the twelfth century, if we
can judge by passages in various *chansons de geste*. The taunting
challenges in the *SR* as well as the vaunting vilification of the
vanquished appear to follow a literary tradition handed down
from ancient times, as the *Iliad, Aeneid,* and *Waltharius* attest.

After right and wrong, perhaps the most important value concepts are good and bad, concepts rendered by *bon* and *malvais*
and by *prod* and *fel*. Blancandrin uses the word *bon* of the advantageous verdict that Marsilie will receive from Charlemagne
(88); and Marsilie's wife, Bramimunde, uses it of some expensive
brooches which she is sending to Ganelon's wife (640). The word
furnishes a standing epithet for swords, horses, saddles, helmets,
spears, and hauberks; and in most cases the "goodness" of an
object is attested by the gold and precious jewels it contains.[35]
The word *bon* is also regularly consociated with *vassal,* in the
sense of "effective warrior". Roland uses the word *bon* in the

---

[34] Rolant enphie den van (*RL,* 3181); Cf. v. 5832. An illustration in the
Heidelberg manuscript of the *Rolandslied* portrays Roland receiving the
banner (Reproduced on the frontispiece of Maurer's edition). Stricker
(3861) also lets Charlemagne give Roland a *van.*

[35] Swords 925, 949, 984, 1325, 1367; horses 1610, 2993, 3064; saddles
1373, 1587; helmets 996; spears 1270, 1285, 1301; hauberks 1277.

sense of valiant in describing the Franks (1080); and the poet uses it similarly in speaking of Roland and Oliver (1097) and of the other Franks (1401). Turpin, for example, says that a *bon vassal* will never cease fighting as long as he lives; and Ganelon is described as brave (*vassals*) and good (*bon*) in defending his arms.[36]

Ganelon warns Marsilie that the Franks will carry him to Aachen on a lowly pack horse (*malvais somier*, 481); and, in a questionable strophe, Roland calls Ganelon a lowly man of base family (*malvais hom de put aire*, 763). The poet later states that Ganelon rendered bad service (*malvais servis*, 1406) through his treachery. When the Emir's messengers report to Marsilie and Bramimunde, they give a bad salutation (*malvais saluz*, 2710), which is an invocation to their heathen gods. It is a moot question whether such a salutation is *malvais* because it is heathen or because it is ineffectual, but the latter is more likely, since the heathen gods later show *malvaises vertuz* (2716). When Turpin sees how many pagans are attacking, he hopes the Franks will fight bravely lest people sing about them deprecatingly (*malvaisement*, 1517).

These examples indicate that *bon* usually means advantageous, useful, or fit for a given function. When applied to men, it means valiant, as one might expect in a military society which evaluates its members by their prowess. On the other hand, *malvais* means not only disadvantageous, but also socially inferior. The word *bon* is never used with reference to moral goodness or Christian righteousness, nor is *malvais* ever used of wickedness or sin. It will be seen that the word *bon* has all the meanings of the English word "good" in combinations like "good fighter" and "good sword". The difference lies in its meaning when applied to men. Taken by itself, the expression "a good man" now suggests a temperate, law-

---

[36] Ja bon vassal nen ert vif recreüt (2088); Vassals est bons por ses armes defendre (3785).

abiding, and altruistic citizen; but in the *SR* it would mean a brave and capable fighter. When Turold says, "the Franks are good," he elucidates the remark by adding that they strike bravely.[37] In other words, they are good as warriors rather than as human beings. In fact Turold seems unaware of the concept of humanity. He classifies human beings as Christians and pagans, heroes and cowards, laymen and clerics, men and women, or nobles and serfs; but he has no word to connote their common humanity. The word *hom* (from Lat. *homo*) most often means "vassal", as when Gualter calls himself Roland's vassal (*Hom sui Rollant*, 801).

Similar in meaning to the adjective *bon* is the noun *prod*, a word derived from Latin *prodest* (it is profitable).[38] Ganelon assures Charlemagne that he is concerned with the latter's *prod* (221), yet Blancandrin assures his Saracens that Ganelon is really working for their *prod* (507). Upon Ganelon's return from his seemingly successful mission, Charlemagne promises him much reward (*prod*, 699), a thought which the *Karlamagnús* poet renders as *gott*.[39] When Charlemagne saves his life, Naimes says that it will be to Charlemagne's advantage (*prod*, 3459) that he has done so. Sansun strikes and kills an opponent whose hauberk is not *guarant prod* (1277), in which context the adjective *prod* seems to mean sufficient or effective. Marsilie uses the word similarly when he says that Ganelon's promise will not be valid (*proz*, 604) until he takes a formal oath.

Because the most useful and advantageous man is the most

[37] *Franceis sunt bon, si ferrunt vassalment* (1080). In *Renaus de Montalban* Naymes tells Charlemagne that, if he attacks them, Aymes, Girart, and their kinsmen will destroy the realm because they are *bone gent et de grant parentés* (p. 4, v. 7).

[38] *prodest* appears with this meaning in the *Carmen*, v. 299. The original meaning of the word still holds in the Middle English derivative *prow*, for example, in the *Song of Roland* (32) when Ganelon says there is no profit in fighting when peace is sought (ther is no prow to pryk þer men pece sought).

[39] Þá skal þér gott af því standa (*KS*, #14).

courageous one, the epithet *proz e vaillanz* (3186) is practically tautological. The adjective *proz* is often attributed to both the Franks and the Saracens, and in most of these cases it retains something of the basic idea of usefulness, as is the case with the Middle High German word *vrum* and the Middle Netherlandish word *vroem*.[40] This is also true of the compound *produme*, which literally meant a useful (i.e., strong and valiant) man, as did the later German expression *frumber landsknecht*. On one occasion *proz* is used in the sense of "fit for combat duty" (1557). The *Rolandslied* (653) uses a unique word *vramchemphen*, which no one has yet been able to explain. Since *vrum* usually equals *prod*, possibly the word should be *vrumchemphen*, which would be an original term coined after the French word *produme*. If so, this would mean that Conrad used the word *kempfe* (fighter) to render the element *hom* in the Old French original, thus showing that he felt the basic meaning of *hom* to be "fighting man".

The *SR* uses the term *produme* not only of the Franks (314, 3875) but also of the pagan Blancandrin (26). In one passage there seems to be some suggestion of moral overtone in the word *produme*, namely when the poet states that the pagan who accepted Ganelon's treacherous promises was not a *produme* (1528). But in all other cases the emphasis is primarily upon physical strength and courage, as is suggested by the statement that Thierry and Pinabel are *produme e de grant vassalage* (3875). As K. J. Hollyman (p. 120) has observed, by Turold's time the words *vassal* and *vassalage* designated military qualities

---

[40] The impossibility of distinguishing between the concepts of utility and courage can be seen when *proz* appears in v. 2905. Charlemagne complains that, now that Roland is dead, he will have no one to defend his honor. He has other kinsmen, but none who is so *proz*. In other words, they are less useful because they are less brave. The meaning of utility, which was the only meaning of MHG *vrum*, is still found in the NHG formula: *zum Nutz und Frommen*. The *Roelantslied* (v. 530) uses the word in this sense in the expression *ter scaden ende vramen*.

such as strength and courage rather than political dependence.

The pagan Blancandrin was both wise and valiant and was a *prozdom* in counseling his king.[41] Here it might appear that a *produme* should be wise; yet wisdom is not a prerequisite for that epithet except in a counselor. Some heroes, like Archbishop Turpin and the pagan Jangleu, are both brave and wise, but the two qualities are usually contrasted, as in the case of Roland and Oliver.[42] Even Chaucer's very perfect gentle knight was worthy *although* he was wise. On the other hand, in being both wise and valiant, Blancandrin could fulfill the two chief functions of a feudal vassal, namely supplying his liege with help and advice (*consilium et auxilium, helfe und rat*); for "help" in this formula generally meant military service, as it does in Stricker's version of the song.[42a] By associating the virtues of wisdom and courage, Turold is probably following the topos of *sapientia* versus *fortitudo;* but direct literary tradition is not required, since it is natural to combine or to contrast the two qualities.[43]

In a note to v. 26, Jenkins says (p. 6): "The *prozdome* at this time is brave, loyal to his lord, and faithful to his word. His merits also include religious devotion, even if, as here, he be an infidel."

[41] Blancandrins fut des plus saives paiens; de vasselage fut asez chevaler, prozdom i out pur sun seignur aider (24). Conrad renders these two epithets as *wise unde chune,* as for example when Roland describes Ganelon with those terms (*RL* 1370).

[42] sages e proz (3691), Vos estes proz e vostre saveir est grant (3509); Rollant est proz e Oliver est sage (1093).

[42a] Stricker says that Turpin gave Charlemagne *helfe unde rât* (676), and he later uses the word *helfe* to designate military aid (7260–7261). For the feudal duty of *consilium et auxilium,* see Ganshof, pp. 58, 87, 90, 100, 185.

[43] For discussion of *sapientia* and *fortitudo,* see Curtius: *Europ. Lit.,* pp. 181–82, and also Battaglia, pp. 122–42. That the Germanic peoples consciously associated these two qualities before being influenced by Roman literary tradition is suggested by names such as Conrad (brave—counsel), Reynold (counsel—power), Renard (counsel—strong), and many others. Rembalt in the *Chanson* (v. 3073) derives his name from *regin* (counsel) and *bald* (brave).

Jenkins does not prove that a *prozdome* had to be faithful to his word. In any case, this was not true of Blancandrin, who advised Marsilie to break his oath to Charlemagne. Also, it is to be remembered that Blancandrin advised the Saracens to abandon their own sons to Charlemagne's tender mercies rather than lose their lands in Spain. In the *Roelantslied* Astromarijs is *vroem,* even though he is a wicked traitor.[44] Some two centuries after the *SR* was written, Joinville claimed that King Philip of France distinguished between a *preu home* (brave man) and a *preudhome* (brave and good man), the latter being one who serves God and keeps himself free of sin.[45] This fanciful distinction was probably based on some learned etymology contributed by Joinville rather than by Philip. In any case, no such ethical overtone can be assumed when the word *produme* appears in the *SR*.

Whether used alone or in the compound *produme,* the word *prod* was equivalent to the word *probus* as used in the *Carmen* (422). Afraid to approach Marsilius's city, Gueno is impelled by *probitas, audacia,* and *virtus* (83). The three words seem synonymous here, and there is no reason to assume that the word *probitas* connotes "uprightness", as Arthur Livingston supposes.[46] Later, when Gueno draws his sword and threatens the entire Saracen court, the Queen asks the courtiers if Gueno is not *probus* and if

---

[44] He is a *fel vroem payen* (134) even though he and Astromoch are *Verraders . . . quaet ende fel* (139).

[45] . . . il a grant difference entre *preu home* et *preudome.* Car il a mainz preus homes chevaliers en la terre des crestiens et des Sarrazins, qui onques ne crurent Dieu ne sa Mere. Dont je vous di, fist-il, que Diex donne grant don et grant grace au chevalier crestien que il seuffre estre vaillant de cors, et que il seuffre en son servise en li gardant de pechié mortel; et celi que ainsi se demeinne doit l'on appeler *preudome,* pour ce que ceste proesse li vient dou don Dieu. Et ceus de cui j'ai avant parlei puet l'on appeler *preuz homes,* pour ce que il sont preu de lour cors, e ne doutent Dieu ne pechié (Joinville, p. 306, #560).

[46] Livingston, p. 64, v. 83. Elsewhere the poet makes a play on the word: In nullo probus es, sed reprobus improbitate, Improbitasque tui te negat esse probum (*Carmen,* 111–113).

his *probitas* should not be approved (143). Here too the word lacks moral overtones. Jules Horrent (p. 113) believes that *probitas* in this passage means loyalty, but it is more logical that the Queen was impressed by Gueno's courage at defying the Saracens than at his loyalty to Charlemagne. Similarly no moral connotation is necessary when Gueno obtains gifts through his *fraus* and not through his *probitas* (176), for that may just mean that he won his gifts through cunning rather than through valor. The fact that Karolus's companion is *probitas* (66) throws no light on the meaning of the word.

Just as the epithet *produme* referred to a warrior's prowess (*proecce,* 1731) or to his deeds of prowess (*proecces,* 1607), the epithet *bon chevaler* referred primarily to courage and military efficacy rather than to noble sentiments or polished manners.[47] Taken alone, the word *chevaler* meant no more than "cavalryman", for Turold used the term to include a man who was not a brave warrior (*s'il ne fust bon vassal,* 2136). The word *chevaler* is most often consociated with *bon, baron, vaillant, hardi,* and *gent,* all of which suggest strength and physical courage. Malpramis, the son of the Emir, is *mult chevalerus* (3176), a quality which seems to depend upon his being *granz* and *forz* (3177). The word *chevalerie* can mean "courage" (960), "knighthood" (3074), or "deed of prowess" (594). It will be noted that the word *chevaler* is used of the pagans, who are elsewhere called wretches and villains. When Ganelon nominates Roland for the

---

[47] According to William Stowell (*Personal Relationships,* p. 400), "In the early Middle Ages *chevaliers* signified simply 'an armed horseman'." G. Gougenheim (pp. 117, 118) maintains that already in the *SR* the word *chevalier* designated "le type unique du combattant avec toute une ambiance de valeurs morales et sociales," but he realizes that these values are primarily valor and nobility. Charlemagne uses the word in this military sense when he says of Roland: Unques nuls hom tel chevaler ne vit Por granz batailles juster e defenir (2888–2889). See also Stowell, "Titles . . .", pp. 78–89.

rearguard assignment, Roland answers him *a lei de chevaler* (752) and thanks him for the dangerous honor and boasts that he will perform it successfully. This arrogant answer is courageous, but it does not exactly accord with modern ideas of chivalry. Later, when the rear guard arms itself *a lei de chevalers* (1143), they are demonstrating courage rather than any other chivalrous quality.

Many persons in the *SR* are called *ber* (acc. *barun*), which is evidently a term of respect. Marsilie addresses his vassals as *seignurs baruns* (70); and Blancandrin calls Marsilie *li bers* (125). Ganelon calls Charlemagne *ber* in a eulogy stressing his strength and courage (530–536); and Roland tells his sword that Charlemagne is *ber e riches* because of the territories he has won for him (2352–2354). Elsewhere the poet says that Ganelon would have been *ber* if he had been loyal.[48] Although this would imply that a man must be loyal to be *ber,* the word is most frequently associated with strength and courage, whether or not they are connected with moral integrity. During their trial by combat, Thierry tells Pinabel that he would like to make peace with him because he is *ber,* and he further qualifies this by telling him that he is large and strong with well-shaped limbs and is known for his bravery.[49] Unless by chance it was of Latin origin,[50] the word *ber* appears to have derived from Old High German *baro,* which meant warrior. The word *baro* had originally referred to any free-born fighter; but the twelfth-century gentry assumed that only wellborn men were brave and therefore they generally restricted the word *ber* to men of good birth, as is the case of the English derivative *baron.* Like the heroes of the *SR*, Saint Giles, Saint

[48] S'il fust leials, ben resemblast barun (3764).

[49] Pinabel, mult ies ber, Granz ies e forz e tis cors ben mollez; De vasselage te conoissent ti per (3899–3901). In one passage of *Raoul de Cambrai* (vv. 3048–49) the word is well illuminated by its consociations: molt bon chevalier, Fort et hardi et nobile guerier.

[50] Robert A. Hall, Jr. endorses A. Wallenskold in deriving *ber* from Old Latin °*baron,* a strong man. See *Studies in Linguistics,* 5, 1947, pp. 65–68.

Silvester, and Saint Seurin receive this epithet (*ber Gilie,* 2096; *baron seint Silvestre,* 3746; *seint Sevrin le baron,* 3685).

Being heathens, the Saracens are doomed to hell regardless of any personal merit. No matter how bravely they die for their cause, their souls go to damnation (1553, 3647). Except for the caliph's violation of Charlemagne's envoys, the Saracens are punctilious in obeying international law, as is shown when the Emir declares war before attacking (2977). In fact, were the Emir a Christian, he would be a true warrior, just as Balaguez would be a good warrior if he were a Christian.[51] It may be noted that, except for their different faiths, the Emir is described much like Charlemagne himself (3140–3175). Turold shows his lack of empathy for his Saracen characters by letting Baligant refer to his troops as pagans.[52]

Because of a peculiar literary practice of Turold's time, the Saracens actually appear more magnanimous than the Christians. Except in their *gabs,* or pre-battle boasts, the Saracens generally speak very generously of their Christian enemies, whereas the Christians always speak disparagingly of the Saracens. For example, Blancandrin calls Charlemagne a marvelous man and says that the Franks are very noble, and Bramimunde says that the Franks are a hardy race who do not fear death and that their emperor is brave and will never flee from battle.[53] Likewise, the Saracens refer to France as *France dulce* and *Tere Major.*[54] The reason for the Saracens' apparent generosity is not hard to guess. It is really Turold speaking, even when he speaks through the

---

[51] Quel baron, s'oüst chrestientet (3164); Fust chrestiens, asez oüst barnet (899).

[52] Venez, paien, . . . (2844); la meie gent averse (3295); mi paien (3136). Cf. al paien Baligant (2725).

[53] Merveilus hom est Charles (370), Francs sunt mult gentilz home (377), Vasselage ad e mult grant estultie; S'il ad bataille, il ne s'en fuirat mie (2606–2607); cele gent hardie Ki si sunt fiers n'unt cure de lur vies (2603–2604).

[54] Dulce France (16, 2773), Tere Majur (952), Tere Major (1659).

mouths of the unspeakable infidels. Certain epithets belong to Charlemagne and the Franks, even when they are being discussed by the enemy.

Another word of praise is *isnel*, which is used of Margariz, Gerin, Gerier, and Pinabel.[55] Boissonnade renders this as *prompt*, and Bédier and others render it as *vite*.[56] This is correct when it is applied to sparrow hawks, falcons, and swallows,[57] but it should be rendered as "courageous" when applied to warriors.[58] In this way it resembles its Old High German source *snël*, which may have acquired its transferred meaning through association with the Latin word *alacer*.[59] It is a moot question whether the ancient Germans associated speed with courage or with cowardice. According to Tacitus, the Chatti considered deliberate action by the infantry better than speed,[60] but in this case he was contrasting them with the other Germanic tribes. The opposite of *isnel* was *lenz*, which implied cowardice, as when Oliver calls down God's wrath upon the *plus lenz* (1938).

Another ambiguous word is *fel* (acc. *felun*). Needing advice, Marsilie calls aside ten of his *plus feluns* vassals (69). No one in Spain is more *felun* than the ruler of Moriane (910); and the exact same thing is said of Abirun (1216) and Abisme (1471). The meaning of the word is sometimes suggested by its consocia-

[55] vv. 1312, 1388, 3840, 3885.
[56] Boissonnade, p. 341; Bédier, trans., *passim*. The glossary to Bédier's commentary says "rapide" (Bédier, *Commentaires*, p. 407).
[57] SR, 1535, 1572, 1616.
[58] This is indicated by its consocations. Margariz is *mult vaillant chevalers, e bels e forz e isnels e legers* (1312); Pinabel is *Granz e forz e vassals e isnel* (3839) and *forz e isnels e legers* (3885).
[59] The complimentary nature of the epithet *snell* is suggested by the opening line of Otfrid's dedication of his *Gospel Harmony*, which is dedicated to *Ludowig ther snello, thes wisduames follo*. These two qualities equal Turold's *prod e sage*. The word *swind* or *swith* (swift) in names like Merswind and Roswitha also shows that speed was a praiseworthy attribute. The *Carmen* calls the Franks *alacres Galli* (271).
[60] (peditum) velocitas iuxta formidinem, cunctatio propior constantiae est (*Germania*, #30). This statement concerns infantry in general, but it implies that the Chatti were of the same opinion.

tions, as when the poet calls Ganelon *li fels, li parjurez* or *li fel, li traïtur.*[61] Roland calls Marsilie a *fels* after he violates Charlemagne's envoys; and Ganelon is called *fels* for having committed treason. Roland says that anyone should be considered a *fel* who does not sell his life dearly, his countrymen later say the same thing of anyone who does not fight to his utmost, and the pagans say the same thing of any of their troops who refuse to attack.[61a] Thus we see that both cowards and traitors were branded as *fel*.

Perhaps the word *fel* first signified social inferiority and only later acquired moral opprobrium,[62] as was the case with the words *villain, varlet, Schalk, Dirne, wench,* etc.; but it may have originally referred to an obscene sexual practice.[63] The SR uses the word most often of the pagans, who sometimes appear to be called *fel* merely because they are not Christians. In return the pagans call the Christians *feluns humes* (2060). The author of the *Karlamagnús saga* often renders *fel* as "malevolent" (*illgjörnust*) and on one occasion as "evil traitor" (*illur svikari,* #5).

The word *fel* is well-defined in the description of the Saracen Abisme, who was the most *fel* in his company: "He had a bad character (*teches*) and committed many *felonies*. He did not believe in God, the Son of Saint Mary. He was as black as pitch and loved treachery and murder more than all the gold of Galicia. No one ever saw him play or laugh. He had courage and temerity

[61] vv. 674, 1024. Sometimes the word is explained by the following action: Guenes li fels en ad fait traïsun (844); Guenes est fels d'iço qu'il le traït (3829). See Dessau, pp. 23–26.

[61a] SR 213, 844, 1024, 1457, 1924, 3559, 2062.

[62] Jenkins (p. 10) believes that this word originally meant "skinner"; and Brüch (p. 109) believes that it meant "whipper". Both of these professions were "dishonorable" in medieval Germany. The word *fillo–fillonis,* meaning "rascal", appeared in medieval but not in classic Latin. See Hollyman, pp. 152–55.

[63] Whereas most scholars assume Germanic origin, Robert Hall suggests in a letter of Jan. 22, 1962, that *fel* derived from Latin *fellâre* ("to perform the obscene action of *fellâtio*"). This action still furnishes a favorite term of abuse among soldiers.

and was therefore a favorite of the *felun* king Marsilie." [64] The word *fel* signifies "publicly censured" or "branded as a coward" in the expressions *tut seit fel* (1924, 2062) and *fel sei* (3757),[65] which mean about the same as the imprecation "God hate!" (*Dehet ait*, 1938). The word *felonie* is nowhere defined, but it seems to mean a morally bad deed, or at least a shameful one.

Although the *SR* is ostensibly a Christian poem, the concept of sin is never fully developed. To be sure, Archbishop Turpin absolves his men before battle to assure them entry into paradise; and he and Oliver and Roland all confess their sins before dying.[66] Likewise, Pinabel and Thierry confess and are absolved before their trial by combat.[67] These heroes have no occasion to prove true contrition, nor do they indicate which of their acts they consider sinful. As we shall see, hate, anger, revenge, mayhem, manslaughter, and pillage were not sins when committed in the Lord's service. The word *colpe* appears most often in connection with confession, but it also appears in a secular sense when Oliver states that Charlemagne is not at fault (*n'i ad culpes*, 1173) for the slaughter caused by Roland's obstinacy.

The word *pecchet* is also used to denote sin by Roland (2370), the archbishop (1882), and the poet himself (1140). When Charlemagne has waged war successfully for seven years against the Saracens, Marsilie calls his advisors together and asks them to hear what *pecchet* has overcome them.[68] Here the word appears to mean calamity, yet the author of the *Karlamagnús saga* renders

[64] Teches ad males e mult granz felonies; Ne creit en Deu, le filz seinte Marie; Issi est neirs cume peiz ki est demise; Plus aimet il traïsun e murdrie Qu'il ne fesist trestut l'or de Galice; Unches nuls hom nel vit juer ne rire. Vasselage ad e mult grant estultie: por ço est drud al felun rei Marsilie (1471–1479).

[65] Bédier correctly translates *tut seit fel* (1924) as "honni à", *Fel seit* (2144) as "Honni . . .", and *fel sei* (3757) as "honte sur".

[66] 1132–1135; 2239; 2014; 2369–2372.

[67] Ben sun cunfès e asols e seignez (3859).

[68] Quel pecchet nus encumbret (15).

the thought as "sin".[69] Naimes uses the word in the sense of "disadvantageous" in telling Charlemagne that it would be *pecchet* for him to prolong his war against Marsilie (240). It is debatable just what the poet meant in saying that the defeated king Marsilie dies loaded down by *doel* and *pecchet* (3646), since he could have been burdened by sin as an unshriven heathen or crushed by calamity as a defeated ruler. Perhaps *pecchet* already had an ambiguous or neutral meaning as in modern Italian *È peccato*, which we can translate as "It's a shame" or as "It's a pity", depending upon whether we wish to follow pagan or Christian tradition.

Another ambiguous word is *pesme*, which is derived from Latin *pessimus*. In warning Marsilie that Charlemagne's heart is *pesmes* (56) and that he will kill his hostages, Blancandrin seems to use the word derogatorily. On the other hand, no insult seems implied when Oliver vetoes Roland as Charlemagne's messenger to Marsilie on the grounds that his heart is too *pesmes* and *fiers* (256). In fact *pesmes* seems almost synonymous with *fiers*,[70] which is generally complimentary. Marsilie would have agreed with Oliver, who also calls Roland *pesmes* for wishing to conquer the world (392). On one occasion the adjective modifies either "battle" or "day". The words *Une bataille lur livrat le jur pesme* (813) mean either that the pagan prince fought a fierce battle on that day or that he fought a battle on that evil day. Since the *SR* most often uses *pesme* in the sense of fierce, the former interpretation is perhaps the better, despite Jenkins' contrary explanation.[71] Be that as it may, the word *pesme* does not always seem derogatory even

---

[69] hvað synd hefir oss komið (*KS*, #2).

[70] This is true in the case of the lion in Charlemagne's dream: mult par ert pesmes e orguillus e fiers (2550). The author of the *Karlamagnús saga* renders *pesmes* as *illir* (#29).

[71] In vocabulary, p. 354. The meaning "evil" probably applies when *pesme* modifies *noveles* (2919), but the meaning "violent" is more appropriate when it modifies *estur* (2122), *bataille* (3304), and *caple* (3404).

when attributed to a Christian knight. In this case it is somewhat like the Middle High German word *übel,* which could mean evil, or else fierce and violent in a complimentary sense.[72]

Virtue and vice do not appear in the *SR* in their Christian and Stoic meanings. Both Oliver and Archbishop Turpin strike with great *vertut* but later Turpin is weak (*fieble*) and has no *vertut* because he has lost so much blood. The Franks attribute all their strength to God and ask Him to give them power (*de Deu aiez vertut*), and Roland compares his own sins (*colpe*) with God's strength (*vertuz*). God shows his power through saints like Saint Giles and also through Charlemagne; and, after the pagans are defeated, Bramimunde sarcastically says that their gods have shown *malvaises vertuz.*[73] There is no reason to translate God's *vertut* in these cases as "miracle", as all translators seem to do, for God's *vertut* differs from that of the pagan gods only by being much greater. The word *vertut* should be understood in the sense in which it is used in the Gospel of St. Mark (5:25–34) when Jesus feels His virtue go out of Himself into the woman with the issue of blood. Before setting out to avenge Roland, Charlemagne blesses himself *de la vertut,* which surely means that Charlemagne received great strength from God.[74] Throughout the *SR* the adjective *vertuus* and the adverb *vertuusement* refer only to physical strength.[75]

The *Carmen* seems to use the word *virtus* to designate courage rather than mere strength; yet it will be noted that courage and strength are nearly always associated in medieval literature.

---

[72] In the *Lay of the Nibelungs* Kriemhild calls Volker *ein übel man* with great admiration for his fighting abilities (*NL,* 1768, 3).

[73] vv. 1246, 1551; 2230; 1045, 2369; 2096, 2458, 2716.

[74] Seignat sun chef de la vertut poisant (3111). Bédier says: "signa son chef du signe puissant". Conrad probably had the idea of *virtus* or *vertut* in mind in letting Roland say: dîne tugent hâstu an mir erzaiget (*RL,* 6898).

[75] This is suggested when the pagan Grandonie is described as *e prozdom e vaillant e vertuus e vassal cumbatant* (1636) and when Roland strikes him so *vertuusement* that he splits his helmet, head, and body (1644).

Physical weaklings with moral stamina rarely appear in secular songs, and *fortitudo* usually designates physical strength. Before gunpowder made all men the same size, self-confidence was difficult for weaklings. In the *Carmen* Queen Bramimunda is magnified by *decus* and adorned with *decor*.[76] Livingston translates *decus* as "virtue", but *decus* is probably a synonym of *decor* and may connote merely physical beauty.[76a] Rollandus later uses the word *decus* in the sense of reputation for victory (238). It is true that moral and philosophical writings like those of Cicero and Seneca sometimes used the word *decus* in a transferred sense to mean moral virtue, which is a man's true adornment. Nevertheless, such works do not seem to have influenced the *SR* or the *Carmen* greatly, even though they were available to anyone able to read Latin.[77]

Just as the *SR* has no word to designate moral virtue, it has none to designate moral vice. The highest virtue being courage, one might say that the worst vice is cowardice (*cuardie*, 1486; *cuardise*, 3531). The *Carmen* uses the word *convicium* (45) in the sense of reproach, that is, it denotes what people say about a person rather than what he really is. One Stoic virtue is mentioned in the *SR*, but only briefly and as a striking exception. This is moderation, a virtue represented by Oliver, who considers discretion the better part of valor. While blaming Roland for

---

[76] Magnificat, decorat hanc decus atque decor (*Carmen*, 94).

[76a] Later Gueno is saved not by his strength but by his *species*, because Bramimunda, moved by his *decore*, persuades Marsilius to spare him (*Carmen*, 140–142).

[77] A good example of Stoic thought is found in the *Formula vitae honestae* by the sixth-century bishop Saint Martin of Braga, who probably followed a text by Seneca. His work was widespread when the *SR* was composed. Many Stoic ideas are found in the *Moralium Dogma*, which was compiled in France probably during Turold's lifetime. The *Moralium Dogma* (#1) says: Virtus igitur et honestum nomina diversa, res autem subiecta prorsus eadem. Notker, an eleventh-century monk of St. Gall, used *êra* to render *decus* in a passage where *decus* designated moral virtue: Neque enim aliena improbitas decerpit probis animis proprium decus (See Jones, *Honor*, p. 5).

their defeat, he says, "Companion, you did it, for courage with prudence is not folly; moderation is better than temerity (*estultie*)." [78]

As we have seen, Turold says that the pagan Abisme has courage and great temerity; and later Bramimunde speaks the exact same words in praise of Charlemagne.[79] The Saracens attack the Franks with such great *estultie* (3528) that they break their ranks and rout them. These examples suffice to show that Turold generally approved of *estultie* as a manly virtue. The pejoration of this word occurred later, no doubt through confusion with the Latin word *stultitia* (folly); for the Old French word *estultie*, which was derived from a Germanic root **stolto*, seems to have had a complimentary sense like its English derivative in "stout fellow" or "stouthearted".

In addition to meaning brave and steadfast, **stolto* also meant proud, like its German derivative *stolz;* and therefore the word *estultie* became debased by clergymen, for whom pride was the greatest folly.[80] It will be noted that Turold uses the word *estultie* in a negative sense only when Oliver equates it with *legerie*, by which he means recklessness.[81] It should be remembered, however, that recklessness is traditionally a virtue in epic heroes. The SR shows little respect for moderation. It is true that Oliver preaches it, but the hero of the song is foolhardy Roland, not prudent Oliver. And even Oliver would appear foolhardy if judged by modern military standards, especially when he gets angry (*irez*, 1558) and, dashing out alone, attacks Climborin, Alphain, and Escabi and then unhorses and incapacitates seven other Arabs (1551–1557).

[78] Cumpainz, vos le feistes, kar vasselage par sens nen est folie; mielz valt mesure que ne fait estultie (1723–1725).

[79] vasselage, mult grant estultie (1478, 2606).

[80] Cf. the German proverb: "Dummheit und Stolz wachsen auf einem Holz."

[81] Franceis sunt morz par vostre legerie (1726). *Legers* is used in a complimentary sense in v. 1313.

With respect to their emotions, Roland and his rear guard may be said to present a youthful ethos. "They are passionate, hot-tempered, and carried away by impulse, and unable to control their passion; for owing to their ambition they cannot endure to be slighted, and become indignant when they think they are being wronged. They are ambitious of honour, but more so of victory; for youth desires superiority, and victory is a kind of superiority." These words, by which Aristotle characterizes youth in general, certainly apply in a large degree to the impetuous heroes of the *SR*. Although Charlemagne is some two centuries old, he too reacts to insult in much the way that Aristotle expected of hot-blooded youth.[81a] Today we condone violent outbursts of anger and grief from infants whose whims are thwarted, but we do not commend such behavior in adults.

[81a] *Aristotle, The "Art" of Rhetoric*, trans. J. H. Freeze, *Loeb*, London, 1926, II, 12.

CHAPTER II

SEMANTIC ANALYSIS
Part Two

A MUCH MISUNDERSTOOD WORD-GROUP in the *Chanson de Roland* comprises the verb *amer* and its cognates. Although derived from Latin *amare*, this verb does not always imply personal affection or emotional attachment. To be sure, it sometimes implies such affection, but this can not be assumed; for in many cases *amer* means "to keep peace with" or "to make peace with," or "to form alliance with." In defying Roland, Ganelon says *Jo ne vus aim nient* (306), by which he means that he is changing from "friendly" to "hostile", and therefore he must also defy the twelve peers *por ço qu'il l'aiment tant* (325). No doubt the peers do feel a personal inclination for Roland, but that is not the issue at stake. Ganelon defies the peers because they are Roland's *ami,* in the sense of allies.

When Ganelon informs Charlemagne that he has defied Roland (*Ne l'amerai a trestut mun vivant,* 323), Faral lets him say that he will detest Roland (*Je le détesterai toute ma vie,* 70). To be sure, Ganelon will hate his stepson, but that is not the crux of the matter. More important is the legal notice that he is proclaiming a state of hostility. In saying that Charlemagne will never

amer him (*ne m'amerat il mie*, 494), Marsilie means that Charlemagne will continue hostilities until the uncle is punished; for
there is no reason to expect any affection between the two
warring monarchs. The same is true when Turold says that Archbishop Turpin will never *amer* the Saracen standard-bearer
Abisme (*ne l'amerat ja mie*, 1481) and when Roland tells the
Saracens that he can never *amer* them (*ne pois amer les voz*,
1591); for here, too, no one would expect him to "love" the
Saracens with any personal devotion.

Other *chansons de geste* frequently use *amer* in its sense of
"to cease hostilities". Guerri, a character in *Raoul de Cambrai*,
swears that he will never *amer* the slayers of his nephew or grant
them peace or truce until he has killed them all,[1] and here it is
obvious that he is not thinking in terms of affection. The word
amer is used again similarly in the same *chanson* when Gautier
swears that he will not *amer* Bernier until he has destroyed or
exiled him;[2] for true love would be difficult after such treatment.
Curtius (p. 277) observed that *non amare*, in the sense of "to
hate", was a stylistic device (litotes) well-known in Roman
rhetoric and poetry and also frequent in the Bible; but he did
not notice that the old formula received an additional legal or
political connotation as used by the Franks. The impersonal or
diplomatic meaning of *amare* is echoed in the international legal
term "un acte peu amical", which denotes not merely an un-
friendly act but an act usually so intolerable as to be a *casus belli*.

When Ganelon promises to betray Roland to the Saracens,
Valdebron gives him a valuable sword *par amistiez* (622); and

---

[1] Qi vos a mort jamais ne l'amerai, Pais ne acorde ne trives n'en prendrai
Desq'a cele eure qe toz mors les arai (*Raoul*, 3169–3171). Cf. "diu suone
wirdet niht alsô: sus kome wir niht ze minnen (*Tristan*, 6825–6826).

[2] Ne l'amerai si l'arai essilié, ars ou destruit ou del regne chacié (*Raoul*,
3616–3617). When the author of *Renaus de Montalban* says that Charlemagne was aided by *li baron qui l'amerent* (p. 26, v. 3), this need mean no
more than that he was aided by his vassals or *ami*. Naturally this did not
include his former *amis* Beuves d'Aigremont, who had recently defied him.

for the same reason Climborin kisses him *par amistiet* (1530) and gives him his helmet and a ruby. In both these cases, *par amistiet* can best be translated as "to confirm their alliance" or "to seal their bargain". It will be noted that *amistiet* generally involves a contract, which is often sealed with a kiss and confirmed with material pledges. In advising Marsilie to feign homage to Charlemagne, Blancandrin says he should offer *fedeilz servises e mult granz amistez* (29). Here he is probably using the two terms synonymously; [2a] for, as William Stowell (p. 393) has shown, the word *amistiet* often designated the relationship between seigneur and vassal. After a vast amount of research, Stowell concludes: "Amistié, the personal bond between seigneur and follower, is radically different from the tie of friendship; *amis* used as a term for the follower does not mean 'friend'. Friendship is a mutual relation."

This feudal or "non-mutual" meaning of the word *amis* holds in the *SR* when it is contrasted with "liege lords" (*lige seignurs*, 2421); and, as we shall see, it may hold when Roland calls to Oliver and the Franks (1113). On the other hand, a mutual relation seems implied when Ganelon calls his kinsman Pinabel *mun ami e mun per* and when Oliver calls to Roland, who is designated as *sun ami e sun per*.[2b] Either or both meanings may apply when Charlemagne mourns his *Amis Rollant* (2887, *et passim*); for his self-commiseration after Roland's death suggests that he misses Roland more as a useful vassal than as a dear nephew.[3] As we shall see, even personal affection in the *SR* is seldom disinterested.

[2a] The verbs *amer* and *servir* are similarly related when Turold states that Marsilie does not love God but serves Mohammed (*ki Deu nen aimet. Mahumet sert,* vv. 7–8). It would seem that Ganelon is actually entering Marsilie's *amistiet* when he gives Climborin *fiance* (1529); for this word is subsequently used to mean homage (2329).

[2b] When used this way, *per* would seem derived from *par, paris;* but in the expression *li duze per* it seems derived from *patricius*. It will be noted that the *Carmen* renders *per* in the latter sense as *patricius* (207, 449, 473).

[3] vv. 839–40, 2890, 2903–5, 2920–29.

In all previous examples the word *amis* is used to close friends or to subordinates, but never to superiors. An exception seems to occur when Roland, regretting Charlemagne's absence from Roncevaux, cries out: *"E! reis, amis, que vos ici nen estes?"* (1697), which is always rendered as "Alas! King, friend, why are you not here?" Since the word *amis* is used elsewhere in the SR only to equals and subordinates, this verse could mean "King, friends . . .". Turold, or the scribe of the *Oxford MS*, seems to have vacillated in his use of the ending *s*. For example, the vocative plural of *ber* appears both as *barons* (1165, 1954) and as *baron* (3366, 3374), and analogy could have caused the vocative plural ending *s* of *barons* to be carried over to the vocative plural of *amis*. If the word *amis* is taken to refer to Charlemagne, rather than to the Franks, then it would contradict William Stowell (p. 394), who says: "The follower is the *amis* of his *seigneur;* the *seigneur* is never the *amis* of his follower. The *seigneur* addresses his follower as *amis*. The follower never thus addresses his *seigneur*." In his footnotes to these statements, Stowell writes that, in the hundreds of examples he has studied, "the *seigneur* is never spoken of as the *amis* of his followers" and "there is not a single example in which the word was used by a follower as a title for a *seigneur*."

Evidence for reading *amis* as a plural may appear in v. 1113 when Roland "shouts to the Franks and calls to Oliver, 'Sir companion, friend(s), do not speak that way'" (*Franceis escriet, Oliver apelat: "Sire cumpainz, amis, nel dire ja!"*). It is generally assumed that *cumpainz* and *amis* both refer to Oliver, perhaps because only Oliver has advised blowing the horn. Nevertheless, it is clear that Roland is addressing the other Franks as well as Oliver, and it is natural for him to wish no one else to repeat Oliver's shameful suggestion. An argument in favor of this reading is that it produces a fine example of chiasm. When Turold says: *Franceis escriet, Oliver apelat: "Sire cumpainz, amis . . ."*, we find the sequence a-b : b-a, which may well have been a conscious use of this impressive rhetorical device. Although there are sound arguments against this reading,[4] it does deserve some consideration.

All critics and translators of the SR render the verb *amer* as "aimer" or "to love", even when it denotes a political or diplomatic relationship rather than a personal or emotional one. The same is true of the noun *amor*. In Charlemagne's statement that he may grant the pagans neither *pais* nor *amor* (3596), the two words are practically synonymous, as is usually the case when Turold pairs two words.[5] To be sure, the verb *amer* could also designate personal affection; but, as we shall see, even family affection was not always disinterested. In telling how Charlemagne loves the twelve peers, Turold uses the words *ad tant chers* (547); and in the following strophe, which is a *duplicatio*, he expresses the same thought as *aimet tant* (560). This suggests that the terms are synonymous and mean "value highly", as the *Karlamagnús* poet seems to have understood.[6] In other words, they do not necessarily denote a selfless or disinterested love, but rather an appreciation of value. Later we shall see that Charlemagne loves his men for the blows they strike.

Critics and scholars rhapsodize about Roland's and Oliver's touching friendship,[7] even though their behavior toward each

---

[4] Perhaps the best contrary argument is that, in all other cases of compound vocatives, both vocatives refer to the same person. For this observation I am indebted to Professor Alfred Foulet. On the other hand, it will be noted that Roland elsewhere calls Oliver *Sire cumpainz* (1546, 1672, 2027) but never *Amis*.

[5] Typical of such nearly synonymous word-pairs are mort – hunte, onur – deintet, honurs – fieus, ami – per, hunte – viltet, dolur – ire, fels – parjurez, doel – viltet, doel – ire, compaign – frere.

[6] fyrir sakir slíkra höggva virðir Karlamagnús konungur oss mikils (#27). The French language can still use the one word *cher* to describe a dear friend or an expensive object. Today there is a definite qualitative difference of emotional overtone in the two contexts, but we cannot assume that this difference was so clearly appreciated in the Middle Ages.

[7] Pauphilet (pp. 177–78) gives a touching picture of the scene between Roland and Oliver, which is endorsed and quoted by Curtius (p. 284).

other would be inexcusable between friends today. It is true that the two peers harbor a strong attachment for each other, the kind of attachment often found between comrades-in-arms who have shared pain and peril. Roland calls Oliver his companion and brother (*cumpaign, frere,* 1456; *bel sire, chers cumpainz,* 1693), which, as William Stowell has shown, means that they were bound by very close social, and one might say political, ties. Because they are sworn to help each other, an enemy of the one is the enemy of the other, and Ganelon must hate Oliver as Roland's *cumpainz* (324). Oliver has sealed his alliance with Roland by giving him his sister, Alde, as a fiancée (1720).

Despite his close alliance with Oliver, Roland endangers him and his other friends rather than risk his own reputation back in France.[8] Although Oliver expresses great love for Roland, he cannot refrain from abusing him for having refused to summon aid while there was still time (1170–1172). As soon as Roland is sure that it will not hurt his reputation, he agrees to blow his horn; but Oliver then reverses himself and warns that it would be a great disgrace (*vergoigne,* 1705) to do so and that his kinsmen would suffer dishonor (*hunte,* 1707) all their lives. Roland insists, and Oliver again reminds him that they would now be safe if he had blown his horn earlier (1715–1718). He adds that, if he lives to see his sister Alde, Roland will never sleep in her arms.[9] This implies that he is hereby terminating their alliance. When Roland asks him why he bears a grudge, Oliver repeats that all the Franks died because of his folly;[10]

Boissonnade (p. 306) shares their enthusiasm: C'est cette même amitié, franche et héroïque, qu'il a immortalisée en une création inoubliable, celle du personnage d'Olivier.

[8] en dulce France en perdreie mun los (1054); Ne placet Damnedeu ne ses angles que ja pur mei perdet sa valur France! Melz voeill murir que huntage me venget (1089).

[9] Se puis veeir ma gente sorur Alde, Ne jerreiez ja mais entre sa brace (1720).

[10] Por quei me portez ire (1722); par vostre legerie (1726).

and their quarrel becomes so bitter that the archbishop must come to reconcile them (1737–1739).

Roland's and Oliver's friendship is illustrated in another scene, which critics often praise for its beauty.[11] Toward the end of the battle, Oliver is sorely wounded and almost blinded with blood. Unable to recognize Roland, he strikes him on his helmet and splits it down to the noseguard, but does not injure him. "At this blow Roland looked at him and asked him gently and sweetly, 'Sir companion, did you do that on purpose? This is Roland who loves you (*amer*) so much! In no way have you defied me.'" [12] Oliver apologizes for the unintentional blow, whereupon Roland vows he is not hurt and pardons him his mistake. Then they nod to each other and part for the last time.

In the fog of battle soldiers often shoot inadvertently at their friends, yet no one today would ask his best friend if he had done so on purpose. Nor would anyone remind his confused friend that he had not declared war on him before shooting. But honor was a fragile thing in the twelfth century, when men of honor had to be punctilious even with their friends. Turold probably considered Roland magnanimous enough for pardoning Oliver's blow as well as his previous reproach. Perhaps Roland was the twelfth-century ideal of a perfect friend, but such a friend would hardly have been appreciated during World War II.

---

[11] John O'Hagan (p. 17) seems to have misunderstood Roland's words. He writes: "There are, I think, few things in poetry more touching than the passage where Olivier, wounded to death and blinded by the blood which streams down his forehead, strikes out darkly and smites the helm of Roland, who had ridden to his side: 'My comrade, thou didst it not wittingly . . . .'" Perhaps even O'Hagan would have found Roland's words less touching if he had realized that they were a question rather than a negation. Strangely enough, he rendered the passage correctly in his translation: "Hast thou done it, my comrade, wittingly?" (p. 157).

[12] Sire cumpain, faites le vos de gred? Ja est ço Rollant, ki tant vos soelt amer (2000–2001). In the *Rolandslied* (6475–6477) Roland asks: Ja du tiuwerlicher degen, hâstuz gerne getân? Warumbe woltestu mich erslân?

When Charlemagne dreams that he is going to lose Roland, his chief regret is that he will be unable to replace him (*ja n'en avrai escange,* 840); and after the massacre he pities himself for having lost his nephew who had conquered so much territory for him.[13] In other words, he seems sadder at being bereft of his defender than at being bereaved of his nephew. By mourning his nephew's death as a peril to his own prestige,[14] Charlemagne proves that Roland was right in believing that Charlemagne loved him and Oliver because of the strokes they struck.[15] In breaking the news to Alde that her fiancé is dead, Charlemagne promises to give her an even better substitute (*Jo t'en durai mult esforcet eschange,* 3714); and here he thinks a good replacement can assuage the sorrow caused by the death of a loved one. As we shall see, after capturing and plundering Saragossa, Charlemagne and his men are full of *joie* (3682), despite the recent death of so many of their friends and relations. Love and friendship in the *SR* are readily subordinated to considerations of honor, as is shown when Roland jeopardizes the lives of his twelve peers and twenty thousand men rather than compromise his own reputation.[16] As an honorable woman, Bramimunde pities herself for having lost her husband so shamefully (*A itel hunte,* 2824), and she later regrets that the Emir has been killed with such shame (*a si grant hunte,* 3643).

When Charlemagne weeps for Roland *par feid e par amur*

---

[13] Morz est mis niés, ki tant me fist cunquere (2920). When Marsilie loses his son, he regrets that he has neither son nor daughter nor heir (Jo si nen ai filz ne fille ne heir: un en aveie, cil fut ocis her seir, 2744–2745). This suggests that he valued his son more as an heir than as a beloved person. This attitude is common in the *chansons de geste;* for example in the *Couronnement Louis* Duke Richard regrets that he has lost his heir: Qui m'a tolu le meillor eritier qui onques fu por terre justicier (2066–2067; cf. 2134–2135).

[14] La meie honor est turnet en declin (2890); N'en avrai ja ki sustienget m'onur (2903).

[15] Por itels colps nos eimet li emperere (1377); Por itels colps nos ad Charles plus cher (1560). Cf. note II, 6.

[16] En dulce France en perdreie mun los (1054).

(2897), this formula may express the liege's concern for his vassal, since it is used elsewhere to connote political rather than emotional ties. During his trial, Ganelon maintains that he has always served Charlemagne *par feid e par amur*, and his kinsmen testify to this fact with similar words.[16a] Marsilie had explained to his men that he would pretend to accept Christianity and become Charlemagne's vassal *par amur e par feid* (86), and Pinabel uses the same words in offering to do homage to Thierry (3893). This suggests that these words were a legal formula like the expressions *par amur e par bien* and *par honur e par ben*, which appear elsewhere in the song (121, 38). By such formulas a vassal acknowledged that he owed both his land and his wealth to his liege.[17] When Blancandrin greets Charlemagne *par amur e par bien* (121), he is announcing that his liege Marsilie is offering homage and wealth to the Christian monarch; for he immediately explains that Marsilie will accept Charlemagne's (Christian) law and will give him rich gifts (123–136). In other words, the *amur* that is offered is not love or friendship, but rather servitude.[17a] Before pursuing the fleeing Saracens to avenge Roland, Charlemagne asks his vassals to grant him his feudal rights (*e dreiture*

[16a] 3770; par feid e par amor (3810); par amur e par feid (3801).

[17] When Pinabel tells Thierry: "Tes hom serai par amor e par feid, a tun plaisir te durrai mun aveir" (3893), the second promise means about the same as the formula *par ben*. The formula *par honor e par ben* may be related to the Latin *beneficium et honor* (See Hollyman, pp. 34–35). In the *Lay of the Nibelungs* (1634) Hagen gives Eckewart six gold rings with the words: *die habe dir, helt, ze minnen, daz du mîn friunt sîst*. De Boor and other scholars assume that he means: "Take these as a sign that you are my friend", but the context and the subjunctive mood suggest that he means: "Accept these as a pledge that you will be my ally."

[17a] Although Blancandrin has not specifically mentioned political subordination, Charlemagne assumes it from his message and tells his court that Marsilie has agreed to accept the Christian law and to receive his lands in fief from Charlemagne (189–190). Where Church and State are one, no distinction is possible between religious and political loyalties. The term *par amur e par feid* seems to have legal as well as emotive meaning even in v. 3460. Along with the other barons, Naimes has just renewed his oath of loyalty to Charlemagne (3416), and the latter has just fulfilled his obligation by saving his vassal in battle.

e honur, 2430), which probably designate the military service the vassals owe him as their feudal lord.

While fully at home in the language of literature, many terms in the SR clearly derive from the language of law, and some of these may still retain their precise legal meanings. Among the terms that probably fit this category are *par feid e par amur, par amur e par ben, par honor e par ben, e dreiture e honur, perdre e del quir e del peil, perdre del sanc e de la char, clamer quite,* and *plevir leial.* Although these terms are expressed in words derived from Latin, they probably descend from, or at least are influenced by, ancient Germanic laws. Someone could render a valuable service by investigating these terms, as Peter Wapnewski has so ably done for the legal terms in the 37th canto of the *Lay of the Nibelungs.*[18]

Hate and anger must be virtues in the value code of the SR, since they are constantly attributed to the most exemplary characters. Even though Turpin is a Christian archbishop, his hate makes him kill Corsablix; and Roland, full of rancor, destroys his sword.[19] As we have seen, when Oliver rebukes Roland for not having blown his horn while there was still time, Roland asks him why he bears a grudge against him (*Por quei me portez ire?*, 1722). It appears that *ire* can mean either anger or hate and that the two emotions are often confounded. Throughout the SR the Christians revel in the enemy's suffering. The poet happily tells how the Saracens drown with great agony (*ahan*, 2474); and he dwells on the social humiliation and mental anguish suffered by Marsilie, who loses his right hand and his only son in battle and lives to see his liege lord slain and all hope of vengeance crushed. The loss of his right hand, which was poetic justice for his perfidy, was an especially great shame for a Mohammedan.[20] Because Charlemagne gains satisfaction from Ganelon's torture (3989), it would seem that malice was more admired than mercy.

[18] Wapnewski, pp. 380–410.
[19] Suz ciel n'at hume que tant voeillet hair (1244); rancune (2301).
[20] Strafe des eidbruchs und falschen zeugnisses war abhauen der meineidi-

Roland considers Oliver praiseworthy because he is so angry; Charlemagne suffers *irur* and *grant ire* upon seeing his nephew dead, and the Franks strike with anger (*par ire*) and are full of wrath (*curoçus*).[21] Anger being a virtuous reaction, there is no reason for Bédier to translate *irur* and *ire* in these passages by "douleur" and "angoisse". Similarly, when Charlemagne pulls his beard like a man who is angry (*cum hom ki est iret*, 2414), there is no reason for Bédier to say "en homme rempli d'angoisse". Charlemagne often exhibits great anger: he writes to Marsilie to remind him of the anger (*dolur e ire*, 489) he feels because his envoys have been violated, and he marches *par irur* (1812) and rides *ireement* (1834). When Margariz swears that Charlemagne will never live a day without *doel e ire* (971), these two emotions stand in the same mutual relationship as the *doel* and *rancune* felt by Roland (2301). As we shall see, the concepts of sorrow and anger were more closely associated in the twelfth century than they are today. In this connection it should be noted that the Modern English word "anger" is derived from Old Norse *angr*, which meant anguish.

Of all words in the *SR*, perhaps the word *honur* has the greatest range of meanings. After the battle of Roncevaux, Charlemagne buries his fallen vassals *a grant honor* (2960), that is to say with the respect due their birth and bravery, in which case the word is closest to the original meaning of its Latin source *honos*.[22] Respect is sometimes expressed with words, as is the case of the *granz honurs* (3181) paid to Charlemagne in the chronicles

---

gen hand (*Deutsche Rechsaltertümer*, II, p. 560). Because the left hand was used for performing bodily functions, it could not be used for eating, and a Mohammedan was disgraced if he had to do so. According to Mohammedan law, the amputation of the right hand was (and in some places still is) the punishment for theft.

[21] 1558–1559, 2877, 1654, 1813.

[22] See Friedrich Klose, *Die Bedeutung von honos und honestus*, Diss. Breslau, 1933. For meanings of *honor* in medieval Latin, see Hollyman, p. 33.

(*gestes*). When Ganelon attributes *onur* to Charlemagne (533) and when Falsaron swears that he will deprive France of her *onur* (1223), the word *onur* equals "fame" or "reputation", which is elsewhere designated as *los* (1194). As Thomas Hobbes later observed, honor is the "opinion of power",[23] and therefore it is won through victory and lost through defeat. That is why Falsaron is sure France will lose her *onur* when she is defeated, regardless of how well her soldiers fight. Honor being the meed of victory, the term "honor of the field" (*onur del camp*, 922) was metonymic for "victory".

Because it designated not only respect but also tokens of respect, the word *honur* could be extended to mean high rank or office or the concomitant tenure of land. This is probably what Blancandrin has in mind when he says that the Saracens should lose their hostages rather than lose their *onur* and *deintet* (45). The honor and dignity to which he refers are goods of fortune rather than goods of the spirit, since it was shameful to betray the hostages one has given. Lucien Foulet's glossary to Bédier's commentary explains *deintet* as "les biens" and then adds that it knows of no other example of this use of the word.[24] Actually, the word *deintet* has not changed greatly from its source, *dignitas*, which often designated rank or position. By *deintet* Blancandrin is clearly referring to the Saracens' ruling status or sovereignty in Spain; and therefore the same idea can be expressed as "beautiful Spain" in the following *laisse similaire*.[25]

Since the word *honur* sometimes connoted land tenure, its meaning could be further extended to designate the land itself, therefore to denote a fief.[25a] Ganelon tells his vassals he has left

[23] *Leviathan*, X.
[24] Nous ne connaissons pas d'autre exemple du mot employé en ce sens (Bédier, *Commentaires*, p. 364)
[25] Que nus perduns l'onur ne la deintet (45); Que nus perduns clere Espaigne la bele (59)
[25a] For the association of *honores* and *beneficia*, see Ganshof, pp. 54–58.

all his *honurs* and *fieus* to his son (315); and the Franks think of their *fius* and their *honurs* (820) upon reaching the frontiers of France. After being defeated, Marsilie wishes to return his *onur* (2833) to his liege lord, Baligant. When fair Alde dies, Charlemagne buries her in a convent and then gives *mult grant honur*. Bédier understands this to mean that he honored Alde greatly, but it is more likely that he donated extensive lands to the convent.[26] Whereas Conrad makes no mention of any donation, Stricker (11,285) says that Charlemagne gave the convent an estate (*ein guot*). Transferred still further, the word *honur* can mean glory, splendor, or power, as when Charlemagne organizes his rear guard *par grant honur* (2774). This meaning is also in the *honur* which Charlemagne shows his fallen vassals (2960).

The opposite of *honur* is *honte*, a word derived from the Germanic word **hauniþa*, which originally meant scorn or disdain, like its modern German derivative *Hohn*. Because he cannot resist Charlemagne, Marsilie asks his counselors to advise him how to avoid death and shame (*mort e hunte*, 21); and Ganelon warns him that he will die with *hunte* and with *viltet* (437), which means almost the same thing.[27] The Saracens eventually rebuke Apollin and desecrate his idol for letting them suffer such *hunte* (2582). Climborin asks Ganelon how he can disgrace France (*hunir*, 631), and later he boasts that he will put France to shame (*metrat a hunte*, 1532). Margariz also boasts that the Franks will die and that France will be disgraced (*France en ert hunie*, 969); and Oliver repeats the exact same words after Roland has refused

---

[26] Mult grant honur i ad li reis dunee (3733). Bédier says: "Le roi l'a hautement honorée." Helmut Hatzfeld has called my attention to the fact that the word *spiritualité* underwent a similar development in acquiring the meaning of ecclesiastical possession.

[27] Roland fears that France will fall into *viltet* (1064), and Climborin boasts that he will put her to *hunte* (1532). Balaguez boasts that the Franks will die *a doel e a viltiet* (904), and Charlemagne declares that it would be *mult grant viltet* to do homage to Baligant (3595). The *Karlamagnús saga* renders *a hunte e a viltet* (437) as *með skömm og haðung* (9).

to blow his horn to summon aid (1734). Roland refuses to blow his horn because he would rather die than suffer *huntage* (1091); and Oliver agrees that it would be better for them to die than to be spoken of shamefully.[28] As we have seen, when Roland finally agrees to blow his horn, Oliver reconsiders and warns him that it would be a terrible shame and reproach for his kinsmen, who would suffer disgrace all their lives.[29]

In most of the passages cited above, *hunte* is caused directly by defeat; and in many cases both the noun *hunte* and the verb *hunir* could be translated as "defeat". No matter how valiantly men fought or against what odds, they were generally defamed when defeated. This view is expressed very succinctly in the *Carmen* when Rollandus asks, "Is it not a disgrace to be beaten? Is it not an honor to win?" When Oliverus falls from his horse after fighting valiantly to the bitter end, the poet exclaims, "What a shame! Behold, he lies. What a shame! Behold, he perishes!" [30] We have seen that Bramimunde feels that Marsilie has died *a itel hunte* and that Baligant has died *a si grant hunte;* and it is noteworthy that both suffered shame through defeat. She seems to have overlooked the fact that Baligant died bravely in battle, whereas Marsilie had fled from the field and died in bed.

Defeat being shameful, the modern concept of a "good loser" would have been meaningless to the twelfth-century knights. Unhorsed and pierced by four spears, Turpin refuses to admit he is vanquished (*Ne sui mie vencut,* 2087), but proceeds to kill four hundred more of the enemy. Roland himself goes to great lengths to prove that he has not been beaten. Aware that he is about to die, he takes up his horn and sword and walks in the direction of Spain so that he will not be reproached (*que reproce n'en ait,*

---

[28] Mielz voeill murir que hunte nus seit retraite (1701).

[29] Vergoigne sereit grant e repruver a trestuz vos parenz; iceste hunte dureit al lur vivant (1705–1707).

[30] Vinci nonne pudor? vincere nonne decus? (238); proh pudor! ecce jacet, proh dolor! ecce perit (416).

2263). Finding him unconscious, an Arab approaches to take his sword. When the Arab says, "Charlemagne's nephew is defeated," [31] Roland refutes him by slaying him with his horn.

Upon reaching the battlefield, Charlemagne remembers Roland's former boast that, should he ever die in a foreign country, he would have penetrated it further than any of his men or peers and that he would be found facing the enemy as a victor.[32] In confessing all the sins that he has committed from the day he was born until the day he was struck down, Roland uses the word *consoüt* (2372). Bédier is correct in rendering this as "abattu" rather than as "battu", since Roland acknowledges being struck down by death but not by his enemies. Oliver had previously urged his men to hold the field and not be defeated (1046), and the Saracens had asked Mohammed to aid them against the Franks, who would rather die than abandon the field (1909). Therefore it gratifies Turpin to be able to assure Roland: "The field is yours, thank God, and mine." [33]

Nearly half a millennium after Turold composed his song, Montaigne argued that it can be just as honorable to fight (*combattre*) as to win (*battre*).[34] This modern view is now so generally accepted that scholars sometimes overlook the fact that Roland was a winner rather than a loser. In his introduction to Scott

[31] Vencut est li niés Carles (2281).

[32] Ja ne murreit en estrange regnet ne trespassast ses humes e ses pers; vers lur païs avreit sun chef turnet; cunquerrantment si finereit li bers (2864–2867).

[33] Cist camp est vostre, mercit Deu, vostre e mien (2183).

[34] Le vrai veincre ha pur son rolle l'estour, non pas le salut; et consiste l'honur de la vertu a combattre, non a battre (Montaigne, II, p. 260). His contemporary, Edmund Spenser, followed the older tradition. In the *Faerie Queene* (II, 24, 4) the pagan Sans Foy fights bravely but unsuccessfully, and the poet adds: "There lies he now with foule dishonor dead." The same point of view appears in *The Lusiads*, which Luis Vaz de Camõens wrote in 1571. When the Castillians were defeated by the Portuguese under King João, they grieved at "the loss of life and wealth, at the shame, the dishonour, the grim affront of seeing themselves defeated and despoiled" (*The Lusiads*, IV, p. 110).

Moncrieff's pseudo-archaic translation of the *SR*, G. K. Chesterton states: "Modern history, mainly ethnological or economic, always talks of a thing like the Norman adventure in the somewhat vulgar language of success. For these it is well to note, in the real Norman story, that the very bard in front of their battle line was shouting the glorification of failure. It testifies to a truth in the very heart of Christendom, that even the court poet of William the Conqueror was celebrating Roland the conquered." [35]

This is sheer nonsense, not only because the accounts left by William of Malmesbury and by Wace were probably apocryphal, but also because Chesterton speaks from a nineteenth rather than from a twelfth-century point of view. The *SR* makes it abundantly clear that Turold also talked of Roland's battle "in the vulgar language of success," as did his imitators. Turold lets a Saracen warn that Roland can not be beaten by any man alive; and the *Rolandslied*, the *Roelantslied*, and the *Karlamagnús saga* have the Saracens admit that Roland has defeated them.[36] Turold insists that Roland was not killed by the enemy: he died of exhaustion after killing so many of the enemy and after bursting his skull by blowing his horn.[37] Thus he realized his hope that Charlemagne and his men would say that he died as a conqueror.[38] Even Oliver was not defeated; for, before dying, he killed the man who had so treacherously wounded him in the back (1957).[39] By and large

[35] *The Song of Roland*, trans. C. K. Scott Moncrieff, Ann Arbor Paperbacks, 1959, p. ix.

[36] Ja n'ert vencut pur nul hume carnel (2153); Roland hât uns uberwunden (*RL*, 6724); Roland ende Olivier hebben ons verwonnen (*Roelantslied*, 1205); Rollant hefir yfirkomið oss alla (*KS*, #34). Priest Conrad states specifically: Mit ir tûwerlichen swerten den sige si wol erherten (*RL*, 6719–6720).

[37] De sun cervel le temple en est rumpant (1765).

[38] qu'il fut mort cunquerant (2362–2363).

[39] The *Lay of the Nibelungs* also uses this stratagem to let a hero die without losing his honor. To avoid an invidious comparison between two superlative heroes, it lets them kill each other; dô vielen beide erslagene, Gêrnôt und Rüedegêr, gelîch in dem sturme, von ir selber hant (*NL*, 2221, 2–3).

Father McNamee (p. x) is justified in his contention that, unlike tragedy, "the epic at its core is a success story and not a tale of failure." According to this criterion, the *SR* is a true epic.

To be sure, in some medieval literary works the dishonor suffered in defeat is somewhat mitigated by the hero's defiant death. In fact his exemplary stand often vindicates him and makes him the object of future veneration, as in the case of Beowulf and Byrhtnoth, and also of Hagen in the *Lay of the Nibelungs*. This is probably true to a certain extent of Gualter and most of the peers in the *SR*, yet Turold seems to consider it insufficient vindication for his three chief protagonists at Roncevaux. As we have seen, Oliver escapes defeat by killing the man who has wounded him, and Turpin and Roland live to proclaim themselves victorious.

Just as defeat brought infamy, surrender proved cowardice, no matter what the circumstances. Turpin expresses the prevailing view in saying that a brave man will never cease fighting as long as he lives, and this explains why the Franks would rather die than surrender.[40] More than four centuries elapsed before a captured French king could maintain that "all is lost, save honor," as Francis I did at Pavia.[41] The ignominy of capture is reflected in the word *caitif*, a derivative of Latin *captivus*, which appears in the *SR* in the sense of miserable wretch. The honor of being free and the shame of being unfree are reflected in the complimentary use of the adjective *franc*, with which both Charlemagne and Baligant address their vassals (274, 2657). The word *franc* naturally implied all the qualities conventionally associated with good birth, such as courage, pride, and liberality. It will be noted that in v. 2657 it is consociated with *vaillant*.

Like the Japanese in World War II, the twelfth-century Franks branded surrender as desertion, irrespective of the circumstances. The verb for "to surrender" was *recreire*, a derivative of Latin

---

[40] Ja pur murir cil n'erent recreanz (3048).
[41] Tout est perdu, fors l'honneur (in 1525).

recredere (to change religion). The original meaning of the word may linger when Roland wishes to make all lands *recreant* (393); for conquered pagan lands were converted to Christianity by fire and sword if necessary. This meaning may hold also when Ganelon dies a shameful death as fits a *recreant* (3973), because he has apostatized by aiding the pagans. During the crusades it was not unknown for Christian units to desert to the enemy and accept their religion, as Alphonse VI of Castile once threatened to do when he joined the Moslem king of Saragossa.

The *SR* sometimes uses the word *recreire* merely in the sense of to tire of fighting. Marsilie asks Ganelon when Charlemagne will tire of campaigning; Marsilie's nephew assures him that he will kill Roland and liberate Spain so that Charlemagne will tire and the Franks will stop fighting, and Balaguer promises to make Charlemagne tire of fighting.[42] Bédier renders the words *si recrerrunt si Franc* as "les Français se rendront", yet surrender is not necessarily implied. This is evident enough during Ganelon's trial when Pinabel offers to become Thierry's vassal and give him his wealth if only he will stop fighting.[43] Bédier translates *car te recreiz* as "reconnais-toi vaincu", but it is unlikely that Pinabel would offer homage to a man who has just surrendered to him. He is not asking Thierry to surrender, but merely to cease fighting.[43a] Nevertheless, Thierry cannot do so for fear of risking reproach.[44] Because it was shameful to break off hostilities without winning, Rollandus in the *Carmen* is indignant (*indignans*, 21)

---

[42] Quant ert il mais recreanz d'osteier (528, 543); Las serat Carles, si recrerrunt si Franc (871); Recreanz ert de sa guerre mener (906). In other words, the meaning of *recreanz* was often close to that of its modern cognate *recru*.

[43] car te recreiz! Tes hom serai par amur e par feid, a tun plaisir te durrai mun aveir (3892).

[43a] Conrad must have understood the passage this way, for he lets Thierry have the upper hand at this point. Pinabel, who has just received a serious head wound, offers to give up his sword if Thierry will reconcile Charlemagne with Ganelon (*RL*, 8929–8945).

[44] Tut seie fel, se jo mie l'otrei (3897).

when Karolus decides to discontinue his Spanish campaign without taking Saragossa.[45] It being understood that people stop fighting through defeat and defeatism rather than through love of peace, the word *recreant* often implied cowardice, as when the pagans say that anyone should be branded a coward for letting the enemy escape.[46]

Victory was not the only requirement for winning honor. Turold seems to express his idea of an honorable man in Ganelon's description of Charlemagne: "No one sees or gets to know him who does not say that the Emperor is brave (*ber*). I could never praise or laud him enough because he has more honor and *bontet* than I could say. Who could tell of his great worth (*valor*)? God has distinguished him with such courage (*barnage*) that he would rather die than abandon his barons (*barnet*)." [47] Because encomiums of medieval rulers invariably stress liberality, I prefer to translate *bontet* as "bounty" or "largess" rather than as "virtues", as Bédier does.[48]

In preferring to die rather than abandon his barons, Charlemagne is practicing the medieval ideal of fealty, a virtue denoted in German texts as *triuwe*. This fealty worked in both directions, from liege to man and from man to liege. Roland extols such devotion twice. He says, "For his lord a vassal must suffer hardship and endure great heat and cold and lose hide and hair"; and later he expresses the same idea in slightly varied words as: "For his

[45] Elsewhere in the *Carmen* the word *indignans* is used in connection with affronts. When Rollandus volunteers to go on the dangerous mission in place of Gueno, the latter becomes insanely furious, fury grieves him, indignation burns him, and anger weighs him down (55–56).

[46] recreant ki les lerrat guarir (2063).

[47] N'est hom kil veit e conuistre le set Que ço ne diet que l'emperere est ber. Tant nel vos sai ne preiser ne loer Que plus n'i ad d'onur e de bontet. Sa grant valor, kil purreit acunter? De tel barnage l'ad Deus enluminet Meilz voelt murir que guerpir sun barnet (530–536).

[48] His translation says "vertus". The glossary to his commentary says "valeur morale" (Bédier, *Commentaires*, p. 342). In v. 2507 *bontet* refers to the bounty of God.

lord a vassal must suffer great harm and endure great cold and heat and lose both blood and flesh." [48a] Priest Conrad praises the Franks' fidelity by saying that Charlemagne's men would seek death rather than desert their lord because of any peril or fail to bring him from the battle with honor.[48b] Turold's barons assure Charlemagne that they will not fail him in battle (3344), and their actions prove their words.

If the word *cumpaignie* in v. 1735 refers to the rear guard,[48c] then Roland is correct in calling it a *leial cumpaignie*, for they later die for him to the last man. The members of a military retinue owed loyalty to each other as well as to their lord, and it is only proper that Turpin, Gualter, and Roland do not wish to leave each other. Turold calls these three respectively a *noble guerrer*, a *bon chevaler*, and a *prozdom* and then adds that "not one of them wished to abandon the other" (*Li uns ne volt l'altre nient laisser*, 2069). This implies that loyalty was a prerequisite of a "noble" or "good" warrior. Ganelon too would have been a good warrior if he had remained loyal to Charlemagne.[49]

Ganelon shows loyalty to his kinsmen in refusing to let them accompany him on the perilous mission to Saragossa, and they later repay his loyalty by standing his bail. Bédier explains the words *.XXX. parenz l'i plevissent leial* (3847) as "Trente parents s'offrent en loyaux otages", but this explanation is not syntactically satisfying, since it is not Turold's practice to interpose a

---

[48a] Pur sun seignor deit hom susfrir destreiz E endurer e granz chalz e granz freiz, sin deit hom perdre e del quir e del peil (1010–1012); Pur sun seignor deit hom susfrir granz mals E endurer e forz freiz e granz chalz, sin deit hom perdre del sanc e de la char (1117–1119).

[48b] Der kaiser erwelte im selbe zehenzec tûsent helde, di sîn in allen cîten huten: di helde wâren sô gemute, daz si ê sûchten den tôt, denne si durch dehainer slachte nôt chômen von ir herren sine brêchten in mit êren von dem volcwîge (*RL,* 7871–7879).

[48c] See note 52 below.

[49] S'il fust leials, ben resemblast barun (3764). This thought is expressed in the *Waltharius* (1411) when Walter says that Hagen is a good warrior (*athleta bonus*) if he keeps the law of faith (*fidei si jura reservet*).

nonlinking verb between a subject and its modifier. One might expect *leial* to be a predicate accusative singular referring to Ganelon, rather than a nominative plural referring to the kinsmen. In other words, they pledged that he would keep his parole. In this case the expression *plevir leial* would fit the pattern *abatre mort* and the verse would resemble the syntax of v. 2531 (*Senefiance l'en demustrat mult gref*). In any case, *plevir leial* seems to be a legal term used in connection with paroling prisoners; for it will be noted that Ganelon is freed on bail, while his bondsmen are kept in custody.[50] The word *leial* appears to have legal meaning in the term *tenir leial prison*, which Chrétien later used of some prisoners who are released from confinement on their word that they will not try to escape or to injure their captors.[51] Even though *leial* had acquired the meaning of *fidelis,* it had not entirely lost its original meaning of *legalis.* Oliver probably intends both the emotive and the legal meanings when he tells Roland that their *leial cumpaignie* will end (1735), whether this refers to the end of their personal alliance or to the destruction of Roland's loyal and legally obligated following.[52]

Despite all his literary pretensions, the author of the *Carmen* actually gives a clearer description of the ideal ruler than Turold does, even if it may not be very original.[53] He calls Charlemagne

[50] Charlemagne releases Ganelon upon the bond of his kinsmen, whom he then puts under guard ("E jol vos recrerai." Fait cels guarder tresque li dreiz en serat., vv. 3848–49). Perhaps they will be chained, as Ganelon was when he was "guarded". See vv. 1826, 1829.

[51] N'en tors n'en fers ne les ont mis, Fors qu'il plevirent solement, Come chevalier leaument, Que il loial prison tendroient Ne ja nul mal ne lor feroient . . . (*Perceval,* vv. 2518–22).

[52] Bédier and most other critics assume that the *leial cumpaignie* refers to the alliance between Roland and Oliver. To judge by the previous *laisse,* it would seem that Oliver is more distressed by Charlemagne's loss of the rear guard (including Roland and himself) than he is by the termination of *compagnonage,* which he himself has implicitly terminated in vv. 1720–21. In v. 1087 Oliver uses the word *cumpaigne* to mean a military "company".

[53] Roland is described somewhat similarly in a complaint by Charlemagne in the *Pseudo-Turpin* (XXVII, 46–53). These attributes, which were com-

"the shield of the empire, protector of the faithful, contemnor of wrong, upholder of right, fierce in war, distinguished in family, outstanding in body, virtuous in mind, blessed with riches, mighty in honors." [54] It is evident that the *SR* also attributes these desirable qualities to Charlemagne.

Charlemagne is a wealthy emperor (*empereres riches*, 718) who can reduce rich kings to poverty.[55] His wealth is reflected in his vassals Ganelon, Roland, and Gaifers, all of whom are designated as *riches;* for a vassal usually held his lands in fief from his liege.[56] It is to be remembered that medieval men drew little distinction between wealth and power.[57] Wealthy men could increase their power by hiring mercenaries as Charlemagne does in the *SR* (*soldeiers*, 34, 133); or, to put the horse before the cart, powerful men were always wealthy as long as club-law allowed them to take as much of their neighbors' property as their power enabled them. The word *riches*, which was derived from Old High German *rihhi*, was cognate not only with *rich, riche,* and *reich,* but also with *Reich* and *rex;* and its basic meaning was rule or power rather than wealth. Clariën speaks redundantly in telling that the Emir is *riches e puisant* (2731). Another complimentary epithet is *poesteïfs* (powerful), which is twice used of Charlemagne (460, 2133).

---

monplaces in encomiums of virtuous rulers, derived from Suetonius and other Roman writers. A fine example of this topos is found in Hartmann's *Armer Heinrich* (vv. 50–74).

[54] Rex Karolus, clipeus regni, tutela piorum, Contemptor sceleris, sanctio juris erat; Marte ferus, stirpe resignis, corpore prestans, Mente pius, rebus faustus, honore potens (*Carmen,* 3–6).

[55] Tanz riches reis conduit a mendisted (527).

[56] *riche* (585, 798, 2720). In offering homage to Thierry, Pinabel says: "Tes hom serai par amur e par feid, a tun plaisir te durrai mun aveir" (vv. 3893–94). As previously mentioned, this practice may be reflected in the formulas *par amur e par bien* (121) and *par amur e par ben* (38).

[57] This confusion is echoed in modern expressions like: "He is a man of means"; "ein vermögender Mann"; "nach meinen nicht sehr grossen Kräften"; etc.

A man owed his power not only to his individual strength but also to that of his family. Ganelon's men tell him that Roland should never have assigned the dangerous Spanish mission to a man of such a great family (*que estrait estes de mult grant parented*, 356). Bédier renders this as "vous êtes issu d'un trop grand lignage," but Mortier comes closer with "Qui êtes né de haute parenté." As we will see, ancestry was considered important, yet *parented* in this passage is better translated as "kindred", since it refers chiefly to Ganelon's living kinsmen who will come to his defense, like Pinabel, who fights for him because he wishes to support the *parented* (3907). What Curtis Watson (445) says of family loyalty in Elizabethan England holds equally well of that in twelfth-century France: "Because the sense of family loyalty was so great, one identified oneself completely with the other members of one's family." Roland's dying thoughts about "the men of his lineage" (*des humes de sun lign*, 2379) are probably directed toward his living kinsmen rather than toward his remote ancestors. The author of *Aliscans*, a somewhat later *chanson de geste*, regrets that the hero will lose his *lin* in the coming battle; and later the hero complains to God that he has lost the flower of his *lignage*.[58] Here the two words obviously refer to the hero's contemporaries rather than to his ancestors.

Roland and his peers are all of good birth, and the adjective *noble* is attributed to him, Turpin, and Naimes (2066, 2237, 3442). The first time it modifies *guerrer*, the second time *barun*, and the third time *vassal*; and thus it appears that the adjective *noble* suggested military qualities rather than any of the Stoic or Christian virtues later associated with the word in didactic literature, which argued that true nobility is nobility of behavior rather than nobility of birth.[59] When Ganelon singlehandedly defies the entire

[58] tot son lin (*Aliscans*, v. 326); De mon lignage ai hui perdu la flor (v. 432). Cf. Car de mon lin ai perdu la clarté (v. 805e).

[59] In his eighth satire, Juvenal had questioned the value of noble birth and claimed that "Nobilitas sola est atque unica virtus." Medieval church-

Saracen court, the pagans say: "This is a noble baron!" (*Noble baron ad ci!*, 467), in which case they are referring primarily to his courage.

Good birth is so prevalent in aristocratic literature that it does not need to be mentioned, as it is when Roland calls Archbishop Turpin a knight of good family (*chevaler de bon aire*, 2252). It being assumed that only wellborn people are courageous, the accusation of humble birth is a most degrading insult; and therefore Roland insults his stepfather Ganelon unpardonably when he calls him "Son-of-a-serf, lowly man of ignoble family" (*culvert, malvais hom de put aire*, 763). When Aelroth insults Charlemagne, Roland kills him and calls him a *culvert* (1207); and Oliver calls Falsaron a *culvert* (1232) in an identical situation. The word *culvert* (from *collibertus*, a freedman) literally meant serf or freedman,[60] but by metonymy it mean coward. In other words, it meant just the opposite of *franc*.

Another word of opprobrium is *bris* (acc. *bricun*) in v. 220, which Jenkins defines as "one who is without wealth or power . . . without honor . . . and incapable of resenting affronts."[61] No amount of Christian virtue would have vindicated such a contemptible creature. If Ganelon uses this deprecating term of himself,[61a] it may be a mere *mea parvitas* formula like those so often used by subjects to their sovereigns; yet in this particular case the term probably has deep psychological import. This is the only time that the *SR* uses this word, or any like it, in the first

---

men and didactic writers repeated this thought in myriad variations, usually with the moral that a truly noble man is one who obeys God's commandments.

[60] See Hollyman, pp. 155–62.

[61] See Jenkins, note to v. 220. This is a far more suitable explanation than the word "drôle", which is given in Bédier's commentary (Bédier, *Commentaires*, p. 343).

[61a] In opposition to most critics, André Burger believes that Ganelon uses the word *bricun* in v. 220 to refer to Roland, since he is paraphrasing his words "Ja mar crerez Marsilie!" ("Le Rire de Roland," p. 8).

person; and this suggests that Ganelon is sensitive about his own dignity, which has recently been threatened by his more successful stepson. Such psychological insecurity would help explain his violent reaction to Roland's ridicule.

People of humble birth being contemptible, it was a grievous indignity to be put into their power; and consequently Charlemagne places the traitor Ganelon into the custody of his cooks with orders to treat him as a *felon* (1819). By setting him on a pack horse to dishonor him,[62] the cooks symbolically eject him from the military élite and thrust him down into the scorned world of the working classes. Ganelon is later whipped by some serfs (*serf*, 3737), a double ignominy because both the agents and the punishment suited a man of low degree. Being dismembered by four horses was grievous not so much because it was painful as because it was degrading. This is suggested by one of the earliest references to Ganelon's death. A loyalty oath inscribed on the wall of the cathedral of Nepi near Rome in 1130 or 1131 is followed by the statement that anyone who breaks his word will suffer the shameful (*turpissima*) death suffered by the traitor Ganelon.[63]

The SR contains several words referring to birth and social status which deserve careful scrutiny. When Roland calls Archbishop Turpin *gentilz hom* (2177), Bédier renders it as "gentil seigneur", which would suggest some of the overtones of the modern English word "gentleman". Actually, this word, in its modern sense, would hardly fit the belligerent archbishop because of his unchivalrous treatment of his victims (1253–1259); and therefore Mortier is wise to translate *gentilz hom* by the less emotive word "gentilhomme". The same holds true when Bédier and Mortier render *li gentilz reis* (2321) as "le gentil roi", since

---

[62] Sur un sumer l'unt mis a deshonor (1828).

[63] item turpissimam sustineat mortem, ut Ganelonem, qui suos tradidit socios (cited by Boissonnade, p. 442).

Charlemagne was far from gentle, genteel, or *gentil*. When Gualter addresses Roland as *gentilz quens, vaillanz hom* (2045), the two adjectives are equivalent, even though Bédier renders *gentilz* with "gentil" as usual.

The SR is so aristocratic in tenor that even the Saracens must all be of royal or at least noble blood in order to be worthy of their foemen's steel. There is no mention whatever of the lower classes, except one insinuation that soldiers of low degree might despoil the dead. Upon leaving the battlefield at Roncevaux to pursue Marsilie, Charlemagne posts a guard to see that the corpses are not molested by beast or lion or *esquier* or *garçun* (2437). These last two terms, which appear nowhere else in the song, must be derogatory. The word *garçun* usually meant "valet" and therefore suggests servile status. Because of the context, the word *esquier* in this passage should be translated as "shield-bearer" or "groom" rather than as "squire", since the latter word now suggests a young nobleman in training to become a knight and not a young man of low degree who would rob a corpse.

The adjective *gentilz* refers directly to good birth rather than to any specific attributes associated with it. If it denoted qualities inherent in good birth, it would refer to wealth, power, and courage rather than to gentleness or gentility, since it most often appears in conjunction with the former qualities. When Oliver is called *proz* and *gentilz* (176), the words are somewhat synonymous, as is the case with *proz* and *vaillanz* (3186). This is certainly the way Blancandrin intends the word when he says that the Franks are *mult gentilz home* (377), for he is in no way concerned with their refinement or amiability. Mortier renders the thought as "vrais gentilhommes", but this too fails to suggest Blancandrin's concern for the Franks' military virtues.

It will be seen that Ganelon's kinsmen call him *gentilz* (3811) even after he is proved a traitor; and this indicates that the epithet was a title of good birth which was not forfeited through questionable behavior.[64] On the other hand, it may only mean that Turold followed the literary convention of using standing epithets without regard to their applicability in a given passage. It is evident that, despite their differences in personality, most of the heroes in the *SR* share the small number of often repeated epithets. Bédier renders *cum chevaler gentill* (1853) as "en gentil chevalier" and Mortier renders it as "en chevalier gentil", even though these modern French expressions suggest attitudes of kindness and courtesy hardly associated with the Old French term. As we have seen, the word *chevaler* referred to any cavalryman.

Where Ganelon calls Oliver *li proz e li curteis* (576), Bédier and Mortier render this as "le preux et le courtois". The modern *courtois*, however, like English "courteous", has acquired overtones of kindness not implied in the word *curteis*, which can better be rendered by "courtly".[65] If we may trust the theory of consociation, the word *curteis* in Ganelon's statement means the same as the *proz;* for strength and courage, rather than polished manners, were the chief requisites of a courtier as long as royal courts were primarily military headquarters. The word *curteis* had little to do with the way in which a Boy Scout is supposed to be "courteous". Turold's Frankish contemporaries were impressed by the refined behavior at the Saracen courts in Spain, yet such courtly conduct does not seem to have flourished in medieval European literature until introduced in the works of Chrétien de Troyes.

The word *gent*, from Latin *genitus*, appears in the *SR* with many meanings, most of which refer to qualities worthy of being

---

[64] In the *Lay of the Nibelungs* Siegfried, in dying, addresses Gunther as "Noble King" (*künic edele, NL*, 996, 2), although aware that he was an accomplice in the treacherous attack.

[65] The same error is made by the Germans who translate *hövisch* as *höflich*.

attributed to, or associated with, people of gentle birth. Among these are strong or handsome (*gent ad le cors*, 118, 1159), mighty (*gente chevalerie*, 594), violent (*gente bataille*, 1274; *colps genz*, 1712), rich (*eschec bel e gent*, 1167), beautiful (*muillers gentes e beles*, 3398), and additional indefinite qualities. The adverb *gentement* in verse 2099 means "violently" or "vigorously".

The heroes of the *SR* show no aversion toward boasters and boasting. Roland brags that he has won many of Charlemagne's campaigns (198–200); and he boasts that he will perform his rearguard action successfully (755–759, 787–791). Charlemagne remembers how Roland promised to surpass both vassals and peers in battle and to end as victor (2864). In praising Oliver's prowess, Roland includes himself by saying that "Charlemagne loves *us* for such strokes." [66] During the battle he constantly boasts that he will destroy the enemy, and he is not too modest to tell Oliver that he has struck hard blows.[67] In fact he has such an excellent opinion of himself that he knows of no higher praise for Oliver than to say that Oliver's deeds may be compared with his own.[68] As we have seen, he is confident that everyone knows that he is unafraid of threats; and he is sure that people think only a fool would try to take his sword.[68a] He tells his sword that it has belonged to a brave hero (*mult bon vassal*, 2310) and adds that there will never be another sword like it (or another vassal like himself?).[69] Even at death's door he gloats over his previous vic-

[66] Pur itels colps nos ad Charles plus cher (1560).

[67] 1058, 1069, 1077–1079; 1712. After Oliver's death Roland boasts to Turpin that Durendal has struck the best blows (Les colps des mielz, cels sunt de Durendal, 2143). Jenkins must have overlooked these last boasts, since he says that v. 1559 is the latest instance of Roland's boasting (note to v. 2311).

[68] Ço dist Rollanz: "mis cumpainz est irez, encuntre mei fait asez a preiser" (1558–1559).

[68a] Ço set hom ben n'ai cure de manace (293); Ne l'orrat hume ne t'en tienget por fol (2294).

[69] Jamais n'ert tel(s) en France l'asolue (2311). The Oxford MS reads *tel*, which would refer to the sword (*espede*). Bédier and most other critics prefer this reading. Gaston Paris preferred *tels*, which would refer to *vassals*.

tories (2322–2334). Charlemagne himself seems compelled to claim credit for his own exploits. After rescuing Naimes from a difficult situation, he tells him that he himself has killed the enemy who has so grievously wounded him. To be sure, he says this in order to console Naimes with the assurance that he has been avenged, yet he does take personal credit for the deed and Naimes does acknowledge his obligation.[70] The *miles gloriosus* was not always a comic character in the twelfth century, as he had been a millennium earlier and as he became half a millennium later.

A major reward for brave deeds was the right to boast of them. Upon mortally wounding Oliver, Marganice says that Charlemagne will have no right to praise himself for the harm he has done the Saracens, because he has been unable to defend his vassal.[71] In turn, Oliver strikes Marganice dead and taunts him that he will never be able to boast to any woman or lady of having killed him.[72] Men have always enjoyed boasting before women, just as stags and cocks strut before does and hens; and it is likely that ladies were present when the Franks boasted at their celebrations of great battles and violent assaults.[73] Just as Oliver kills Marganice to prevent him from boasting of his victory, so must Charlemagne execute Ganelon to keep him from boasting of be-

---

The author of the *Pseudo-Turpin* seems to have preferred the former thought. He writes: A spata felicissima, acutissimarum acutissima, cui similis non fuit nec erit amplius (XXVI, 24–25).

[70] "Bel sire Naimes, kar chevalcez od mei! Morz est li gluz ki en destreit vus teneit; El cors li mis mun espiet une feiz." Respunt li dux: "Sire, jo vos en crei. Se jo vif alques, mult grant prod i avreiz" (3455–3459).

[71] nen est dreiz qu'il s'en lot (1950).

[72] ne a muiler ne a dame . . . n'en vanteras (1960–1961). The same motif appears in the *Waltharius* when Walter resists the Franks to keep them from boasting to their wives that they have despoiled him (v. 562) and later when he kills Randolf to keep him from boasting to his bride (vv. 979–80).

[73] See George F. Jones, "Lov'd I not honour more," *Comparative Literature*, XI, pp. 131–43; se vanterent . . . de granz batailles, de forz esturs pleners (2861–2862).

traying Roland.[74] It should be remembered that, for Turold, the word *vanter* lacked the negative overtones of our word "to boast", even though the Christian Church had been preaching *vanitas vanitatum* for centuries. There was nothing shameful in boasting, but only in failing to carry out one's boasts. The vaunt before the attack was crowned by the taunt after the victory.

Boasts served the military purpose of goading men to even greater endeavor. By boasting of his past deeds, a successful warrior exalted himself and thus spurred his less conspicuous or still untried comrades to emulate him in future engagements. By boasting of his future deeds, a warrior staked his honor on a fulfillment of his boasts and thus committed himself irrevocably to the battle. This principle is well-illustrated in the *Battle of Maldon*, an Anglo-Saxon ballad that somewhat resembles the *SR* in ethos.[75] Because they have boasted during battle, Byrhtnoth, Ælfwine, and Leofsunu must carry out their boasts or die in the attempt, just as the twelve Saracen peers must do in the *SR*. Ælfwine even announces that they will now have a chance to justify the boasts they have previously made during their drinking bouts.[76] In like manner Roland must justify the boast he made at a high festival that he would advance further than any of his men and that he would die as a conqueror (2860–2867). In other words, the morale and performance of the troops in battle are enhanced by their boasting over their cups.

One of the *SR*'s most frequent epithets is *fiers*. Both Roland and Anseis are *fiers* (28, 105, 796), Ganelon and Charlemagne speak

---

[74] Hom ki traïst altre, nen est dreiz qu'il s'en vant (3974).

[75] Frederick Whitehead is rather exceptional in detecting a great difference of outlook between Turold and the *Maldon* poet. He feels that the former condemns Roland's *desmesure* whereas the latter did not condemn Byrhtnoth's *ofermod* (pp. 115–17). However, he does see that the military ethos is similar: "Il est vrai que l'arrièregarde constitue en quelque sorte le *comitatus* de Roland et que les barons qui la composent font preuve d'un dévouement aussi aveugle que celui des compagnons de Byrhtnoth" (pp. 116–17).

[76] *Battle of Maldon*, vv. 45–61, 212–24, 246–53.

fierement (219, 2984), and Charlemagne rides *fierement* (739, 3316). The Franks ride with *grant fiertet* (1183), and Roland is *de tant grant fiertet* (2152) that no mortal man will ever defeat him. These random examples indicate that the word *fiers* does not designate pride, as most critics assume. Rather it designates fierceness or ferocity, as one might expect of a development of the Latin word *ferus*.[77] This is obvious when Roland makes himself more *fiers* than a lion or a leopard (1111), when the Franks fight as fiercely as lions (*si fiers cume leuns*, 1888), and when Charlemagne dreams that he sees a leopard attack *fierement* (729). *Fiers* probably means "fierce" when Turpin says that a knight should be *forz e fiers* in battle (1879) and when Charlemagne looks *fierement* at Ganelon for nominating Roland for the dangerous rearguard mission (745).

The word *fiers* means fierce even when it describes Charlemagne's countenance (*cuntenant fier*, 118; *mult par out fier lu vis*, 142); for it was fitting for an austere emperor to have a withering glance, like many chieftains in Germanic literature.[78] Roland too could be recognized by his *fier visage* (1640), even by a total stranger like the pagan Grandonie, who at once attempts to flee. Because neither our Christian nor our Stoic tradition recognizes ferocity as a virtue, critics have tended to misconstrue the word *fiers* and to render it by "fier" or "proud" in all cases except where

---

[77] The *Carmen* uses *ferus* in much the way that the SR uses *fiers*. For example: Corde tumens, ira succensus, cede cruentus, Rollandus magis est quam fuit ante ferus (*Carmen*, 323–324). As we have seen, Karolus is *Marte ferus* (v. 5).

[78] See also vv. 895, 1111, 2802, 3161. In *Raoul de Cambrai* (v. 3579) Guerri's countenance is more *fiers* than a wild boar, and it is obvious that wild boars are more noted for their ferocity than for their pride (Par contenance fu plus fiers d'un sengler). Cf. plus fiers que un sengler (*Aliscans*, v. 2565). In the *Lay of Ríg* Jarl has a glance as fierce as that of a snake. In the *Lay of the Nibelungs* Volker has such *swinde blicke* that the Huns dare not attack him (*NL*, 1795, 4. Cf. 413, 3; 1734, 4). Tacitus himself had commented on the Teutons' *truces et caerulei oculi* (*Germania*. #4).

this would be absurd.[79] The word *fiers* clearly retains its older meaning in the name Fierabras, the hero of a *chanson de geste* of that name; for a man's arm is more likely known for its ferocity than for its pride.

Ganelon accuses Roland of being haughty (*orguillos*, 474, 1774) and predicts that his *orgoilz* (389) will cause his downfall; and he disapproves of haughty counsel (*cunseill d'orguill*, 228). Roland dislikes men who are *orguillos* (2135) and accuses Ganelon of that fault (292). Escremiz accuses the Franks of *orgoill*, and Roland makes the same accusation against the pagans (934, 1592). Since everyone attributes this quality to his enemy (28, 2978, 3132), it appears that *orgoill*, unlike *fiertet*, was sometimes contemned. Whereas it was always praiseworthy to be proud and fierce, it was sometimes blameworthy to be haughty or arrogant.

Nevertheless, this professed disapproval of arrogance must have been largely theoretical; for most of the characters of the epic behave arrogantly, especially the most admirable ones. Certainly Roland's braggadocio is the epitome of haughtiness (2316–2334). The avowed contempt for haughtiness was a recent and still unassimilated attitude, no doubt of Christian origin and based on clerical condemnation of *superbia*. Although hard to prove, it seems that the Franks understood *orgoill* to mean self-glorification that can not be backed up by deeds.[79a] While the Saracens often call the Franks *orguillos*, the poet does not. On the other hand he does attribute the fault to the Saracens, who are unable to carry out their threats.

[79] For example, Bédier says *hardi* (1111, 1879), *hardiment* (799), *de si fière hardiesse* (2152), *durement* (745), and *menaçant* (1162) in the cases where *fier* would be meaningless, but in most other cases he says *fier*, even where the context implies ferocity (56, 256, 2125).

[79a] When Ganelon threatens to get even with Roland for nominating him to the rear guard, Roland calls his threat *orgoill* and *folage* (292). This does not imply that he thought it wrong for a warrior to threaten his enemy, but only that it was folly for Ganelon to threaten him.

The Saracens also dislike *orgoill*, at least on the part of the Franks; and Escremiz boasts that he will lay low their *orgoill* at Roncevaux.[79b] This does not prove that he rejects *orgoill* in principle, but merely that he does not think the Franks justified in their confidence, since they will soon meet defeat. Because *orgoill* often denoted vainglory that could not be supported by action, it was naturally "wrong" in a society that accepted trials by combat as proof of right. If a contestant lost after boasting that he would win, his defeat proved that his opponent had *droit* while he and his own boasts were wrong;[80] and consequently Roland associates *orguilz* with *torz* (1592). Whereas the word *orgoill* generally has pejorative meaning in the SR, it seems to be complimentary on one occasion, namely when Baligant is described as wise (*saives*) but also *orgoillus* (3175). The adverb *orgoillusement* is distinctly complimentary in v. 3199, since the pagan Malpramis is speaking very favorably of the Franks.

During the battle Roland looks fiercely toward the Saracens and humbly and gently toward the Franks.[81] This thought is clearly a *topos* handed down from the time of Euripides, which was especially popular during the Middle Ages and traveled as far as Iceland.[82] But this is learned lore rather than national behavior, for people considered humility a sign of physical cowardice rather than of moral courage. The word *humilitet* (73) is used only of the surrender or homage promised by the Saracens.[83] This would

[79b] En Rencesvals irai l'orgoill desfaire (934). In his eulogy, Roland says that no man was ever better than Oliver at defeating proud men (*orgoillos veintre*, 2211).

[80] This point of view is well illustrated in Gottfried of Strassburg's *Tristan* when the hero exults at having brought low his victim's arrogance: "der rehte und der gewære got und gotes wærlich gebot die habent din unreht wol bedaht, und reht an mir ze rehte braht. der müeze min ouch vürbaz pflegen! disiu hohvart diust gelegen" (*Tristan*, 7075–7080).

[81] Vers Sarrazins reguardet fierement e vers Franceis humeles e dulcement (1162–1163).

[82] See Jones, "Grim to your Foes . . .".

[83] According to Werner Betz, the Christian concept of *humilitas* was

have caused them great humiliation, just as it would have been *viltet* if Charlemagne had done homage to Baligant (3595).

Admission of inferior worth would have indicated cowardice rather than Christian humility or Stoic modesty, and for that reason the heroes of the *SR* must constantly struggle to maintain their status. This explains the psychological motivation for Ganelon's indignation when Roland nominates him for the mission to Saragossa. Most critics assume that Ganelon resents the danger inherent in the mission, but his bravado at the Saracen court belies that charge. Robert A. Hall, Jr. has correctly recognized that Ganelon is offended because his stepson has nominated him "after Charlemagne has indicated that Roland, Oliver, and the other Peers are too valuable to send on this mission—thereby implying that whoever is sent is obviously 'expendable' and inferior in worth to the Twelve Peers." [84] By endorsing Roland's choice, Charlemagne publicly confirms Ganelon's inferiority and thus lowers his prestige.

A warrior enhanced his prestige most by bragging in the face of the enemy. Such boasting, called *gab,* raised the morale of the boaster and also committed him to the combat.[85] It also induced psychological superiority and shamed the enemy into attacking without caution. When the word *gab* appears in Old French literature, translators often render it as "pleasantry" or "joke", even when the original meaning of bragging clearly predominates. At the sound of Roland's horn, Ganelon tries to convince Charle-

---

rendered in Old High German as *diomuoti,* which meant the disposition of a vassal (*Gesinnung eines Gefolgsmannes*). See *Deutsche Wortgeschichte,* ed. F. Maurer & F. Stroh. Berlin, 1959, I. 115.

[84] Hall, "On Individual Authorship . . .", p. 298.

[85] Das Bedürfnis des Deutschen, sich bei feindlicher That zu steigern und dem Gegner überlegen zu erweisen, macht den Helden vor dem Kampfe beredt; er strebt danach, den Gegner zornig zu machen. Deshalb reizen einander die Krieger vor der Schlacht, die Helden der Sage vor dem Kampf. Der grimme Hohn, welcher den Gegner traf, bevor der Speer ihn erreichen konnte, wurde höchlich bewundert (Freytag, I, p. 204). This custom, which seems to have been international, also appears in Latin literature.

magne that Roland is not summoning help but merely showing off before his peers (*Devant ses pers vait il ore gabant,* 1781). Bédier explains this as "c'est quelque jeu qu'il fait devant ses pairs," and Mortier explains it as "Devant ses pairs, il s'en va plaisantant." Teissier (p. 47) renders it even more freely by saying "il est sans doute en train de rire avec ses pairs." It is of note that Roland is showing off before his peers, in both meanings of the word *peers* (both *patricios* and *pares*). Hearing Charlemagne's horns, the pagans know he is coming and at once cease their *gab* (2113). This probably means that they stopped boasting of slaying Turpin, rather than that they stopped laughing, as Bédier and Mortier explain.[86]

As we have seen, an individual's honor depended upon his family's power and was therefore a family matter. As Franz Settegast (p. 4) says of the *chansons de geste:* "The honor or dishonor of the individual does not remain restricted to him but is imparted at once to the whole kinship. Thus the honor of the kinship forms a common treasure zealously guarded by its members, who endeavor diligently to increase it." This is borne out in the *SR* when Pinabel says that he wishes to protect his entire kinship.[87]

In offering to fight Pinabel, Thierry tells Charlemagne that he is obligated to prosecute the case *par anceisurs* (3826). Bédier explains this as "faithful to the example of my ancestors", and Ruggero Ruggieri says in the most thorough study of this episode: "Through his ancestors, that is to say, through the nobility of his forebears." [88] Nevertheless, the context in the song and the customs of the time indicate that Thierry had to prosecute the case

---

[86] Bédier renders *nel tindrent mie en gab* as "ils n'ont garde d'en rire", and Foulet's glossary renders *gab* here as "plaisanterie" (Bédier, *Commentaires,* p. 395). Mortier says, "de s'en rire ils n'ont garde."

[87] Sustenir voeill trestut mun parentet (3907).

[88] Fidèle à l'exemple de mes ancêtres (Bédier); Voglio far notare che Tierry no in grazia di un proprio particolare ufficio giuridico attesta il suo diritto, ma semplicemente 'per gli antenati', cioè per la nobilità dei suoi avi (Ruggieri, p. 66). Mortier says, "Par mes aïeux au plaid ai droit venir."

"as a matter of family obligation". Although the poet fails to say so, Thierry must be a member of Roland's and Charlemagne's family, just as Pinabel is a member of Ganelon's. The song mentions that Thierry is the brother of Jeffrey of Anjou (*dam Geifreit*, 3806); and perhaps Turold expected his twelfth-century public to know that the latter was Charlemagne's kinsman. Possibly this was verified by Jeffrey's position as the emperor's standard bearer (*le rei gunfanuner*, 106). Thierry himself believes that family ties are the best grounds for defending someone in a trial by combat, as he shows by asking whether Ganelon has any kinsman who will fight on his behalf.[89] Feudal obligation alone would authorize Thierry to champion his liege, but it must be kinship that gives him precedence over the other vassals. In any case, Priest Conrad surely understood this to be the reason; for his Thierry claims the honor on these grounds: "Roland has reared me. I was born of his kinship. I am his nearest-born kinsman." [90]

Honor being a family concern, the Saracens act dishonorably in giving their sons as hostages to Charlemagne while knowing he will kill them (40–46). The Franks, as their contrast-types, are ever mindful of their kinsmen, ancestors, and descendants. When Oliver asks Roland to blow his horn, Roland refuses to do so lest he bring reproach upon his kinsmen; [91] and later, in reproaching Roland for not blowing his horn, Oliver reminds him that his defeat will bring disgrace upon his relatives all their lives.[92] Roland asks God to confound (i.e., to disgrace) him if he is un-

[89] S'or ad parent ki m'en voeille desmentir (3834).

[90] Rolant hât mich gezogen. Uzer sînim chunne bin ich geboren: ich bin sîn næchister geborn mâc (*RL*, 8823–8825).

[91] Ne placet Damnedeu que mi parent pur mei seient blasmet (1062); Ja n'en avrunt reproece mi parent (1076).

[92] Vergoigne sereit grant e repruver a trestuz voz parenz; iceste hunte dureit al lur vivant (1705–1708). The same incentive appears in *Aiol* (307–311): Or vous plevi ge bien ma loiauté, Ne ferai couardie en mon aé, Ne felonie, traison porpenser, Ne ja a mon linage n'iert reprové C'on i truisse boisdie ne lasquetés. It also appears in *Couronnement Louis* (vv. 788–89) when Guillelm asks Saint Mary to help him so that: Par coardise ne face lascheté, Qu'a mon lignage ne seit ja reprové. See note III, 76.

worthy of his lineage, and in dying he thinks of the men of his family line.[93] The inheritance of physical characteristics is alluded to in the description of Malpramis, who is large and strong like his ancestors.[94]

During the fatal battle Roland hopes that "sweet France" will not be disgraced by him and his peers, and he asks God to keep France from being shamed.[95] His dying thoughts are not only of the men of his lineage but also of "sweet France" (2379). Oliver regrets that France will be disgraced, a misfortune which Marsilie's nephew Aelroth had previously predicted.[96] As we have noted, the Saracens as well as the Franks call France *dulce*, just as they both call her *Tere Major*.[97]

The Franks fight not only for their country, but also for their God and their faith. The concept of faith, which was expressed by the word *lei* (from Latin *lex*), meant both law and religion. Just as God was the source of right, he was also the source of law; and this explains why Raoul de Cambrai swears by God "who made the laws" and why Conrad calls God the "Highest Lawgiver".[98] Whereas there was one "law" for all Christians (*la lei de chrestiens*, 38, 471, 2683), this law applied differently to the various orders in accordance with the principle of gradualism. Today we profess the Old Testament ideal of one law for all, even for the stranger without the gate; and efforts are actually made to realize this ideal. In the twelfth century, on the other hand, it

[93] se la geste en desment (788); des humes de sun lign (2379). Some critics believe *geste* in v. 788 to mean "chronicles" as in vv. 1443, 1685, 2095, 3181, 3742, and possibly 4002.

[94] Granz est e forz e trait as anceisurs (3177).

[95] Que dulce France par nus ne seit hunie (1927); n'en laiser hunir France (2337).

[96] France en ert hunie (1734); Enquoi perdrat France dulce son los (1194).

[97] dulce France (16, 2773); Tere Major (952, 1659).

[98] Dieu qui fist les lois, *Raoul*, v. 731. Cf. Puis que diex eut establies les lois (v. 2475). Cf. den unseren oberisten êwart; Der aller oberiste êwart (*RL*, 3485, 5250).

was generally agreed that each order had its own law, just as each had its own *recht* or *dreit*. A vestige of this attitude may appear in the expression *a la lei de chevalers,* since physical courage was an obligation for a knight but not for a priest or peasant. To be sure, this term may have been weakened to a mere *façon de parler,* but it does reflect the belief that law is relative to social class, caste, or order.

Charlemagne calls Christianity the "most saving law" (*lei plus salve,* 189); and Blancandrin calls it "the law of salvation" (*lei de salvetet,* 126 cf. 649). Roland asserts that no one ever maintained the law and attracted men to it as Turpin did (*lei tenir . . . humes atraire,* 2256). To become Charlemagne's vassal, Marsilie must accept *la chrestiene lei* (85) and swear to serve Charlemagne *par amur e par feid* (86). It would seem that the twelfth-century Franks drew little distinction between fealty and religious faith, both of which were rendered by the Latin word *fides.* It is significant that the dying Roland proffers his right-hand glove to God when dying, for it was a feudal custom for a vassal to offer his glove as a pledge when submitting himself to his lord's jurisdiction.[99] Another act with either secular or religious symbolism was joining hands in doing homage to God or feudal lord.[100]

Roland promises his men that Charlemagne will bless them if they die fighting, and Charlemagne blesses his men with his right hand.[101] Here a Germanist might detect a vestige of the king's *heil,* a mysterious power inherent in Germanic kings which brought their subjects health, prosperity, or victory.[102] It is more

---

[99] Pur ses pecchez Deu en puroffrid li guant (2365); Sun destre guant en ad vers Deu tendut (2373); Sun destre guant a Deu en puroffrit (2389). Thierry presents his glove to Charlemagne as a pledge before the trial by combat (Sun destre guant en ad presentet Carle. Li emperere l'i recreit par hostage, 3851–3852). See also v. 3845.

[100] Homage to liege: 223, 696; supplication to God: 419, 2240, 2392.

[101] Ne lesserat que nos ne beneïsse (1931); Sis beneïst Carles de sa main destre (3066). Whereas Charlemagne can bless his men himself, his vassal Oliver can only pray to God to bless Charlemagne (2016–2017).

[102] See Walter Baetke, *Das Heilige im Germanischen,* Tübingen, 1942.

likely, however, that the *SR* merely echoes Old Testament ideas of the king as the Lord's annointed.[103] In fact, the pagan Germans may have acquired their belief in the king's *heil* from their Christian enemies, whose military successes proved the *heil* or charisma of their kings. Christian origins are obvious when Charlemagne absolves Ganelon by making the sign of the cross over him with his right hand.[104] With this gesture he says, "Go in Jesus's name and in mine" (*Al Jhesu e al mien!* 339). Today such a remark would sound presumptuous, if not blasphemous.

Turold apparently intends his emperor to hold both the spiritual and the secular swords with a firm hand; and this may imply a protest against the policy of the popes who, during the investiture conflicts, were trying to gain both swords for themselves. Turold probably composed his poem within a generation after Gregory VII humiliated Henry IV at Canossa in 1077. His Charlemagne shows independence of clerical advice by abruptly silencing Archbishop Turpin when the latter tries to speak at his council. "Go sit down on that white cloth," he commands, "Speak no more about it unless I command you!" [105]

Roland's most holy (*seintisme*) sword contains one of Saint Peter's teeth, some of Saint Basil's blood, and a bit of the Virgin Mary's clothing (2344). Similarly, Charlemagne's sword contains the head of Longinus's spear, which, having been touched by Christ's blood, makes its bearer invincible in battle (2503–2511). The power of such amulets lay in their own magic properties rather than in the faith with which they were used. Turold did not consider it incongruous for Ganelon to swear his treacherous

---

[103] See I Samuel 10:1; 16:13.

[104] De sa main destre l'ad asols e seignet (340). A. H. Schutz (p. 458–60) argues that *asoldre* here means only to dismiss, yet the similarity of v. 337 with v. 2957 seems to confirm the prevailing view that *asoldre* should be understood in its ecclesiastical sense.

[105] Alez sedeir desur cel palie blanc! N'en parlez mais, se jo nel vos cumant (272).

oath to the Saracens over the relics in his sword,[106] yet the author of the *Karlamagnús saga* must have seen the discrepancy, for his Ganelon swears on the Koran.[107] In similar manner Conrad's Ganelon swears by an idol.[108] When the Franks say that the archbishop's crozier (*croce*) is *salve* (1509), they must be speaking humorously. A symbol of holy office, the crozier should lead men to salvation; but here the Franks are probably alluding to Turpin's sword, with which he is protecting them. The word *salvament* is used elsewhere to designate the security offered by Roland's twenty thousand troops (786).

The Franks accuse the Saracens of worshiping idols (*ymagenes*, 3664; *ydeles*, 2619, 3664). This is ironic, for the Mohammedans, like the Jews, eschewed graven images, whereas the Christians bowed down to them and worshiped them. The Franks also charge the Saracens with polytheism and ascribe to them the gods *Apolin, Tervagan,* and *Mahumet* (3490, 3267); but the Mohammedans really worshiped one God, Allah, whereas the Christians not only gave God three persons but also delegated much divine power to his Mother and to a host of lesser saints.[109] Just as Ganelon would have been *barun* if he had been loyal, Balaguez would have had *barnet* if he had been a Christian.[110] Here there is no question of moral value. Turold merely meant that Balaguez would have been an effective warrior if he had been on the right side and enjoyed God's patronage. The *Karlamagnús* poet says that Balaguez would have had power (*ríki*) if he had been a Christian, and Margariz would have been a good

[106] Sur les reliques de s'espee Murgleis la traïsun jurat e si s'en est forfait (606–607).

[107] Á þeirri bók voru lög Maúmets og Terrogants (*KS*, #12).

[108] *RL*, 2363–2366.

[109] Chief among the saints in the *SR* are Peter, Michael, and Giles: Perre de Rume (921), La dent seint Perre (2346), l'apostle de Rome (2998), Seint Piere (3094); Seint Michel (date, 37, 53, 152; place, 1428; person, 2394); Li ber Gilie, por qui Deus fait vertuz (2096).

[110] Fust chrestiens, asez oüst barnet (1899).

hero (*Góður drengur*) if he had been a Christian.[111] Judging by the similarities in the descriptions of Charlemagne and Baligant, it would seem that there were no essential physical, mental, or moral differences between them. Religious allegiance alone made one of them right and the other wrong.

The SR presents allegiance to both temporal and spiritual liege lord as a matter of *do ut des*. In explaining Roland's success, Ganelon says that the Franks "love him so much that they will never fail him. He gives them much gold and silver, mules, horses, clothes, and accoutrements." [112] It is easy to detect a causal relationship between these two statements, which is attested later when Roland spurs his men on with promises of booty.[113] Charlemagne also eggs his men on by reminding them of the lands and wealth he gives them for their aid, and he thanks God when he sees how much plunder they gain from the Saracens.[114] This plunder is indispensable, since some of his men are mercenaries (*soldeiers*, 34, 133). Because the Franks based their feudal loyalty largely upon a pecuniary basis,[115] they assumed the same of their enemies. Consequently, the Emir reminds his men that he has supported them for a long time, and he wins their help with promises of women and fiefs.[116] Priest Conrad clearly indicates the chief bond between feudal lord and vassal in using the term

[111] og ef hann væri kristinn maður, þá ætti hann ærið ríki (*KS*, #19; *KS*, #26).

[112] Il l'aiment tant ne li faldrunt nient; or e argent lur met tant en present, muls e destrers e palies e guarnamenz (397).

[113] Encoi avrum un eschec bel e gent (1167).

[114] Mult grant eschec en unt si chevaler (2478).

[115] The word feudal is derived from Old High German *fihu* (cattle or wealth), which was cognate with Latin *pecus*. Medieval literature often reveals that feudal obligation was validated by the gifts or lands with which it was contracted. The *Lay of the Nibelungs* shows this in Rüdiger's attempt to return his lands to Etzel to free himself of his obligation to fight against his Burgundian friends (*NL*, 2157, 2–4). See Jones, "Rüdiger's Dilemma," pp. 7–21.

[116] nurrit vos ai ling tens (3374); Je vos durrai muillers gentes e beles, Si vos durai feus e honors e teres (3398–3399).

"gold-friends" (*goltwin*) in speaking of Targis of Tortolose's followers, who are devoted to him because he rewards them liberally.[117]

Like a true liege, God rewards his faithful vassals in this world. By taking Saragossa, Charlemagne confirms Turold's claim that "He succeeds who has God's help" (*Mult ben espleitet qui Damnes deus aiuet*, 3657). Yet God helps not only in this world but also in the next. Whenever the archbishop exhorts his men to fight the pagans, he reminds them of the heavenly reward they will win (1135, 1522, 2197). When the angel Cherubim and Saint Michael and Saint Gabriel fetch Roland's soul (2393–2396), we find a belief similar to the pagan Germanic superstition that the souls of brave warriors killed in battle are taken to Valhalla by the Valkyries. It might be supposed that the pagan superstition had prepared the Frankish converts to accept the doctrine that angels fetch the souls of those Christians who die fighting for the Faith. Nevertheless, it is more likely that the Germanic belief, if it ever really existed, was modeled on the Christian one. The Christian belief was the source of the Mohammedan dogma of *shahid*, which declares that warriors who die for their faith are taken to heaven.[118] This dogma, backed by the Koran,[119] gave Mohammedan fighters reckless courage; and their fanaticism may well have encouraged the Christian hierarchy to propagate the same belief among their Christian soldiers.

Upon capturing the Saracen city of Cordres, the Franks gain much booty and kill or convert every pagan in the city; [120] and the sequence of these two activities probably reflects their order

[117] vil willic wâren si im, want er milticlichen gab (*RL*, 4676–4677).

[118] A. J. Wensinck (pp. 147–74) shows that Islamic belief in shahid derived from primitive Christianity. The idea of martyrdom had been developed already in the Maccabaean age under the influence of Greek Stoicism.

[119] "Consider not those slain on God's path to be dead, nay, alive with God; they are cared for" (*Sura* iii, 166. See also iii, 156; xlvii, 4–6).

[120] Mult grant eschech en unt si chevaler d'or e d'argent e de guarnemanz chers. En la citet nen ad remés paien ne seit ocis u devient chrestien (99–100).

of importance for the Christian soldiers. Later the Christian soldiers are again rewarded for their religious fervor (2478), and thus we see that the heroes of the SR can expect tangible rewards for performing their religious duty. But men of honor valued their reputations even more than wealth; and therefore appeal was also made to their pride. Although he is a churchman, Turpin goads his men to greater effort by admonishing them that it is better to die fighting than to have brave men sing scurrilous songs about them.[121] Notwithstanding his reference to God, his appeal is made directly to his men's solicitude for their worldly fame. Turpin's hope of favorable songs and fear of unfavorable ones was very real. This mode of thinking is illustrated in *Raoul de Cambrai* when Bernier calls shame upon the first to flee from the approaching battle; for the writer intervenes to say that an eye-witness, Bertolais de Loon, declared that he would compose a song about the event.[122]

Charlemagne's prestige is heightened by his conquests in Spain, but then it is threatened when his vassal, Oliver, is fatally wounded by Marganice. This explains what Marganice means in boasting that, because he has mortally wounded Oliver, Charlemagne can no longer praise himself for the harm he has done the Saracens.[123] Fortunately for Charlemagne, Oliver vindicates his emperor's honor and his own by killing Marganice before dying (1957). But in general, honor was a fragile and perishable thing. Salvation, on the other hand, was a much simpler matter. The

[121] Pur Deu vos pri que ne seiez fuiant. Que nuls prozdom malvaisement n'en chant. Asez est mielz que moerium cumbatant (1516–1518).

[122] "Diex!" dist B., "quel fiance ci a! Mal dehait ai qi premiers requerra, Ne de l'estor premerains s'enfuira!" Bertolais dist que chançon en fera, Jamais jougleres tele ne chantera (*Raoul,* vv. 2439–43). Guillaume, the hero of *Aliscans,* also fights bravely so that minstrels will not sing disparagingly of him: Mes ains ke muire, ferai une envaïe, Ke ja jugleres, s'il en chante, ne die, Ke j'aie feite traïson ne boidie; Ja en chançon ki de moi soit oïe, N'avra retret, se dieu plet, vilenie" (vv. 450–55).

[123] Tort nos ad fait, nen est dreiz qu'il s'en lot, kar de vos sul ai ben venget les noz (1950).

Franks receive general absolution just before the battle and therefore need no individual confession. *Laisse LXXXIX*, in which Turpin absolves his men, gives a classic example of absolution under battle conditions. As Thomas Thornton has observed, it contains confession, prayer to God for remission, absolution, benediction, and provision for penance.[124]

When Ganelon sets out for Spain, Charlemagne absolves him (*l'ad asols e seignet*, 340) even though he has not confessed and cherishes murderous hatred toward Roland. Today this might be explained as a *benedictio itineris*, or a wish for God's absolution; but Charlemagne's apparent position as priest-king must have made Turold's lay public understand this to be an absolution. Archbishop Turpin promises the Franks absolution in return for the *penitence* of fighting the Saracens (1138), and this seems guarantee enough of heaven. The word *penitence* obviously means "penance", and there is no proof that Turpin's idea of penitence included much more than the formality of beating one's breast and reciting certain formulas. Charlemagne has enough bishops, abbots, monks, canons, and tonsured priests to absolve and bless all the dead at Roncevaux,[125] regardless of whether or not they have followed Turpin's injunction to join the general confession.

Perhaps the religiosity of the *SR* is best illustrated in Archbishop Turpin, who was a clergyman by profession but a warrior by calling. When Turpin dies, the poet says: "Dead is Turpin, Charlemagne's warrior. Through great battles and many beautiful sermons he was always a champion against the pagans."[126] Thus

---

[124] Clamez voz culpes, si preiez Deu mercit; Asoldrai voz pur voz anmes guarir. Se vos murez, esterez seinz martirs, Sieges avrez el greignor pareïs. Franceis descendent, a tere se sunt mis. E l'arcevesque de Deu les beneïst: Par penitence les cumandet a ferir (1132–1138).

[125] Asez i ad evesques e abez, Munies, canonies, proveires coronez, Sis unt asols e seignez de part Deu (2955–2957).

[126] Morz est Turpin, le guerreier Charlun. Par granz batailles e par mult bels sermons cuntre paiens fut tuz tens campiuns (2242).

he is characterized first as a soldier of Charlemagne and only secondly as a soldier of Christ, provided that priority of position indicates priority of emphasis.[127] Likewise, he served the cross primarily by fighting and only secondly by sermonizing; and it may be assumed that his "sermons" were merely harangues inciting his troops to annihilate more pagans. To inflame the Franks' courage, Turpin reminds them that Charlemagne has left them there; and then he adds: "For our king we must die well. Help support Christianity." [128] Here he frankly places fealty before religious duty.

Charlemagne too appeals primarily to his men's secular emotions, even though he is the champion of Christendom against Islam. In his chief exhortation before the final battle he reminds his troops that he loves them for their services and repays them well. Next he calls upon them to avenge their sons, brothers, and heirs; and only then does he remind them that he is in the right against the pagans (3406–3413), which may mean no more than that he is bound to win. Because Charlemagne's battle against Baligant suggests the spirit of the Crusades, it seems surprising that there is no reference to crosses as standards or insignia on their arms. Modern illustrators usually assume that the Crusaders had crosses on their chests, banners, and shields, yet the *SR* does not justify this belief.[129] Even Conrad's more clerical version of the song makes little mention of crosses. Roland has a dragon on his chest, birds and beasts on his banner, and a lion on his shield; and thus his insignia differs little from that of the pagans.[130]

Roland calls Turpin *gentilz hom* (2177, 2252) and *chevaler de*

---

[127] In a letter of October 17, 1961, Thomas Thornton writes that in Roman rhetoric, "in the naming of two or more virtues, the position of most importance is the last, not the first."

[128] Pur nostre rei devum nus ben murir. Chrestientet aidez a sustenir! (1128).

[129] When Conrad says of the Christians: *si zeichinoten sich mit chrucen* (v. 167), Ruth Hoppe (p. 116) explains this as: "Die christlichen Ritter hängen sich das Kreuz um." However, Conrad more probably meant that they made the sign of the cross.

[130] Von sinen brusten vorne scain ain trache von gold (*RL*, 3284–3285),

bon aire (2252), and the poet calls him *nobilie barun* (2237); and this suggests that they admired him more for his worldly status than for his spiritual office. Roland also calls him a *mult bon chevaler* (1673) because he can well strike with lance and spear.[131] Being no conscientious objector himself, Turpin maintains that anyone who shirks fighting is not worth four-pence and should be a monk in a monastery praying for their sins.[132] In other words, prayer is a fitting activity for those not worthy of fighting. Turpin seems to have profited from warfare, for he rides a horse taken from a king he has killed in Denmark (1488). Since he is the special champion of the faith, we may assume that the Danish king was a pagan.

As we have seen, Turpin taught a strictly utilitarian religion: good works, in the form of military service, are performed in exchange for eternal life in paradise. He could scarcely have appreciated a bootless *amor dei purus*. Whereas the Bible says you should not swear by your head (*neque per caput tuum, Matth.* 5, 36), this is precisely what Turpin does (*par mun chef,* 799). Likewise, whereas the Bible teaches forgiveness, the archbishop is most anxious to be avenged; and he not only hates but even wishes to hate.[133] His concern for his men's immortal souls seems matched by his concern for their mortal remains, since he prom-

---

ain wîzzen van er an bant: dâ wâren tiere unt vogele mit golde unterzogene (*RL*, 3325–3326), ain lewen fûrt er an sînem schilte, ûzer golde ergrabin (*RL*, 3986–3987). Paligan has a dragon on his banner (*RL*, 8125). Beringer's troops seem to be the only ones that carry the sign of the cross (*RL*, 4980), unless we interpret literally the expression *daz crûce an sich nemen* (*RL*, 3447, 5823). Apparently Charlemagne has no cross on his person until an angel brings him one (*RL*, 7475–7477).

[131] ben set ferir e de lance e d'espiet (1675).

[132] Einz deit monie estre en un de cez mustiers, si prierat tuz jurz por noz peccez (1881). Similar contempt for monasticism appears in *Le Couronnement de Louis* when Charlemagne, believing his son to be a coward, declares that they should cut off his hair and put him in a monastery: Or li feson toz les chevels trenchier, si le metons la enz en cel mostier (vv. 96–97). This is precisely what was done to Charlemagne's illegitimate son Pippin, in whose favor some vassals rebelled (*Vita Karoli,* #20).

[133] nus purrat venger (1744); bien nus vengerat (2145); Suz ciel n'at hume que tant voeillet haïr (1244).

ises Roland and Oliver that Charlemagne will remove their bodies to a minster so that they will not be eaten by wolves, swine, or dogs.[134] Although he assures his friends of the joys of paradise, he himself is sorry to die because he will not be able to see his mighty emperor again.[135]

The contradiction between Christian ethics and worldly honor is nowhere more conspicuous than in matters of revenge. The New Testament proclaims a God of peace and forgiveness, but the twelfth-century Franks preferred the Old Testament's God of vengeance, whom they served by avenging His name whenever it was insulted. Nevertheless, the *SR* usually presents revenge as a matter of personal satisfaction. When an archangel urges Charlemagne to gain vengeance, it is to avenge his own troops; and Charlemagne asks God for personal satisfaction.[136] In Priest Conrad's adaptation of this song, which is more clerical in ethos, Charlemagne invokes God to defend His own good name: "Gracious God, now think of Thy honor and show Thy strength." [137] Because the Franks were God's chosen people, any insult to them was automatically an insult to God, and therefore its vengeance enjoyed divine sanction.

Roland entreats Charlemagne to continue the war against Marsilie in order to avenge the murder of his two ambassadors, Basan and Basil (201–209), it being disgraceful for a feudal leader to fail to avenge his followers. This motivation is first revealed when Charlemagne sends Marsilie his ultimatum commanding him to surrender his uncle who killed the Frankish en-

[134] Enfuerunt nos en aitres de musters; n'en mangerunt ne lu ne porc ne chen (1750–1751).

[135] La meie mort me rent si anguissus! Ja ne verrai le riche empereur (2198).

[136] La flur de France as perdut, ço set Deus. Venger te poez de la gent criminel (2455); Par ta mercit, se tei pleist, me cunsent que mun nevold poisse venger Rollant (3107).

[137] Gnædeclicher herre, nu gedenke an dîn êre. erzaige dîne tugende (*RL*, 8417–8419).

voys (488–494). Priest Conrad clarifies this reason for the Spanish campaign by letting Charlemagne explain that he has been insulted by the envoys' murder.[138] Oliver asks God to help him gain revenge, and he still strives to avenge himself when mortally wounded.[139] Because no one ever wished vengeance as much as Roland, Turpin can persuade him to blow his horn by promising that it will help Charlemagne avenge them.[140]

Charlemagne has already offered his men rich rewards to avenge their fallen comrades (3406–3412), yet his vassal Oger shames him into even speedier action by saying, "See, the pagans are killing your men. May it not please God for you to wear your crown if you do not strike to avenge your shame!" [141] In this passage revenge results from a point of honor, since Oger is goading Charlemagne to avenge his shame. But elsewhere revenge is usually motivated by the hope of gaining pleasure through inflicting pain, as is the case when Charlemagne urges his men to avenge their grievances and soothe their hearts.[142] Here it is a matter of retribution rather than of vindication. Whereas the Christians often ask God to avenge them, the Mohammedans ask Mohammed that favor only once.[143]

As long as reputation was the greatest of worldly goods, its loss caused the greatest sorrow. The word *doel* is often used in the *SR* to denote the dismay or chagrin felt by the victim of an insult or injury. Ganelon feels *doel* (304) when Roland laughs at him, and Falsaron feels *doel* when he sees his dead nephew (1219). Likewise, Roland feels *doel* when he sees that Sansun has been

---

[138] dâ er mich mite scande (*RL*, 818).

[139] Deus le me doinst venger (1548); De lui venger ja mais de li ert sez (1966).

[140] Jamais n'iert home plus se voeillet venger (1873); nus purrat venger (1744).

[141] Veez paien cum ocient vos humes! Ja Deu ne placet qu'el chef portez corone, s'or n'i ferez pur venger vostre hunte! (3537–3539).

[142] vengez voz doels, si esclargiez voz talents e voz coers (3627–3628).

[143] 1548, 3013, 3109; Aie nos, Mahum! Li nostre deu, vengez nos de Carlun! (1906–1907).

slain (1581) and later on when he sees most of his troops lying dead at Roncevaux (1867). When Aelroth slanders Charlemagne, Rolands feels such *grant doel* (1196) that he attacks and slays him; and Charlemagne urges his men to avenge their *doels* (3627) by attacking the Saracens. Balaguez boasts that the Franks will die *a doel e a viltiet* (904), and Margariz boasts that France will suffer shame (*en ert hunie*, 969) and that Charlemagne will suffer *doel e ire* (971).

Although *doel* is sometimes consociated with pity or affection, it is more often consociated with anger and shame; and therefore the deeper meaning of the word must be shame, humiliation, or indignation more often than sorrow, as most translators have believed.[144] When Charlemagne feels *doel* because his vassals have failed to convict Ganelon (3817), he probably feels indignation and chagrin because they have failed to uphold his honor. Here and elsewhere in this study the word "chagrin" is used in the sense of "acute vexation, annoyance, or mortification, arising from disappointment, thwarting, or failure", as it is explained by the fourth definition in the *New English Dictionary*. Where Turold says that Roland felt great *doel* because of Aelroth's slander, the *Karlamagnús* poet says that he raged.[145] The meaning of *doel* can

[144] de doel e de pitet (1749), le doel e la pitet (2206); de doel e de tendrur (1446), tendrur . . . doel (2217–2219); doel e ire (971), dol . . . ire (2936–2944); par doel e par rancune (2301); a doel e a viltiet (904); e doel e hunte (929). Tears are often shed in connection with *doel*, but that does not prove sorrow, since they also appear where chagrin is the dominant affection. This meaning is noted in Foulet's glossary to Bédier's commentary: "il indique un chagrin violent causé par une affection blessée, l'indignation ou la honte" (Bédier, *Commentaires*, p. 370). Nevertheless, critics and translators seem to have overlooked this observation. The *chansons de geste* constantly use the word *doel* to denote the frustration and disgrace an offended person feels until he can avenge himself: De duel morrai, se ne le puis vengier (*Girart*, v. 1868); Jà i morrai de duel, se ne somes venjant! (*Renaus*, p. 42, v. 24); De duel morrai se ne me puis vengier! (*Raoul*, v. 5083). Raoul's mother, who feels especial *duel* because her son has been slain by a bastard, states that it would be only half as bad if he had been slain by a powerful count: se l'eüst mort un quens poesteïs, De mon duel fust l'une motiés jus mis (*Raoul*, vv. 3597–98).

[145] En Rolland reiddist mjög við illyrði hans (*KS*, #23).

be extended to include not only the chagrin one feels but also the offense or affront which causes the chagrin. Therefore the expression *doel e damage* in v. 2983 means about the same as our expression "insult and injury". In this regard it is of interest to note that the word "injury" itself first meant an offense or wrong (*in-iuria*).

An overtone of indignation or resentment is also attached to the word *dolur*, for example in Charlemagne's mention of the *dolur* and *ire* caused him by the violation of his envoys (489). In the *SR* Naimes urges Charlemagne to avenge his *dolur* (2428), but in the *Roelantslied* he urges his men to avenge their anger (*Laet ons wreken onsen toren,* 1647). Indignation and resentment are even more apparent in the participial form of the word. Estramariz says that Charlemagne will be *dolent* when he sees the Franks die, and Roland is *dolent* when he sees Oliver dead (951, 2023). While hastening to Roncevaux to aid or avenge the rear guard, the Franks are *dolenz* and *curoçus* (1813), a thought repeated in the next strophe (1835). Baligant feels *dolent* upon seeing his vassal Marsilie's humiliation (2835), and Bramimunde calls herself *dolente* when disgraced by the loss of her husband (2823). These examples show that the word *dolent* often implies shame, humiliation, or resentment.[146]

It is significant that even the classical Latin word *dolor* had designated an emotion arising from injury and equal to anger and indignation.[147] It should also be noted that the Old High German

---

[146] Whereas Bédier missed this meaning in his translation, it is noted in Foulet's glossary to his commentary (Bédier, *Commentaires*, p. 370). In *Girart de Viënne* (vv. 1625–27) Aymeri is so offended that he is *dolant* and *mautalant* and speaks loudly *par grant aïroison*. When offended, Charlemagne says: Dolanz serai se ne m'en puis vengier (v. 4021). The word is used similarly in *Aliscans* (vv. 693–94): Li quens Guillaumes ot molt le cuer dolant, Molt fu iriés et plains de mautalant.

[147] "orta ex iniuria, saepe prope i.q. ira, indignatio" (*Thesaurus Linguae Latinae*, Leipzig, 1910, V. pt. 1, col. 1841). Many examples are cited from classical sources. This meaning is probably present when Seneca says: "Pater caedetur, defendam; caesus est, exsequar, quia oportet, non quia dolet" (*De Ira*, I, xii, 2). John Basore (*Seneca Moral Essays*, New York, 1928, Loeb, I, p. 136), renders *dolet* as "grieve".

word *leid* could mean both sorrow and resentment as well as insult or injury.[148] The older meaning of the word *leid* may linger in its Old French derivative *laidement* when the Saracens desecrate their idols (2581). Ganelon feels such *doel* at Roland's ridicule that he almost bursts with *ire* (304); and Charlemagne reminds Marsilie that the death of his envoys has caused him *dolur* and *ire* (489). The two words are also consociated when Margariz boasts that he will disgrace France (971). In all these passages the word *ire* connotes an anger that calls for revenge, as is the case when Charlemagne feels *ire* because his men have fallen at Roncevaux (2944) and because Ganelon has betrayed the rear guard (3989). This meaning also predominates in the word *irur* when Charlemagne feels *irur* (2877) at seeing his nephew dead. Bédier and Mortier render this as *douleur*, but resentment and indignation actually predominate as they also do in verse 1224, in which Oliver feels *mult grant irur* and strikes Falsaron dead for having boasted that he would disgrace France. As in the case of *doel* and *dolur*, it is clear that *irur* can mean both grief and grievance.

When Guenes threatens Rollandus in the *Carmen* (45–50), the threats incite him (*mine tante urgent*) and the reproaches sadden him (*convicia tanta mestificant*). Rollandus rages at the reproaches (*hinc furit*) and swells up at the threats (*inde tumet*). He bears the threats and the threatener with difficulty (*grave fert*) and decides to destroy them. Nevertheless, at Karolus's urging, his fury, ferocity, and anger diminish (*furor, feritas, minor ira sui*). This would suggest that the reproaches had really made Rollandus feel resentment or chagrin rather than gloom, as Livingston renders it.[149] When Rollandus is *mestus* at being defeated,[150] he is probably more chagrined than saddened, since

---

[148] See Friedrich Maurer: *Leid,* Bern, 1951.

[149] Rollandumque mine tante, convicia tanta Urgent, mestificant: hinc furit, inde tumet (*Carmen*, vv. 45–46). "By so many threats Roland is provoked, by so much insult he is filled with gloom" (Livingston, p. 63).

[150] Marte . . . vinci mestus (*Carmen*, v. 364).

defeat was disgraceful. Thus, like the French words *doel, dolur,* and *irur* and the Latin word *dolor* and the German word *leid,* the Latin word *maestitia* could mean either sorrow or resentment. An echo of these mixed emotions may appear in the English cognates *grief* and *grievance.* Today we wish to mourn our grief and avenge our grievance, whereas twelfth-century Franks, like the Kwakiutl Indians, scarcely distinguished between these emotions.[151]

The opposite of *doel* is *joie.* Just as *doel* most often resulted from defeat or failure, *joie* most often resulted from victory or success. The Saracens feel *grant joie* (1627) when Grandonie kills several Franks, so Roland naturally feels *grant doel* (1631). Having felt *doel* as long as they had not attained satisfaction for the death of their men, Charlemagne and his barons return from the capture of Saragossa with joy and good spirits (*a joie e a baldur,* 3682). Charlemagne receives Thierry *a joie* (3944) after the latter has defeated Ganelon and thus repaired his emperor's honor. It is to be noted that Turold uses the word *joie* only in the sense of triumphant exultation, and that Charlemagne can feel this emotion so soon after the death of his beloved nephew. Turold's only other words for "joyful" are *balt* and *liet,* which also appear only in cases of victory and revenge.[152] Since *balt* meant "joyful" mostly in the sense of jubilant with victory, it implied optimistic self-assurance and thus resembled its English cognate "bold". That *baldur* was more respected than meekness or humility is suggested by the frequency of the syllable *bald* in Christian names like Baldewin, Tedbald, and Rembalt, all three of which appear in the SR.

[151] See Ruth Benedict: *Patterns of Culture,* Mentor Books, New York, 1936, pp. 221–22.

[152] Turpin wishes Charlemagne to avenge the rear guard so the Saracens will not return *liez* to Spain (1745); and Baligant is *joüs e liet* at the very thought of getting revenge (2803). In *Renaus de Montalban* (p. 34, v. 39) Bueves says that he will never be *lies* until Charlemagne pays for killing his nephew; and in *Raoul de Cambrai* (v. 5016) Bernier says that he will never be *liés* unless he avenges himself (Se ne me venge, jamais liés ne serai).

Just as Charlemagne experiences *joie* and *baldur* upon taking Saragossa, he feels *balz* and *liez* upon plundering Cordres and massacring its inhabitants (96). Between these victories, however, he has his moments of dejection, for example upon realizing that he will always suffer *dolur* and will lose his *force* and *baldur* after Roland's death because he will have no one to sustain his honor.[153] Thus one could almost say of him and his men what Ruth Benedict says of the Kwakiutls: that they recognize "only one gamut of emotion, that which swings between victory and shame." [154]

The word *blasmer*, from Latin *blasphemare*, originally meant to blaspheme or to speak evil of. In common American usage the word "blame" has almost lost this original meaning of social censure and generally implies objective responsibility or guilt, or else accusation of guilt. For example, the sentence "He is to blame" means "He is responsible" or "He is at fault" rather than "He should be reproached". This transferred meaning of guilt or incrimination may be present in the word *blasmer* the first time it appears in the *SR*, namely when Blancandrin asks Charlemagne to pardon Marsilie for not sending his uncle to be punished,[155] but in all other cases the word refers to social censure. For example, Oliver says that the knights who are with Charlemagne should not be reproached for being absent from Roncevaux, and he repeats this thought later with slightly different words.[156] The poet says that one should not reproach the twelve peers who have fought so well; and he questions whether Roland will be reproved or approved for killing both rider and horse.[157] Oliver advises Roland that he will not be criticized for blowing his horn,

---

[153] Jamais n'ert jurn de tei n'aie dulur. Cum decarrat ma force e ma baldur! N'en avrai ja ki sustienget m'onur (2901–2903).

[154] *Patterns of Culture*, p. 198.

[155] De l'algalifes nel devez pas blasmer (681).

[156] Cil ki la sunt ne funt mie a blasmer (1174); Cil ki la sunt n'en deivent aveir blasme (1718). Strangely enough, Bédier seems to think these two passages refer to the members of the rear guard.

[157] Li .XII. per n'en deivent aveir blasme (1346); ki quel blasme ne quil lot (1589).

and Roland hopes that his kinsmen will not be reproached because of his defeat.[158] In this last instance it is clear that the word *blasmer* does not mean "to blame" in the modern sense of the word, since no one can be blamed for what his ancestor has done.

While in Spain, Ganelon is afraid that the emperor will *say* that he has died without selling his life dearly (*dirat*, 447). Roland refuses to blow his horn lest someone might *say* that he was afraid of the pagans (*Que ço seit dit*, 1074); and he determines to fight hard so that the man who gets his sword can *say* that it belonged to a brave man (*dire poet*, 1122). His last act is to face Spain so that Charlemagne and his men will *say* that he died as a conqueror.[159] He expresses this same concern in the Middle English version of the *Song of Roland* (378–379) by saying: "For men will tell charls this full sone, when we haue slayn the fals, & the feld won." Earlier in the SR Roland, like Turpin, had urged his men to make greater efforts so that no one would sing scurrilous songs about them.[160] All in all, it is easy to see that Roland was worthy of the first and more significant syllable of his name, which was derived from the Germanic word *hroþi*, meaning fame.

Roland refuses to blow his horn for fear of losing his own fame in France (*mun los*, 1054); and he is also afraid that France will lose her *los* too (1194, 1210). In other words, he is socially advanced enough to identify his own reputation with that of his group. His concern for his reputation is a concern for what people will say, for a man's reputation consists of what people say about him. Turold rewards Turpin's great efforts by predicting that Charlemagne will *say* that he spared no one (2091); and Thierry

---

[158] D'iço ne sai jo blasme (1082); Que mi parent pur mei seient blasmet (1063).

[159] Que Carles diet e trestute sa gent . . . qu'il fut mort cunquerant (2362–63).

[160] Que malvaise cançun de nus chantet ne seit (1014); Male chançun n'en deit estre cantee (1466); Que nuls prozdom malvaisement n'en chant (1517).

undertakes Ganelon's punishment because not a day will pass that people do not talk about it.[161]

The heroes of the SR thus appear sensitive to what other people say; and they could hardly have agreed with Montaigne, who maintained that "a man's value and estimation consists in heart and will: there lies his true honor." [162] For them, a man's honor lies in other people's opinions, particularly in the public expression of those opinions. Their fear of disapproval explains to what ends they go to escape reprobation. When Roland boasts that he will not be reproached (ne me reproverunt, 768) for dropping Charlemagne's arc as Ganelon dropped his glove, he seems less afraid of dropping the arc than of being seen and censured for doing so. Roland refuses to blow his horn more through fear of public disgrace than through aversion toward cowardice as such. This is how the author of the Carmen motivated Rollandus, who refuses to blow because it would be not only cowardice (ignavia, 227) but also a disgrace or shame (dedecus, pudor, 228). Later Oliverus says: "Desist, feel shame! Desist, for what a shame! Will it not be for you and yours an intolerable opprobrium, a perpetual disgrace, and the greatest shame?" [163]

When the hero of the SR brags of the havoc he will wreak among the Saracens, he expressly boasts that Oliver and his other comrades will see his sword covered with blood.[164] What counts most is not the death of the Saracens, but rather the public display of his courage. In the Karlamagnús saga a pagan king named Kossablin expresses knightly sentiment by saying that he would not wish to be called a coward for all the gold in the world, and

[161] dist, 2091; Jamais n'ert jur que il n'en seit parlet (3905).

[162] The Essays of Montaigne, trans. E. J. Trechmann, Oxford, 1927, chapter 31.

[163] Desine, te pudeat! desine, namque pudor! Num tibi, nonne tuis erit intolerabile, perpes, Maximus, obprobrium, dedecus, atque pudor? (vv. 366–68).

[164] Tut en verrez le brant ensanglentet (1067); De Durendal verrez l'acer sanglent (1079).

one of Roland's friends boasts that heathen men will *say* that they have bought him dearly.[165]

An untarnished reputation being better than gold, the word *maldire* may retain some of its original meaning of "to speak evil of", which was the only meaning of its Latin source *maledicere*. To be sure, the newer meaning of "to curse" in the sense of "to wish evil upon" is usually attached to the word (as for example in v. 1659), since abusive language was considered an injury as well as an insult. In general, the word *maldire* has the same overtones as the *mals moz* (1190) spoken by Aelroth against the Franks, which serve as both calumny and malediction. Like the ancient Stoics, many modern men maintain that "sticks and stones may break my bones, but names will never hurt me"; but this attitude was unfeasible in an age in which passive acceptance of insult proved cowardice and thus undermined one's dignity and security. After Marsilie's defeat, his wife and men "wish evil upon" or "speak evil of" Charlemagne and sweet France (*si maldient Carlun e France dulce*, 2579). This is certainly an imprecation, yet the idea of abusive language is present too. They also use abusive language toward their god Apollo, whom they call a "weak god" (*malvais deus*, 2582) because he has let them suffer shame (*hunte*, 2582).

When the Saracens desecrate Apollo, they ask: *Cest nostre rei por quei lessas cunfundre* (2583). Bédier explains this question as "Pourquoi as-tu souffert la ruine de notre roi?"; and elsewhere he renders the word *cunfundre* as "confondre", "détruire", or perdre".[166] Nevertheless, in view of its use in the *SR*, these translations do not seem adequate. To Marsilie's prediction that Charlemagne's advisors will *cunfundre* him (380), Ganelon re-

---

[165] Sá hefir mælt að drengmanns lögum, að fyrir allt veraldar gull vill hann eigi vera kallaður regimaður (*KS*, #19). og það skulu heiðnir menn segja, að þeir hafa mig dýrt keypt (*KS*, #34).

[166] Lucien Foulet renders *cunfundre* as "ruiner" and "détruire" (Bédier, *Commentaires*, p. 358).

torts that only Roland will suffer shame (*avrat hunte*, 382).
Climborin swears that he will put France to shame (*metrat a hunte*, 1532) and that the Franks are good to *cunfundre* (1542).
These consociations suggest that the verb *cunfundre* implied shame as well as ruin, an ambiguity to be expected in a heroic work that damned defeat as worse than death. The Bible associates the two ideas similarly when Isaiah says that the makers of idols will "be shamed, and also confounded".[167]

When Blancandrin predicts that Roland's pride will *confundre* him (389), he may be predicting his disgrace rather than his death, as Jenkins supposes.[168] In warning Basbrun that he will be *morz e confunduz* (3955) if any of Ganelon's kinsmen escape, Charlemagne probably means that he will suffer some shameful death like hanging or quartering. The *Rolandslied* renders *cunfundre* with *schenden*, the usual Middle High German word for "to put to shame".[169] The author of the *Roelantslied* may have had the word *confunduz* in mind in letting Oliver say that Charlemagne's power is destroyed (*gheschant*, 877) and in having Ganelon disgraced (*ghescant*, 1015) by being turned over to Charlemagne's cooks for punishment.

The ratio between imprecations to God and threats of public disgrace gives a clue to the relative motive power of religion and shame in the SR. There are but two imprecations invoking God's hate: to wit, when Oliver twice calls down God's hate upon any who flee from the approaching pagans.[170] In contrast there are six

---

[167] Confusi sunt et erubuerunt omnes, simul abierunt in confusionem fabricatores errorum (*Isaiah*, 45, 16).

[168] Jenkins (p. 39) says: "Should certainly some day be the death of him", yet Blancandrin has just finished saying that Roland will be shamed (*avrat hunte*, 382).

[169] *scenden*, (*RL*, 411). Medieval writers often used *confusio* as the antonym of *honor*. A doctor is wrongfully imprisoned with *plagis et iniurijs maximis et contumelijs* but is later proved innocent. Saint Thomas, his guardian saint, says: "*Cum confusione es introductus cum honore exibis*" (*Exempla*, p. 61, vv. 2, 34).

[170] Dehet ait ki s'en fuit (1047); Dehet ait li plus lenz (1938). Bédier renders both these as "honni soit".

threats of public disgrace: Roland cries shame upon any who show fear and declares anyone a coward (*fel*) who does not sell himself dearly, Turpin invokes public opprobrium upon any who do not strike well, Ganelon calls shame upon himself if ever he should try to hide his vengeance on Roland, Thierry calls shame upon himself should he concede to Pinabel, and the pagans call anyone a coward who lets the Christians escape.[171] Perhaps the Franks were concerned with righteousness and God's law too, but it is everywhere evident that they feared "the reproach of men" and that they were "afraid of their revilings", despite the teachings of the Church as recorded by Isaiah (51:7). To borrow a *bon mot* from Helen Adolf, one might say that they were more afraid of losing face than losing grace. This was certainly true of Roland, who kept his face pointed toward the South during his final prayer instead of turning it to the East, as a good Christian should,[172] so that Charlemagne and his men might know that he died as a conqueror.[173]

Roland makes every effort to avoid *reproece* for himself (2263) and for his kinsmen (1076); and Pinabel sacrifices his life so as not to be *reprovet* (3909). This solicitude for public approval is echoed in an obscure and apparently meaningless passage. Roland splits Valdabrun in half and cleaves his saddle and horse as well, and thus he kills both rider and mount. The poet then adds: "Let him who wishes censure or praise him" (*ki quel blasme ne quil lot*, 1589). This may imply that it was praiseworthy to kill an enemy but blameworthy to kill a horse, or else it may just mean that the pagans censured him while the Franks praised him.[174]

---

[171] Mal seit del coer ki el piz se cuardet (1107); tut seit fel cher ne se vende primes (1924); Fel seit ki ben n'i ferrat (2144). Fel sei se jol ceil (3757); Tut seie fel, se jo mie l'otrei (3897); recreant ki les lerrat guarir (2063).

[172] Cf. Turnet sun vis vers le soleill levant (3097).

[173] Turnat se teste vers la paiene gent: Pur ço l'at fait que il voelt veirement que Carles diet e trestute sa gent, li gentilz quens, qu'il fut mort cunquerant (2360–2363); Envers Espaigne en ad turnet sun vis (2376).

[174] The same expression is used in the latter sense when Guineman kills a pagan king and Turold adds: ki qu'en plurt u kin riet (3364). Cf. v. 1279.

In the long run, it was hope of fame and fear of shame that motivated the whole fight. The Middle English *Song of Roland* (211–
213) summarizes Roland's motivation with the words: "For dred
of dethe, he hid neuer his hed, with hym is worship euer-mor in
ded, ther men may wyn worship for euer."

Ronald Walpole (p. 14) believes that Roland is a hero who
"serves a cause, or rather many causes—Emperor, companions,
country, religion, fidelity, loyalty, patriotism, faith," yet he realizes
that Roland "cannot eradicate from himself that vestige of bar-
barian heroism, his pride, which remains potent within him as the
determining source of integration providing the motive force for
all his acts." Roland was serving his various causes not directly
through any sense of absolute duty, but rather to indulge his self-
esteem, which in turn depended upon the approval of his peers.
As Ruth Hoppe (p. 59) has remarked, the actions of Turold's
heroes are almost exclusively determined by regard for public
opinion.[174a] Concerning Roland, Alain Renoir (p. 578) states:
"The pride with which he serves his cause is understandable, and
his willingness to die for it is admirable." This statement is correct, if the antecedent of "it" is pride, but we may assume that
Renoir meant the word "it" to refer to the cause. He documents
his statement with vv. 1089–1091, in which Roland prays to God
and the angels that France will not lose her fame "through me"
(*pur mei*) because he would rather die than be put to shame
(*Melz voeill murir que huntage me venget,* 1091). This implies
that his immediate preoccupation is his own individual honor,
which will be besmirched if he allows France to be defeated.

A good reputation was vital as long as men judged others by
public repute more than by personal observation. For example,
when Roland kills twenty-four of the most praised and prized

[174a] Das Rolandslied bietet eine lange Reihe von Beispielen dafür, wie der
Gesichtspunkt der vorschriftsmässigen Haltung, der Meinung der andern,
fast ausschliesslich die Handlungsweise der Helden bestimmt.

Saracens (*les melz preisez*, 1872), the poet does not tell us what kind of men they really were, but only what people thought about them. The Saracens assure Ganelon that he is reputed to be a noble warrior; and Bramimunde loves him greatly because her husband and his men praise him.[175] In describing Charlemagne, Ganelon can do no more than tell how everyone praises him (530–534). Balaguez is renowned for his courage, and Thierry wishes to be reconciled with Pinabel because his peers recognize his courage.[176] Baligant respects Charlemagne for being mentioned with honor in the chronicles; and he refers to France as "France the praised".[177] Such examples suggest that the heroes of the SR avoid making personal judgments and merely accept and transmit the opinions shared by the group. It will be noted in this connection that *valur* can mean either "valor", as in v. 534 and and v. 1877, or else "reputation for valor", as in v. 1090.

[175] Noble vassal vos i solt hom clamer (352), Car mult vos priset mi sire e tuit si hume (636).

[176] De vasselage est il ben alosez (898), De vasselage te conoissent ti per (3901).

[177] En plusurs gestes de lui sunt granz honurs (3181), France la loee (3315).

CHAPTER III

ETHICAL ORIGINS AND IDEOLOGICAL ENVIRONMENT

THE PRECEDING INVESTIGATIONS have revealed the heroes of the *SR* as constantly motivated by concern for public opinion. Roland utters lofty sentiments about fighting for the honor of his family and fatherland (1062–1064), but he soon adds his hope that it will never be said he blew his horn through fear of the pagans (1074–1075). Later he expresses a desire that France will not lose her good name because of him, but then he explains that he does not wish to suffer shame (1088–1091). When he praises the virtue of fealty and says that a vassal should suffer for his liege, he adds that he will strike so well with his sword that the man who inherits it can say that it belonged to a brave warrior (1117–1123). Later he prays for his peers and then for himself; but at once he tries to avoid reproach to himself by destroying his sword so that it will not fall into the enemy's hands (2261–2264). Pinabel sounds selfless in his determination to defend his kinship, until he explains that he would rather die than be reproached (3906–3909). To make his men stand and fight, Turpin first appeals to their sense of shame by warning that they will be reviled if they flee, and only then does he remind them that fighting is a religious duty for which they will be paid with paradise (1515–1523).

These and other passages indicate that the heroes of the SR are what modern sociologists call "other-directed" men: they have a group morality and strive to please their peers rather than to follow the decrees of their own conscience.[1] What society admires is honorable, what it scorns is dishonorable. "Inner-directed" men, in contrast, accept certain broad and absolute values, usually early in life; and these they follow to the best of their ability even when they conflict with social conventions. As long as they are sure of the merits of their actions, inner-directed men are morally independent of the opinions of society. Inner-direction scarcely appears in the SR.

Although the SR often refers to heavenly reward, most of its actions are motivated by fear of shame; and therefore it expresses a way of life known as a "shame culture".[2] To be sure, Turold mentions repentance and remission of sins, which belong to a "guilt culture"; but sin may have meant little more to him than culpability in its sense of liability to divine retribution. Perhaps he knew the theological distinction between attrition and contrition, but he does not distinguish these in his song. Of course such problems would be out of place in a martial epic; yet Turold's great concern with heavenly rewards suggests that he was not deeply troubled by the sense of sin and guilt that plague so many modern Christians and Jews who are weighed down more by consciousness of moral inadequacy and wrongdoing than by fear of punishment.[3] He was evidently more concerned with heavenly

[1] For discussion of "other-direction", see David Riesman, *The Lonely Crowd*, New York, 1953.

[2] "In anthropological studies of different cultures the distinction between those which rely heavily on shame and those that rely heavily on guilt is an important one" (Ruth Benedict, *The Chrysanthemum and the Sword*, Cambridge, 1946, p. 222).

[3] Following the sentence quoted above, Ruth Benedict continues: "A society that inculcates absolute standards of morality and relies on men's developing a conscience is a guilt culture by definition. . . ."

reward than with sin itself, and this reward was earned more through military prowess than through the avoidance of evil. It is true that his archbishop preaches heavenly grace; yet even he surpasses most of his lay companions in his fear of being shamed.

It is to be noted that Turpin is afraid of being shamed, not *a*shamed; for shame was a public rather than a private consideration. Because Western civilization now stresses an inner sense of shame, modern scholarship often assumes such an attitude among medieval men, even though they generally understood shame as a matter of social disgrace. Le Gentil believes that Ganelon, having let the Franks see his anguish at being nominated for the dangerous mission, "feels a need of showing himself that he is not a coward"; [4] and he also believes that Roland is afraid of "sinking in his own eyes and in the opinion of his peers." [5] Perhaps such inner qualms played a role, but it must have been a relatively minor one; for Ganelon clearly states that he would not wish Charlemagne to *say* that he died in a strange country without selling himself dearly (447–449), and Roland nowhere mentions any fear of "sinking in his own eyes", whereas he frequently refers to "the opinion of his peers". In fact the SR presents little introspection and almost none of the psychological analysis so typical of the works of Chrétien of Troyes only a few decades later. It may lack these because it is an epic dealing with action rather than with speculation, yet this lack does indicate that the author and/or his public were little concerned with psychological problems.

In a shame culture the poet's chief function is to distribute

[4] Il a, devant les Francs, laissé voir son angoisse et il éprouve le besoin de se démontrer à lui-même qu'il n'est pas un lâche . . . (Le Gentil, p. 99).

[5] C'est que l'honneur est son grand souci: par dessus tout, il redoute de déchoir à ses propres yeux et dans l'opinion de ses pairs; il aimerait mille fois mieux mourir que de voir, si peu que se soit, pâlir sa réputation et sa gloire (Le Gentil, p. 122). Here Le Gentil mentions Roland's self-esteem first, even though he comments longer on his external reputation.

praise and blame where due; and Turold has surely performed his task well. Except for the traitor Ganelon, all his Frankish heroes personify the warrior ideal. By immortalizing their deeds he inspired his public to emulate them and thus win everlasting glory. William of Malmesbury relates that a minstrel sang of Roland to William the Conqueror's troops before the Battle of Hastings "so that the warlike example of the hero would enflame those who were about to fight." [6] Whether true or apocryphal, this account does show that William of Malmesbury's contemporaries believed that to have been the purpose of the song.

Roland was often cited as a model of courage. Raoul of Caen's *Gesta Tancredi* describes two crusaders at Dorylaeum with the words: "Seeing them, you would have thought Roland and Oliver had been brought back to life." [7] Ordericus Vitalis quotes Robert Guiscard as saying: "Noble warrior Bohemond, comparable in martial valor to the Thessalian Achilles and to the French Roland. . . ." [8] This commonplace lasted for centuries and even reached the New World with Pizarro's conquistadors in Peru, who, when hard pressed, swore that they would each do more than Roldán. [9] The *SR* gives not only models to emulate but also a model to shun: the previously mentioned inscription on the wall of the cathedral at Nepi warns against the *shameful* death suffered by the treacherous Ganelon.

Although the heroes of the *SR* show more concern for their

[6] tunc cantilena Rollandi inchoata, ut martium viri exemplum pugnaturos accenderet . . . praelium consertum est (*De gestis regum Anglorum,* ed. William Stubbs, London, 1889, Vol. II, p. 320).

[7] Rollandum dicas Oliveriumque renatos (Cited by Fawtier, p. 67).

[8] Nobilis athleta Buamunde, militia Thessalo Achilli, seu Francigenae Rollando aequiparande (*Orderici Vitalis, Historiae Ecclesiasticae Libri* XIII, ed. A. Le Prévost, Paris, 1845, III p. 186).

[9] *The Conquest of Peru,* trans. Joseph H. Sinclair, New York, 1929. Apparently the translator did not recognize the Spanish form of the name. There were marked similarities in ethos, particularly with regard to righteous rapacity, between the eleventh-century crusaders in Spain and their successors five centuries later in the New World.

worldly reputations than for their eternal salvation, most critics emphasize the "Christian" nature of the song. John O'Hagan says that it "displays a deep and tender faith," and Robert Fawtier maintains that it "is profoundly inspired with Christian spirit." [10] Giuseppe Chiri believes that "from beginning to end the song is full of those traits that reveal in the poet an ardent flame of Christian religiosity," and Boissonnade calls Turold a "fervent Christian".[11] Although aware of the Franks' pride of conquest and will to victory, Boissonnade considers religious faith the primary incentive of the warriors of the SR; [12] and Dorothy Sayers (p. 19) says that "it is not only Christian in subject; it is Christian to its very bones." Ronald Walpole, Alain Renoir, and others also stress the Christian nature of the song, especially with regard to Roland's humility and penitence after the battle of Roncevaux.[13]

Many critics who call the SR a "Christian" epic mean that its values concur with those of most twelfth-century Christians in Western Europe. But such a view implies that "Christian" is a relative or progressive term which depends upon contemporary social views, rather than upon an absolute or divinely revealed law. To be sure, there are as many interpretations of Christianity as there are Christian denominations, sects, and confessions—or perhaps one might say there are as many confessions as there are confessors. Yet there are a few tenets that most Christians, and even many non-Christians, consider basic to Christianity

[10] O'Hagan, p. 29; "La *Chanson de Roland* est profondément inspirée d'esprit chrétien" (Fawtier, p. 137).

[11] "Dal principio alla fine tutto il cano è pieno di questi tratti che manifestano nel poeta un'ardente fiamma di religiosità cristiana" (Chiri, p. 127); "fervent chrétien" (Boissonnade, 489).

[12] "Avec la foi religieuse, c'est la fierté de la conquête, l'affirmation de leur personnalité et de leur supériorité qui déterminent leurs actions. On sent chez le chef suprême de la croisade, à côté de la conviction de la mission divine qui lui a été assignée, la joie qui lui donne le triomphe d'une volonté consciente de ses desseins et de la victoire, appelée à couronner ses efforts." (Boissonnade, p. 276).

[13] R. N. Walpole, "The *Nota Emilianense*", Romance Philology, X, 1956, pp. 1–18; A. Renoir, "Roland's Lament", Speculum, 35, 1960, pp. 572–83.

because they are recorded in Scripture and have been accepted, at least in theory, by most Christian cults. Among these are the tenets that humility is better than pride, that love is better than hate, and that forgiveness is better than vengeance. Such tenets are not expressed in the *SR*.

In view of the preceding investigations, it is evident that the word "Christian" must be more precisely defined before being attributed to Roland and his colleagues. If the word "Christian" means "Christlike" or "following the teachings and tenets of Christ", then it should not be applied to those brutal and fanatic conquerors. On the other hand, it is appropriate if it means "professing to be a follower of Christ" or "belonging to a political-religious organization that bears His name". The difficulty is semantic. There should be at least two words for "Christian", just as there are two German words for "Lutheran": *Lúther(i)sch*, which refers to the reformer, and *luthérisch*, which refers to the church named after him.

The ethos of Christianity is perhaps best formulated in the Gospels, particularly in the Sermon on the Mount. This sermon summarizes Christ's ethical principles in the beatitudes, among which are:

Blessed are the poor in spirit; for theirs is the kingdom of heaven.	Beati pauperes spiritu, quoniam ipsorum est regnum caelorum.
Blessed are the meek; for they shall inherit the earth.	Beati mites, quoniam ipsi possidebunt terram.
Blessed are the merciful; for they shall obtain mercy.	Beati misericordes, quoniam ipsi misericordiam consequentur.
Blessed are the peacemakers; for they shall be called the children of God.	Beati pacifici, quoniam filii Dei vocabuntur.
Blessed are they which are persecuted for righteousness' sake; for theirs is the kingdom of heaven.	Beati qui persecutionem patiuntur propter justitiam, quoniam ipsorum est regnum caelorum.

Blessed are ye, when men shall revile you, and persecute you, and shall say all manner of evil against you falsely, for my sake. (Matthew 5:3–11)	Beati estis, cum maledixerint vobis et persecuti vos fuerint et dixerint omne malum adversum vos mentientes propter me.

This sermon differs from those of Archbishop Turpin, who won so many people to the faith. There was no place in Turpin's company for the meek or the poor in spirit, no place for the merciful or the peacemakers. The peacemaker Ganelon is the villain of the song; the warmonger Roland is its hero. God sends special angels for Roland's soul, but not for that of his more reasonable friend Oliver. For the heroes of the *SR*, being persecuted or reviled would only prove cowardice and weakness; and failure to achieve revenge would bring everlasting shame. They would have ostracized any man who turned his other cheek.

When Christ advises doing alms and saying prayers in secret (Matthew 6:1–7), he is clearly teaching a theocentric ethos; for good and bad depend upon love of God and obedience to divine command rather than upon public opinion. In the *SR*, on the other hand, society is the arbiter of good and bad; and men make their supreme effort to win public approval and to avoid public censure. Except for the theme of holy war, the ethos of the *SR* often resembles that of the *Iliad*. In fact it may be argued that martial epics inherently stress the glory won through deeds of daring. A heroic ethos based on fame and shame is present to some extent in the *Aeneid* too, even though Aeneas is chiefly motivated by moral virtue (*pietas*) and, like Charlemagne, is ultimately led by divine destiny.[14]

Whereas Turold may have received some ideas on honor and

[14] Curtius (*Eur. Lit.*, pp. 181–82) shows that Virgil presents an ideal of peace rather than of war and stresses the virtues of *iustitia* and *pietas* rather than the warlike virtues. Nevertheless, Aeneas is outstanding in military as well as moral virtue: *pietate insignis et armis* (*Aeneid*, VI, 403), and Virgil often stresses worldly fame as the purpose of courage in battle.

glory from classic literary sources, he most likely used only those that fitted the values held by his public. As we shall see, the values he emphasized were mostly of Germanic origin. It is easy to agree with Gaston Paris in believing that the *chansons de geste* have a "Germanic spirit in a Romance form." [15] There are many parallels between the attitudes and actions of the SR and those of various Germanic songs and sagas, especially in the sagas of Iceland. Such parallels, however, are questionable proof that the SR has a Germanic spirit, since most Germanic literature was first recorded by clerics familiar with classic writings and prone to flaunt their erudition by including scraps of Latin wisdom. Moreover, many of the Norse parallels were first written down after the SR appeared and could therefore show its influence. This may be true, for example, of the classical commonplace that you should be good to your friends but stern to your enemies, which is echoed in both the SR and the Icelandic *Njáls saga*.[16] It will be noted that the thought appeared also in the *Karlamagnús saga*, which acquired it from the SR.[17] Having preceded the *Njáls saga*,[18] the *Karlamagnús saga* may well have supplied it with this thought.

Whereas one can not prove Germanic origins for the ideas and attitudes in the SR by comparing them with similar ideas and

[15] "l'esprit germanique sous une forme romane" (*Revue Critique*, V, 1868, p. 385). This thought was probably influenced by Uhland's dictum: "Das karolingische Epos . . . ist in einem germanischen Volksstamme, dem fränkischen, erzeugt, aber abgefasset und ausgebildet in einer romanischen Mundart" (*Uhlands Schriften*, VII, 1868, p. 654).

[16] Vers Sarrazins reguardet fierement e vers Frances humeles e dulcement (1162–1163). In the *Brennu-Njáls saga* Snorri was good to his friends but grim to his enemies: hann var góðr vinum sínum en grimmr ovinum (cxiv, 4).

[17] The *Karlamagnús saga* (#22) follows the SR quite closely: og mælir hermilega við alla heiðna menn, en blíðlega og hælega við sína menn. For classical examples of this topos, see Jones, "Grim to your Foes . . .".

[18] According to Stefán Einarsson (pp. 162, 145) the *Karlamagnús saga* was written in the second half of the 13th century and the *Njáls saga* in the last quarter of the 13th or the first quarter of the 14th.

attitudes expressed in contemporary or later Germanic works, such origins are indicated by similarities in the *Germania* of the Roman historian Tacitus, which gives a convincing picture of Germanic morals and manners prior to 98 A.D. Tacitus made some errors in interpretation, yet his compact little area-study has generally proved to be a reliable work.[19] Tacitus especially emphasizes the Germanic warriors' courage and loyalty in battle. In time of war the chief social unit is the *comitatus,* a band of young warriors serving a famous leader (#13). The leader supports his followers in time of peace, and they fight for him in time of war. As Tacitus expresses it, "the leaders fight for victory, and the followers fight for their leader." It is disgraceful for the leader to be surpassed in battle by his followers, and it is disgraceful for the followers not to keep up with their leader. The followers not only defend their leader but also give him the glory for their own deeds (#14); and it would bring them shame and disgrace all their lives to survive his death in battle (#6).

This military society is clearly founded on the principle of service and reward, for the followers serve their leader in return for daily food and gifts, as well as for a chance to win plunder and martial fame. Because of his followers' demands, the leader must wage constant war in order to win enough booty to support the system (#14). Offenses are usually avenged, yet even murder may be atoned by compensation paid to the entire family of the victim; and an individual must assume both the feuds and the friendships of his father (#21). A man's influence depends upon the number and power of his kinsmen, and men honor their sisters' sons as much as their own (#20).

Excepting material rewards, the greatest motivating factor here is plainly hope of fame and fear of shame. Followers must die with their leader or live a life of shame (#14), and they recover

[19] For reliability of *Germania,* see *Cornelii Taciti de Origine et situ Germanorum,* ed. J. G. C. Anderson, Oxford, 1938, pp. xxvii–xxxvii.

the bodies of their companions even when the battle is still un-decided (#6). Throwing away one's shield in battle brings ever-lasting shame, and fear of shame often impels survivors of battle to hang themselves (#6). Even sexual morality is enforced chiefly through threat of public disgrace (#19).

The barons of the *SR* manifest an ethos much like that of the ancient Germans described by Tacitus approximately a millen-nium earlier, for example, when they assure their leader that not one of them will fail him in battle.[20] Charlemagne resembles the older and renowned Germanic chieftain defended by loyal followers whom he has long supported. Like their Germanic forebears, his men must serve their liege in return for the suste-nance he has given them, even if it costs them their lives. That probably explains why Roland laments: "Alas that the Emperor has nourished (i.e., retained) you!" (*Li empereres tant mare vos nurrit!*, 1860).[21] Even while dying, Roland thinks of Charle-magne, who has retained him (*kil nurrit*, 2380). The *SR* also attributes this type of obligation to the Saracens, who are cul-turally the Franks' counterparts: in trying to urge his men to aid his son, Baligant reminds them that he has supported them for a long time (*nurrit vos ai ling tens*).[22] Germanic literature often denounces the ungrateful follower who fails to repay his liege's generosity. The author of the *Battle of Maldon* reproaches the warriors who desert Byrhtnoth in his need by saying that they have forgotten the many favors he has done for them;[23] and in the *Lay of the Nibelungs* Hagen reviles the cowardly Huns who

[20] Dient Franceis: "Icist reis est vassals. Chevalchez, bers! Nul de nus ne vus falt!" (3343–3344). Compare this with *Germania*, #14.

[21] Bédier renders this as "L'empereur vous a nourris pour son malheur", and Jenkins renders it as "Your stay in the Emperor's household, alas! is a thing of the past".

[22] *SR*, 3374. The *Rolandslied* alludes to this obligation twice. Baligant reminds his men: Ich hân iuch gezogen (7199), and Thierry wishes to avenge his kinsman Roland in part because: Rolant hât mich gezogen (8823).

[23] ed. Gordon, vv. 196–97.

refuse to fight for their lord: "Those who have eaten their prince's bread so shamefully and now fail him in his need, I see many of them standing around like cowards even though they would like to be thought brave. They must always suffer disgrace because of it." [24]

Also of Germanic origin is the custom of sealing friendships or alliances by giving gifts.[25] When Marsilie, Valdabrun, Climorin, and Bramimunde give their gifts to Ganelon, they are following the ancient Germanic tradition of validating an agreement, and Valdabrun and Climorin patently specify that they are giving Ganelon the gifts to obligate him to aid them against Roland.[26] Turold lets each of the donors emphasize the value of his gift, yet it was the symbolic rather than the monetary value of the gifts that made them binding.[27] By accepting these gifts openly and before many witnesses, Ganelon has become beholden and will forfeit his honor if he does not carry out his part of the agreement.

Charlemagne's retinue thus has much in common with the *comitatus* described by Tacitus. It is tempting to suppose that Tacitus chose the word *comitatus* to render the Germanic word *gasinþs, which literally meant "fellow-travelers" and was used

[24] Die hie sô lasterlîchen ezzent des fürsten brôt unde im nu geswîchent in der grœzesten nôt der sihe ich hie manigen vil zagelîche stân, und wellent doch sîn küene: si müezens immer schande hân (NL, 2027).

[25] In the *Germania* (#18) Tacitus observes this fact only in connection with the gifts exchanged at weddings, but later Germanic literature shows that it was a customary way of sealing any bargain. Surprisingly, Tacitus maintains that hosts and guests exchanged gifts without demanding credit or admitting obligation (*Germania*, #21).

[26] Par amistiez, bel sire, la vos duins, que nos aidez de Rollant le barun (622–623); Si nos aidez de Rollant li marchis (630).

[27] meillur n'en at nuls hom; entre les helz ad plus de mil manguns (620–621); unches meillor ne vi . . . (629). Jan de Vries (p. 59) says that the ancient Germans considered a gift more than just an object: "eine Gabe ist nicht nur die Darreichung eines Gegenstandes, sondern sie stiftet zwischen dem Gebenden und dem Empfangenden ein innigeres Verhältnis, das gegenseitig verpflichtet."

of a chieftain's retinue. Yet it is perhaps more likely that the Germanic word acquired its precise political and military nuance as a semantic borrowing from Latin, because most cultural influences between Romans and Teutons were from the former to the latter. Nevertheless, although more often the recipients than the donors, the Teutons did contribute some thoughts and words to the Latin language. This is obvious in the case of medieval Latin terms based on words borrowed from the various Germanic dialects and used to designate Germanic weapons, customs, and institutions. Many of these terms are represented in the *SR* by their Old French derivatives.[28]

Whereas it is easy to recognize Germanic loan-words in the *SR*, it is more difficult to recognize loan-translations and semantic borrowings. A good example of a loan-translation from Germanic is the word *cumpainz,* a derivative of the Medieval Latin word *cumpanio,* which in turn seems to have been formed through analogy with the Old High German word *gileibo.*[29] The word *gileibo* literally meant "one who shares bread", but it also designated a fellow retainer of a common liege. The designation of a liege lord as a "bread-donor" must have been a Germanic concept, since there were words to express the idea in various Germanic languages but not in classical Latin. The English word "lord" is derived from Anglo-Saxon *hláfweard,* which literally meant a "loaf-ward"; and *æt-gifa,* an Anglo-Saxon kenning for "liege", literally meant "food-giver".[30] Whereas classical Latin had

[28] In the area of arms alone we find: *algier, brant, bronie, dard, espiet, halbercs (osberc), helme, helz, targe, wigre.* Similar lists could be made of military equipment, formations, actions, and virtues. For very early Romance borrowings of Germanic military terms, see Brüch, pp. 99–105.

[29] Related to Gothic *gahlaiba,* from *hlaifs* (loaf). Bédier denies that there is anything Germanic about the word *compagnon* (Bédier, *Commentaires,* p. 306).

[30] For *æt-gifa,* see H. Marquart, *Die altenglischen Kenningar,* Halle, 1938, p. 256.

no word designating a seigneur in his function of *Brotherr*, medieval Latin had the word *nutritor*.[31] The immediate mental association between nourishment and obligation is suggested by Tacitus's remark that the followers' meals were looked upon as pay.[32]

The Germanic languages enriched Old French not only with loan-words and loan-translations but also with semantic borrowings, which are considerably more difficult to prove. This study has previously shown that the word *amis* could mean ally without connoting affection and that *amur* could mean peace or alliance. Such change in meaning may have resulted from semantic borrowing from Old High German. The Frankish invaders derived their noun *fridu* (peace) from the same root as their verb *frijôn* (to love), from which the noun *friund* (friend) was also derived. The word *fridu* meant "peace", not in the sense of absence of war, but rather in the sense of absence of hostility between two or more parties who are bound by birth or oath to protect one another. Such pacts were often guaranteed through marriage. This seems to have been the case between Oliver and Roland; for, by marrying her brother's friend, Alde plays the role of *friðu-sibb*, as the Northmen would have called the person used to seal such a bond.[33] As we have seen, when Oliver becomes angry with Roland, he immediately threatens to end the engagement.

The *fridu* can be explained as a state of amicability sanctioned by blood or treaty; and it can be likened to a mutual defense pact, even if formed for the purpose of waging a joint offensive against nonmembers. Its purpose is not peace, but protection. The *fridu* had originally bound members of a clan or kindred, and consequently the word *friund* designated kinsmen as well as

[31] See Hollyman, p. 55. The Old High German word *gimazzo* (literally, a "co-eater") also meant a companion.

[32] Nam epulae et quamquam incompti, largi tamen apparatus pro stipendio cedunt (*Germania*, #14).

[33] Grönbech, II, p. 55.

friends. As we have seen, the word *amis* in the SR connotes both kith and kin as well as friend and ally. When Charlemagne refuses to show either *pais* or *amor* to Baligant, the mental association of these words may reflect a tradition handed down from the days when the Franks still spoke their Germanic dialects, and therefore still expressed peace and love with cognate words. Germanic institutions may have influenced the meaning of all three words for friend in the SR. The word *drud* is clearly a loan-word derived from Old High German *drût;* the word *cumpainz* is, as we have seen, a loan-translation based on *gileibo;* and the word *amis,* in its sense of a member of a common *amistiet,* may have acquired its technical meaning through semantic borrowing from the word *friund.* Although derived from Latin *comes,* the Old French word *quens,* in the sense of count or military retainer, probably owes more to Germanic than to Roman tradition.

Like their Germanic forebears, Roland's men all die for him in battle; and he is ready to follow them once he has recovered their bodies for burial. Just as fear of shame kept the Germanic warrior from throwing down his shield in battle, fear of shame makes Roland prevent his sword from falling into his enemies' hands. He does not fear that the enemy will harm his fellow Christians by using the sword, but rather that they will besmirch his posthumous fame by getting possession of it. When Roland declares that a follower must be ready to lose hide and hair (*perdre e del quir e del peil,* 1012), his choice of words may reflect the old Germanic legal term *hût und hâr;* for loss of hide and hair was a common form of punishment.[34]

Like the Germanic chiefs before him, Charlemagne must seize booty and accept gifts from neighbors in order to buy the loyalty

---

[34] *Deutsche Rechtsaltertümer,* II, pp. 287–88. Tacitus mentions that women were punished thus for adultery: abscisis crinibus nudatam coram propinquis expellit domo maritus ac per omnem vicum verbere agit (*Germania,* #19).

of his warriors. He agrees to overlook his envoys' murder in return for rich gifts, which correspond to the blood moneys paid
by ancient Germanic offenders; and he is expected to distribute
this compensation to his retinue like the chiefs of German antiquity.[35] In advising Charlemagne to refuse the gifts and to
avenge his envoys, Roland resembles the virtuous heroes of the
Icelandic sagas who think it dishonorable "to carry a kinsman in
one's purse". Whereas the SR does not make it clear that Marsilie's
gift is a blood money, the fact is a bit more apparent in the
Rolandslied.[36]

The ancient Germans' respect for men with large kindreds
is echoed in the SR when Ganelon's kinsmen assure him that
Roland has acted foolishly in provoking a man with so many
relatives. Although in no way responsible for Ganelon's treachery,
they must nevertheless defend him or else be publicly shamed.
As we have seen, Pinabel proudly avows that it is fear of shame
that causes him to undertake the trial by combat.

The heroes of the SR feel as much affection for their sisters'
sons as the barbarians described by Tacitus did. Both Pauphilet
and Curtius recognize that Roland is Charlemagne's nephew, yet
they believe that Turold failed to specify whether he was a
sister-son or a brother-son.[37] Even though Turold's public would
have taken it for granted that Roland was a sister-son,[38] Turold

---

[35] luitur enim etiam homicidium certo armentorum ac pecorum numero
recipitque satisfactionem universa domus (Germania, #21). After listing
the compensation (SR, 30–33, 127–132), Blancandrins assumes that Charlemagne will give it to his soldeiers (34, 133).
[36] Marsilie hiez in die houbet abe slahen. Swer nu golt welle haben, der
entphâhe iz dar ubre. Der rât gevellet mir uble: man nimt iz âne gotes êre
unde gerûwet uns hernâch vil sêre (RL, 1148–1153). Conrad attributes
Roland's unwillingness to his fear of offending God's rather than Charlemagne's honor.
[37] Certes Roland est le neveu de Charlemagne; mais de quelle manière?
Fils d'un frère, ou d'une soeur, du roi, ou de la reine? (Pauphilet, p. 181);
Roland ist Karls Neffe—ob von Vater- oder Mutterseite, sagt uns der
Dichter freilich nicht (Curtius, p. 311).
[38] This is indicated by the numerous passages cited by W. O. Farnsworth
in his Uncle and Nephew in the Old French Chansons de Geste, New York,

does clarify the relationship, namely by stating that Roland is the step-son of Ganelon and that Ganelon is the husband of Charlemagne's sister.[39] This certainly indicates that Turold meant Roland to be the son of Charlemagne's sister by a previous marriage, as seems to have been assumed by the authors of later *chansons de geste* revolving around Charlemagne.[40] The author of the *Karlamagnús saga* entertains no doubt and makes Roland his *systurson* (#17); and in like manner the author of the Middle English *Song of Roland* makes Roland the Emperor's *sostir son* (180) or *sistir son* (186). The *Pseudo-Turpin* is more specific in saying that Roland is the son of Charlemagne's sister Berta;[41] and the *Nota Emilianense*, a recently discovered Spanish reference to the battle at Roncevaux, makes all twelve peers Charlemagne's nephews.[42]

The relationship between uncle and sister-son also requires Falsaron to avenge his nephew Aelroth,[43] who appears to be the son of his sister.[44] In fact, whenever Turold mentions the uncle-nephew relationship, we may assume that he is referring to uncle and sister-son, for he does not even mention the relationship when an uncle tries to avenge his brother's son.[45] Although

---

1913. See also F. B. Gummere, "The Sister's Son" in *An English Miscellany Presented to Dr. Furnivall*, Oxford, 1901, pp. 132–49.

[39] Rollant, cist miens fillastre (743); ensurquetut si ai jo vostre soer (312). The *Rolandslied* says: dîn swester ist mîn wîb (1444).

[40] For example, in *Fierabras* (v. 2278) Namles says: "Rollans est vostre niés et de vo sereur nés."

[41] nepos Karoli, filius ducis Milonis de Angulariis natus ex Berta sorore Karoli (*Pseudo-Turpin*, XIII, 8–9).

[42] In his diebus habuit duodecim neptis (*Nota Emilianense*, v. 2).

[43] asez ad doel quant vit mort sun nevold (1219).

[44] Aelroth is a nephew of Marsilie (*Li niés Marsilie*, 860) and therefore also of Marsilie's brother Falsaron, who calls him *Bel sire niés* (881) just as Charlemagne calls Roland (784). Since the SR does not imply that Marsilie and Falsaron have another brother (who would certainly have taken part in the battle), it is a safe assumption that Aelroth is the son of their sister, as the *Karlamagnús* poet assumes (*systurson*, KS, #18, 23).

[45] Turold does not mention the relationship when Canabeus tries to avenge his brother's son Malprimes (3421–3433). Canabeus is *le frere a l'amiraill* (3430) and Malprimes is *Ses filz* (3176). It is a justifiable assumption that

Turold fails to mention it and no critics seem to have noted it, this relationship also plays a role when Marganice slays Oliver. By slaying Oliver, Marganice avenges his nephew Falsaron, whom Oliver had previously slain.[46] Since Falsaron had lost his life in trying to avenge his own nephew Aelroth, whom Oliver had killed, we can see that Turold pursued the point of avuncular honor to its ultimate fulfillment. In only one case does anyone disregard his avuncular duty, namely when Charlemagne executes Ganelon to avenge his nephew Roland; for Ganelon's shameful death naturally brings disgrace on his son Baldwin, who is just as much Charlemagne's sister-son as Roland was. Whereas the SR never ascribes a nephew to Roland, the Roelantslied does so, perhaps only in order to explain why it is he who avenges Sanson.[47]

Scholars may have misinterpreted Tacitus's remark about the bond between Germanic uncles and nephews: "Sororum filiis idem apud avunculum qui apud patrem honor" (Germania, #20). This is generally understood to mean that men held their nephews in the same honor as they held their sons, although it is unusual in most societies for seniors to hold their juniors in honor.[48] This may be what Tacitus meant to say; but, judging by later Germanic literature, it would seem that his Germanic informants or sources had meant that uncles shared a common

---

Turold uses the word uncle only in the original sense of avunculus (mother-brother) and not in the sense of patruus (father-brother).

[46] As Marsilie's uncle (mun uncle l'algalife, 493), Marganice is also uncle of Marsilie's brother Falsaron (Icil ert frere al rei Marsiliun, 880). When Oliver kills Falsaron (1229), he offends Marganice, who later causes his death (1943). Becker (p. 9) denies that the algalife mentioned in vv. 453, 493, 505, and 681 is the same person as mentioned in vv. 1914, 1943, 1954; but the relationship remains the same in either case, since Marganice too is an uncle of Marsilie (Se fuït s'en est Marsilies, Remès i est sis uncles, Marganices, 1913–1914).

[47] Hi hadde rouwe wter maten groot, om dat hi sinen neve soe sach ligghen doot (Roelantslied, vv. 731–32).

[48] Guinemer honors his nephew Ganelon by holding his stirrup (348), but that is only because Ganelon is the head of the kindred.

honor with the sons of their sisters. That is to say, an offense against a nephew was publicly regarded as an offense against his mother-brother, who had to avenge it or else suffer public shame. To be sure, honor was a common possession of the entire clan, but the relationship of uncle and nephew was especially strong and helps explain why Marsilie sends important hostages to certain death at Charlemagne's hands rather than surrender his guilty uncle (488–494).

The common honor of uncle and sister-son is illustrated in the *Waltharius* when Walter kills Patafrid, for Hagen must then avenge his nephew even though Walter is his best friend and sworn ally.[49] The duty of revenge devolved not only upon the uncle of a slain nephew, but also upon the nephew of a slain uncle; and therefore it was axiomatic that nephews avenge better than brothers.[50] In the *SR* Charlemagne invokes God to help him avenge his nephew,[51] and this suggests that the descendants of the Germanic converts assumed that God sanctified the mutual obligation between uncles and nephews. Charlemagne's great determination to obtain revenge at Ganelon's trial also reflects awareness that his honor has been impugned through his nephew's death. It is, of course, debatable whether or not avuncular affection was really as dear to twelfth-century men as it was in their literature. In either case, it gradually lost its importance even in literature. This may explain why some poets believed Roland to be Charlemagne's son as well as his nephew, for they may

[49] *Waltharius*, vv. 846–77, 1272–75. It is to be noted that it is *dolor* that requires Hagen to demand satisfaction from Walter (v. 1272), just as it is *doel* that makes Falsaron wish to avenge his nephew (*SR*, 1219). The *Waltharius* is rather exceptional in having satisfaction demanded by a brother-son when Scaramundus demands his uncle's life: Et dum nepos conspexerat hoc Camalonis, Filius ipsius Kimo cognomine fratris . . . (vv. 686–87).

[50] The hero of *Folque de Candie* (v. 537) says: "toz jors l'oi dire: ainz venge nies que fraire."

[51] Par ta mercit, se te plaist, me cunsent, Que mun nevold poisse venger Rolland (3108–3109).

have felt that some stronger tie than avuncular affection was needed to explain the emperor's great grief at Roland's death. For this purpose they made Roland the result of the Emperor's incestuous relationship with his sister.[51a]

Just as binding for the ancient Germans as the uncle-nephew relationship was the oath-brotherhood (*Schwurbruderschaft*), a close personal alliance voluntarily established by two or more individuals. Members of these alliances accepted all the obligations normally incumbent upon blood brothers, particularly the obligation of avenging the death of any other member. Since every free man was a sovereign power, such alliances were just as formalized as international treaties are today, and any breach of contract brought lifelong ignominy. The *SR* presents a relic of this Germanic institution in the companionship between Roland and Oliver, a relationship which William Stowell (p. 410) has named the *Compagnonage of the Higher Degree*. Gerins and Geriers also stand in this relationship to each other,[52] a fact which may explain why they join forces to kill Timozel and why they die together; but their companionship is less important for the song than that between the two chief protagonists at Roncevaux.

Turold did not explain how Roland and Oliver became companions, but Bertrand de Bar-sur-Aube did so a century later in his *Girart de Viënne*.[53] Even before the *SR* appeared, the formation of a personal relationship was well described in the *Ruodlieb*, an eleventh-century German romance in Latin hexameters. Ruodlieb, a knight errant, makes a pact with a royal hunter and seals it with a handshake and a kiss in a scene somewhat like that in *Girart de Viënne*.[54] The *Waltharius* had already

---

[51a] Rita Lejeune, in "Le péché de Charlemagne . . .", argues that Turold alludes to this accusation.

[52] Li quens Gerins . . . e sis cumpainz Geres (1379–1380). Cf. vv. 107, 794.

[53] *Girart de Viënne*, vv. 5935–67. Note that, at the conclusion of their friendship-pact, the author adds: "Einsi fu lor pais fete."

[54] *Ruodlieb*, I, vv. 114–21.

alluded to a pact of this kind; in fact it is "the often sworn pact" between Walter and his former friend Hagen which furnishes the dramatic moment of the poem.[55]

To appreciate personal friendships and hatreds in the Middle Ages, we must liken medieval individuals to modern sovereign states. Now that the state protects its citizens or subjects from each other, private individuals are no longer in such constant fear of aggression as they were in the Middle Ages, when every free man was obliged to defend his own life, property, and honor. Kings and other rulers protected their subjects from foreign enemies but not from each other, since all free men had the right to settle their own disputes by feud. When Ganelon believes himself abused by Roland, he must seek redress with his own hands, because there is no law to which he can appeal as long as Roland has the right of self-help.

Life, liberty, and property were not inalienable rights guaranteed by the state, they were inherited possessions that had to be jealously guarded. Men were constantly on the alert against real or supposed aggressions, as is the case today among sovereign nations that maintain a delicate balance of power by recourse to alliances, standing armies, fleets in being, and threats of instant atomic reprisal. Consequently, medieval men protected themselves with all sorts of personal and political alliances in addition to their natural ties of kinship. Although these alliances were conventionally negotiated in terms of the words *amer, amis, amor,* and *amistiet,* they were often a matter of practicality rather than affection.

Tacitus relates that the ancient Germans would predict the outcome of a serious war by having one of their warriors fight an enemy captive, each being equipped with his own arms.[56] As

---

[55] fides saepissime pacta (*Waltharius,* v. 1259). Cf. sponsa plerumque fides (vv. 1089–90), pactum almum (v. 1275).

[56] est et alia observatio auspiciorum, qua gravium bellorum eventus explorant. eius gentis cum qua bellum est captivum quoquo modo inter-

we have seen, similar prognostication occurs in the *SR* when Rabel and Guineman fight individually with two Saracen warriors prior to the main engagement; for their victory is taken as proof of a successful outcome for the entire army.[57] To be sure, a similar duel occurs in the Old Testament between David and Goliath,[58] but this duel is unique in the Bible whereas such duels were common in Germanic song and saga. Individual combats also play a large role in the *Iliad* and the *Aeneid,* and also in Prudentius's *Psychomachia,* but their outcomes are not presented as divine revelations.

Hans Kuhn states that trials by combat were not originally concerned with reward and punishment.[59] Later, when the Christian missionaries taught that God rewards the righteous, it was only natural to assume that He helps the righteous contestant in a duel and that the duel therefore proves who is right. Hence, it is not surprising that a Burgundian law code of 502 A.D. applied the words *Deo judicante* to a trial by combat.[60] The belief that God aids in battle was no Christian innovation. Tacitus relates that the ancient Germans propitiated the god "whom they believe to aid them in battle" (quem adesse bellantibus credunt, *Germania,* #7). This would suggest that the Christian missionaries, justified by Old Testament precedents, merely accommodated themselves to the traditional beliefs of the converts. When Pinabel and Thierry make pious donations before their combat (3861), they are behaving much like their heathen ancestors.

---

ceptum cum electo popularium suorum, patriis quemque armis, committunt: victoria huius vel illius pro praeiudicio accipitur (*Germania,* #10).

   [57] Carles ad dreit (3359, 3367).

   [58] I Samuel 17.

   [59] Er hat in der germanischen Zeit nichts mit dem sittlichen Lohngedanken zu tun gehabt. Er war ein Mittelding zwischen Fehde und Prozess, eine Austragung des Streites mit Waffengewalt, jedoch in öffentlich geregelten Formen (*Germanische Altertumskunde,* p. 178).

   [60] Cited by Dill, p. 73.

Unlike the Germanic peoples described by Tacitus, the heroes of the *SR* constantly invoke God, whose cause they claim to champion. As we have seen, however, this consideration was usually secondary to motivations of material reward and worldly fame. In fact it might be argued that the pious invocations in the *SR* owe as much to literary tradition as to deep religiosity on Turold's part, for he found frequent examples in the *Aeneid,* which in turn may have derived them from the *Iliad.* Moreover, as the Franks understood religious duty, it was no more than a projection of the duty they owed their secular leader who nourished them in time of peace and shared the plunder with them in time of war.

In giving God credit for their personal strength and success, as they so often do, the Frankish barons are doing no more than their heathen ancestors had done in giving their leader credit for all their courageous deeds.[61] Although boasting of the many lands he has conquered for Charlemagne, Roland nevertheless gives the credit to his liege,[62] just as Germanic warriors had been expected to do. This point of view is well expressed in the *Ruodlieb,* in which a defeated king says he does not need to praise or glorify the king who conquered him, since the latter has received enough praise and honor from his victorious general.[63] In the *Rolandslied* the pagan prince Alterot asks Marsilie for the boon of being allowed to kill Roland. He explains: "People will tell the tale about me. You will have the honor, and I shall be indebted to you ever afterwards." [64]

---

[61] illum defendere, tueri, sua quoque fortia facta gloriae eius adsignare praecipium sacramentum (*Germania,* #14).

[62] When Roland says: E li emprereres en est ber e riches (2354), the word *ber* suggests that Charlemagne's personal worth is enhanced by his vassal's conquests.

[63] "In cuius parma uictricia tu geris arma, ille tibi laudis sat praestat et omnis honoris; non opus est hinc te laudare uel amplificare" (*Ruodlieb,* V, vv. 47–49).

[64] daz ich Rolanten erslahe unt man daz maere von mir sage; sô hâstu sîn êre, und dîn iz iemir mêre (*RL,* 3559–3562).

The ethos of the twelfth-century Frankish warriors differed from that of the ancient Germans chiefly through an extension of the in-group. Between wars the primitive Germans had owed peace and justice only to their family and kinship and to those people allied to it. That is to say, they had owed peace only to their *friunde,* or members of their *fridu.* In war time they owed loyalty to their leader and to his other followers as well. Caesar relates in his *Gallic War* that the Germans did not consider brigandage wrong as long as it was performed beyond the tribal boundaries.[65] The same was true of the Franks a millennium later, provided the brigandage was performed outside of the borders of Christendom, or rather of Roman Christendom, since all other Christian denominations were damned as heretical. Just as Charlemagne has divine sanction to seize land and booty in Spain, William the Conqueror received Pope Hildebrand's blessing on his conquest of Christian England, and his Norman kinsmen in Sicily enjoyed papal support in their designs on the Christian empire of Byzantium. The *SR* may echo the Pope's support of William the Conqueror in the statement that Charlemagne crossed the salt sea to England and conquered Peter's Pence.[66]

Although the Spanish campaign in the *SR* is overlaid with Christian purpose, its deeper motivation still resembles that of Charlemagne's real Spanish campaign of 778, which was waged for purely practical reasons. Even the clerical biographer Einhard states that Charlemagne entered Spain to help one Mohammedan ruler against another. It is ironic that he destroyed the Christian city of Pampluna but not the pagan city of Saragossa and that his rear guard was annihilated by Christian Basques rather than by pagans. It is perhaps significant that most of the lands that

[65] Latrocinia nullam habent infamiam, quae extra fines cuiusque civitatis fiunt (*Gallic War*, VI, 23).

[66] Vers Engletere passat il la mer salse, ad oes seint Perre en cunquist le chevage (372).

Roland conquers for Charlemagne in the *SR* had been Christian long before he conquered them.

Believing the *SR* a compilation of folk ballads or *cantilènes* produced by the collective soul of the Frankish people and later joined together into an epic, Jacob Grimm, Ludwig Uhland, Gaston Paris, and other "romantic" scholars proved transmission from Frankish times by citing many customs of Germanic origin. It is undeniable, for example, that the code of honor in the *SR* shows more affinity with old Germanic than with late Roman codes, even if it does sometimes express its views on honor in terms borrowed from Latin authors.

It could be argued that some Frankish attitudes were holdovers from the earlier Celtic population of Gaul, but these cannot have been significant because the Gauls had been largely assimilated into Latin culture before the Franks arrived. In any case, it would be hard to distinguish between Celtic and Germanic attitudes because, as Caesar and other Roman historians have shown, the two peoples had not differed sharply in ethos. Caesar states that the uprising under Vercingetorix was partly due to the Gauls' desire to recover their martial fame,[67] and he also gives some illustrations of military loyalty among the Gauls which resemble that of the Germanic invaders and of their Frankish descendants depicted in the *SR*.[68] I say "their descendants", because the French warriors of the twelfth century were patently the spiritual successors of the Germanic invaders, re-

---

[67] Tamen tanta universae Galliae consensio fuit libertatis vindicandae et pristinae belli laudis recuperandae . . . (*Gallic War*, VII, 76).

[68] quorum haec est condicio, ut omnibus in vita commodis una cum eis fruantur, quorum se amicitiae dediderint, si quid eis per vim accidat, aut eundem casum una ferant aut sibi mortem consciscant; neque adhuc hominum memoria repertus est quisquam qui, eo interfecto cuius se amicitiae devovisset, mori recusaret (*Gallic War*, III, 22). Litaviccus cum suis clientibus, quibus more Gallorum nefas est etiam in extrema fortuna deserere patronos, Gergoviam profugit (VII, 40).

gardless of how much Gallo-Roman blood the latter may have absorbed from the occupied population.

Historians may disagree as to whether the Germanic invaders largely displaced the native population of northern France or whether they merely formed a thin upper-crust and left the bulk of the native population racially intact. In either case it is clear that the military aristocracy of medieval France retained many of the attitudes and outlooks of their Germanic forebears, attitudes and outlooks that were self-perpetuating in times of turmoil. As the ruling class, they set a social pattern that was emulated by those below them on the social ladder, and their social prestige and cultural continuity are indicated by the adoption of their Germanic names by all social classes in France. The majority of the Christians in the SR have names of Germanic origin, most of which have to do with war, weapons, or renown.

Even if Ramón Menendez Pidal and his fellow traditionalists are correct in believing that many themes and narrative details in the SR had been handed down from ancient times along with the historical subject matter,[69] we may be sure that Turold expressed only those moral values acceptable to his public. The song's impact was direct. It stirred the hearer's heart and did not merely appeal to his aesthetic tastes or antiquarian interests. According to Italo Siciliano, the Germanic uses and customs found in the SR "may have persisted in the life of the people or in the memory of the French writers." [70] It is probable that ethical values remained not only in the memory of the poets, but also in the

---

[69] Cada refundición conserva mucho de su predecesora . . . en las refundiciones del Roland de los siglos XII y XIII subsisten en general la mayoría de los versos y de las tiradas de la versión de hacia 1100; y esta versión, a su vez, sabemos que conserva varios temas existentes en el siglo X, y aun sabemos que conserva pormenores narrativos (Menendez Pidal, pp. 466–67).

[70] . . . il peut s'agir aussi d'us et de coutumes germaniques qui ont persisté dans la vie du peuple ou dans la mémoire des écrivains français (Siciliano, p. 59).

life of the people, at least of the public for whom the song was composed.[71] This public was a military élite that endorsed an heroic code and cherished worldly fame as man's worthiest goal.

While desirous of posthumous fame, the Hellenistic Greeks and the Romans of the declining Empire do not seem to have longed for it as intensely as the ancient Germans did. By the time the Germanic tribes invaded the Roman Empire, the Roman will to glory was on the wane; and leading philosophers discredited posthumous fame as a meaningless vanity. The invaders, on the other hand, still yearned to leave good reputations behind them in the memories of men; for lasting praise was the only form of immortality they knew. As Andreas Heusler states: "Renown or good reputation after death was for the heathen what eternal salvation is for the Christian." [72] Hans Kuhn confirms this opinion: "The greatest possession of the ancient German and the decisive yardstick for everything that he did and left undone was his honor and the fame which was to survive him." [73] The Franks inherited their hope of future fame largely from their Germanic ancestors, even though classical literature had also stressed it.[74]

[71] C. L. Barber (*The Idea of Honour in the English Drama*, 1591–1700, Göteborg, 1957) has shown that the code of honor portrayed in Shakespeare's historical dramas was that of Elizabethan England, not that of their literary sources. This principle holds of ethical values in most historical fiction, even where the author has attempted to retain historical settings and local color.

[72] Der Ruhm, die 'gute Nachrede nach dem Tode' ist dem Heiden, was dem Christen die ewige Seligkeit: das höchste Gut (*Germanentum*, p. 103).

[73] Der höchste Besitz des Germanen und der entscheidende Maßstab für alles, was er tat und ließ, war seine Ehre und der Ruhm, der ihn überleben sollte (*Germanische Altertumskunde*, p. 215).

[74] The *Aeneid* expresses several sentiments typical of Germanic poetry. Euryalus assures Nisus that honor is well bought with life (vita bene credat emi honorem, IX, 204), Pallas tells Turnus that he will soon be praised for royal spoils or for a distinguished death (aut spoliis ego iam raptis laudabor opimis aut leto insigni, X, 449), and Jupiter says: "Everyone has an appointed day. The span of life is short and irretrievable for everyone; but the task of virtue is to lengthen one's fame through deeds" (stat sua cuique dies, breve et inreparabile tempus omnibus est vitae; sed famam extendere factis, hoc virtutis opus, X, 467–469).

In classic Greek dramas an ancestor's guilt often lingers as a curse upon his descendants. Being concerned with shame rather than guilt, the ancient Germans considered shame the most pernicious blight transmitted from father to son. In reproving Beowulf's cowardly vassals for deserting their leader in his peril, Wiglaf reminds them that their families will suffer because of their shameful deed.[75] When the Burgundians in the *Lay of the Nibelungs* strike Siegfried from behind, he tells them that they have committed a grievous injury against their kinsmen for which even their future descendants will be reproached.[76] In the *Battle of Maldon* Ælfwine gives the following reason for refusing to flee: "I will tell everyone of my noble birth and that I am of great family in Mercia. My grandfather was called Ealhelm and was a wealthy alderman. No heroes in this troop shall ever reproach me for wishing to flee from this army and seek my home, now that my liege lies dead in this battle. For me that is the greatest of evils: he was both my kinsman and my lord." [77]

The SR often preaches that men should avoid infamous deeds in order to protect their families from shame. As we have seen, Roland hopes God will confound him if ever he brings reproach upon his family (788), and Oliver warns him that blowing the horn will bring life-long reproof upon his family (1705–1707). In their earlier and more expansive period some Romans seem to have taken an intense pride in family too, if we can judge by

---

[75] Nû sceal sincþego ond swyrdgifu, eal êðelwyn êowrum cynne, lufen âlicgean; londrihtes môt þaere mægburge monna æghwylc îdel hweorfan, syððan aeðelingas feorran gefricgean flêam êowerne, dômlêasan dæd (*Beowulf*, 2884–2890).

[76] ir habt an iuwern mâgen leider übele getân (*NL*, 989, 4). Die sint dâ von bescholten, swaz ir wirt geborn her nâch disen zîten (990, 1). This attitude was not exceptional in the *chansons de geste*. In the *Chançun de Willame* (1326–1328) Guiburc tells William that she would rather see him die fighting than bring dishonor on his family and descendants: Mielz uoil que moergez en l'Archamp desur mer, Que tun lignage seit par tei auilé, Ne apres ta mort a tes heirs reproué. See note II, 92.

[77] *Battle of Maldon*, vv. 216–24.

an epitaph on the tomb of one of the Scipios: "By my behavior I have increased the virtues of my family; I have produced children and strived after the deeds of my father. I have maintained the glory (*laudem*) of my ancestors so that they are happy that I was born to them. My honors have ennobled my family." [78] Some Roman sentiments like this reached medieval men via literary channels, but it is unlikely that they would have decisively influenced the behavior or ideals of the Northern peoples. Tacitus reported that young boys were often made chiefs because of their conspicuous ancestry and the great merits of their fathers,[79] and this would suggest an indigenous respect for ancestry.

The Franks must have inherited their intense fear of other people's tongues from their Germanic ancestors, since the Roman world had largely lost its sensitivity to slander before the invasions had progressed very far. This was true even of those public figures who desired status, prestige, power, and posthumous fame. Suetonius relates that Julius Caesar let people sing ribald songs about his baldness and lechery and that Tiberius "was quite unperturbed by abuse, slander, or lampoons on himself and his family." [80] Germanic heroes and Frankish crusaders would have spurned such shamelessness as proof of cowardice.

It is hard to estimate how much of its ethos the *SR* owed to classical Latin and how much to Gallo-Roman civilization. Considering the *SR* a compilation of folk ballads born of the untutored soul of the Franks, the romantic scholars underestimated the Latin contributions to the song. Yet, as more scholars began to recognize the *SR* as an art-epic (*Kunstepos*) rather than as a popular epic (*Volksepos*), they began to note more classic in-

[78] virtutes generis mieis moribus accumulavi; progeniem genui, facta patris petiei. maiorum optenui laudem, ut sibi me esse creatum laetentur; stirpem nobilitavit honor (cited by Clarke, p. 3).

[79] insignis nobilitatis aut magna patrum merita principis dignationem etiam adulescentulis adsignant (*Germania*, #13).

[80] Suetonius: *The Twelve Caesars*, trans. Robert Graves, *Penguin Books*, 1957, III, 28 (p. 125).

fluences. Becker did not doubt "that Virgil helped at the birth of the epic," and Pauphilet asserted that "the *Aeneid* and the *Pharsalia* were distant but certain models of the *Chanson de Roland*." [81] Turold certainly knew something of Homer and Virgil, whom he mentions in his song (2616).

Classical influence was transmitted more through literature than through popular memory. Although the Gauls were thoroughly Romanized before the Empire fell, Roman civilization was only skin-deep and remained a monopoly of a small element of the population. According to C. E. Stevens (p. 80), Roman civilization in fifth-century Gaul was an essentially artificial culture founded on a very narrow base, since the middle classes, which might have given it stability, had been decaying throughout the past two centuries . . . Therefore ". . . from one point of view it would not be wrong to call Sidonius the last of the Romans in Gaul, for with him the Roman tradition was broken" (p. 18). Once this small intellectual élite was submerged by the Germanic invaders, Roman culture was too effete to assimilate the more vigorous foreigners. As a result, ancient civilization gradually disappeared except in Latin manuscripts and in the minds of those few clerics able to read them. It was only later, through the efforts of vernacular poets like Turold, that ancient ideas began to have any real effect on the bulk of the population. And even then the populace accepted chiefly those ideas that fitted their own traditional attitudes.

Among the Roman concepts that survived were those appropriate to an heroic culture, such as ideas concerning renown and victory. Almost overlooked were Stoic ideas of inner values, which had developed in Greece and had been adopted in Latin

---

[81] Dass Virgil bei der Geburt des Epos Helfer war, steht für mich ausser Zweifel (Curtius, p. 281); *L'Énéide, la Pharsale,* sont les modèles lointains mais certains de la *Chanson de Roland* (Pauphilet, 197). Bédier, *Commentaires,* p. 60, believes that the *chansons de geste* would have been impossible without the *Aeneid, Thebaid,* and the *Ilias Latina.*

literature by Cicero, Seneca, and other writers. Whereas classic ideas concerning glory and victory appealed to twelfth-century society at large, the ideas of the Greek Stoics and their Roman imitators found far less reception. The public fancy of the day was more heroic than Stoic, and whatever inner-directed men did exist were mostly withdrawn from the world and immured in monasteries with other "four-penny" monks.

Although Cicero spent most of his life struggling for fame and glory,[82] he denied their value in his *Offices*, which was based largely upon the Greek philosopher Panaetius. In this work Cicero declared that true honor (*honestum*) does not lie in the opinions of other people, but in disinterested performance of duty. Seneca too adopted and popularized similar Stoic ideas in his *Moral Essays*. The ideas of the Stoics, as compiled by Cicero and Seneca, were never entirely lost during the Middle Ages. The *Offices*, which was often copied, served as a popular text in monastic schools; and many of its ideas were incorporated into the writings of the church fathers. Stoic philosophy had much in common with the wisdom of the Old Testament, particularly with that found in the books of Proverbs, Ecclesiastes, Sapientia, and Ecclesiasticus, except that the Stoics valued virtue on its own merits whereas the Hebrew preachers valued righteousness as pleasing to God. Surprisingly enough, the Hebrew preachers placed more value on a good name than most of the Stoics did.[83] Although the standards of good behavior set by the Stoics often concurred with those preached by the Christian Church, it must be remembered that they were differently motivated; for the Stoics sought self-realiza-

---

[82] "The longing for glory, the desire to leave a name to posterity, was a marked feature of the Roman temperament and was present to an abnormal degree in Cicero himself" (Clarke, p. 63).

[83] The following sentiments are typical: "Melius est nomen bonum quam divitiae multae" (Proverbs, 22, 1); "Melius est nomen bonum quam unguenta pretiosa" (Ecclesiastes, 7, 2); "Corpora ipsorum in pace sepulta sunt, et nomen eorum vivit in generationem et generationem" (Ecclesiasticus 44, 14).

tion, whereas the Christians sought the greater glory of God.

While the Goths and Vandals were ransacking the moribund Roman Empire in quest of gold and glory, Saint Augustine denounced the love of human praise thus: "It is, therefore, doubtless far better to resist this desire than to yield to it, for the purer one is from this defilement, the liker he is to God; and, though this vice be not thoroughly eradicated from his heart,—for it does not cease to tempt even the minds of those who are making good progress in virtue,—at any rate let the desire of glory be surpassed by the love of righteousness. . . . But since those Romans were in an earthly city, and had before them, as the end of all the offices undertaken in its behalf, its safety, and a kingdom, not in heaven, but in earth,—not in the sphere of eternal life, but in the sphere of demise and succession, where the dead are succeeded by the dying,—what else but glory should they love, by which they wished even after death to live in the mouths of their admirers?" [83a] According to this definition, it is apparent that Roland and his companions at Roncevaux found their incentives more in an earthly city than in the City of God.

Love of glory (*gloriae cupiditas*) was universally damned by the Church. Saint Martin of Braga, a sixth-century bishop of the Suebi in Spain, illustrates this tradition in his *Formula de vitae honestae;* for this treatise, which he may have taken directly from Seneca, devotes a whole chapter to the problem of repelling vainglory, or *iactantia*.[84] While Turold was composing his song, the official view of the Church was like that subsequently expressed by Thomas Aquinas: "a man is not really virtuous who does virtuous deeds for the sake of human glory." [85] Nevertheless, human glory was the chief purpose of most of the virtuous deeds in the SR.

[83a] *The City of God by Saint Augustine,* trans. & ed. M. Dods, New York, 1948, V, 14.

[84] *Martini Episcopi Bracarensis, opera omnia,* ed. C. W. Barlow, New Haven, 1950.

[85] Non tamen est vere virtuosus qui propter humanam gloriam opera virtutis operatur (*Summa Theologiae,* II, II, 132, 1, ad. 2).

Although the Church endorsed the Stoics' contempt for worldly glory, most churchmen could not overcome their admiration for and envy of worldly honor. As we shall see, Otfrid of Weissenburg praised rather than condemned his nation's military renown. In general, medieval churchmen rejected the Stoics' view that worldly honor was of no value. To the contrary, they recognized it as the world's greatest good and damned it precisely because it distracted men from their task of preparing for heaven.[86] Despite the attitude professed by the Church, most laymen and many churchmen failed to distinguish between celestial glory and worldly honor. A typical example of their confusion appears in Rollandus' apostrophe to his sword in the *Pseudo-Turpin:* "Through you perfidy has been destroyed, the Christian law has been exalted, and God's praise and glory and great fame (*celeberrima fama*) have been won." [87] The *Karlamagnús* poet confuses earthly and celestial glory by letting Turpin promise the Franks that they will win good names in paradise.[88] Charlemagne's lament at Roncevaux echoes Christian disdain for worldly fame, but exactly in reverse. Upon reaching the battlefield, he asks: "Where are you, fair nephew? Where is the archbishop? and where Count Oliver? Where is Gerins? and his companion Gerers? Where is Otes? and Count Berenger, etc." (2402). This lament clearly follows the literary *topos* of *ubi sunt;* yet the poet is not damning the vanity of worldly endeavor, rather he is showing the great honor the fallen heroes receive from this royal lamentation.

Only one Stoic virtue plays a prominent role in the *SR*, namely when Oliver urges Roland to overcome his pride and blow his horn. "Prudent courage," he says, "is no folly. Moderation is worth

---

[86] This tradition lasted unbroken until modern times. A typical example is given by Bossuet: La Gloire! Qu'y a-t-il pour le chrétien de plus pernicieux et de plus mortel? quel appât plus dangereux? quelle fumée plus capable de faire tourner les meilleures têtes? (*Oraison funèbre d'Henriette d'Angleterre*).

[87] Per te gens perfida destruetur, lex christiana exaltabitur, laus Dei et gloria et celeberrima fama adquiretur (*Pseudo-Turpin*, XXVI, 23–24).

[88] þer skuluð eignast nafn í hinni góðu paradísu (*KS*, #22).

more than temerity." [89] Oliver's idea of prudent courage (*vas-selage par sens*) seems to be the golden mean between *cuardise* and *estultie*, the latter of which Turold presents as undesirable in this passage, but not everywhere else. Turold most probably acquired his concept of moderation from literary sources, for philosophers had praised moderation ever since the days of Aristotle and the Stoics. He could have found this idea, for example, in the *Disciplina Clericalis* of Petrus Alfonsi, a converted Spanish Jew who wrote at about the time that the *SR* was composed.[90] The concept of the golden mean was preserved in Latin manuscripts throughout the Middle Ages; yet it does not seem to have been appreciated in popular literature, which usually dealt with foolhardy heroes like Roland rather than with prudent ones like Oliver. To prove that Oliver's caution is not cowardice, Turold must let him take as many risks as the other heroes. Besides that, he enjoys prestige as Roland's closest friend.

Whereas the Stoics admired men who control their passions, the *SR* extols heroes like Roland and Charlemagne who give vent to all emotions, particularly to indignation and anger. As we have seeen, it draws no distinction between hate and anger, both of which are virtues. Turold's heroes are goaded into battle by violent hate and anger, which blind them to the risks they run; and it is ironic that the Christians display even more anger than the pagans do. This admiration for hate and anger is clearly a legacy from the ancient Germanic warriors rather than from the Romans, who had prided themselves on their cool and calculated military operations.[91] Like the Northern barbarians a millennium

[89] vasselage par sens nen est folie, mielz valt mesure que ne fait estultie (1724).

[90] Qui dat quibus dandum est et retinet quibus retinendum est, largus est. Et qui prohibet quibus prohibendum est et quibus non est prohibendum, auarus est. Et qui dat quibus dandum est et quibus non est dandum, prodigus est (*Disciplina Clericalis*, XXI). This follows Aristotle (*Nicomachean Ethics*, II, 7). It is possible that Turold's idea of moderation in courage was in some way derived from Aristotle, too (See *Nicomachean Ethics*, II, 9).

[91] Wenn die Germanen zur Schlacht zogen, so thaten sie dies in einer

earlier, Charlemagne's warriors attack individually and without any military plan or concert of action, except when Gerin and Gerier co-operate in attacking Timozel. These individual combats probably owe much to literary tradition, for the warriors of the *Iliad*, the *Aeneid*, the *Psychomachia*, and the *Waltharius* all fight individually. Single combats are by nature more dramatic than mass actions, and they are easier for the poet to depict and for his audience to visualize. Nevertheless, it is quite clear that Turold's barons, like their crusading contemporaries in real life, have not yet learned the discipline that Tacitus found so wanting across the Rhine [92] and that they follow their own tempers rather than their commander's orders. Roland, we are told, had previously attacked and destroyed the city of Noples against orders and had tried to hide the evidence by washing away the blood.[93] The Book of Proverbs (16:32) teaches that he who is slow to anger is better than the mighty, and he that ruleth his spirit is better than he that taketh a city, yet Turold and his public preferred a city-taker, even one who acted out of anger and against the orders of his lawful sovereign.

Roland and his company lack the self-control required of a Greek phalanx or a Roman legion. Just as the Germanic barbarians enflamed their courage by shouting their war-cry, so too their Frankish descendants increase their martial ardor by shouting theirs.[94] In discussing the vice of wrath (*ira*), Seneca ex-

---

Kampfeswuth, welche stark abstach von der harten Ruhe des krieggeübten Römers (Freytag, I, p. 204). In Norse literature berserkers were particularly admired.

[92] Tacitus distinguishes the Chatti from all the other Germanic tribes because they more nearly resemble the Romans in military discipline: multum, ut inter Germanos, rationis ac sollertiae: praeponere electos, audire praepositos, nosse ordines, intellegere occasiones, differe impetus, disponere diem, vallare noctem, fortunam inter dubia, virtutem inter certa numerare, quodque rarissimum nec nisi Romanae disciplinae concessum (*Germania*, #30).

[93] Ja prist il Noples seinz le vostre comant (1775).

[94] The Frankish *enseigne* (war cry) "Monjoie!" seems to have served the same purpose as the *barditum* mentioned in the *Germania* (#3).

pressly mentioned the Germans. "The Cimbrians and the Teutons who poured over the Alps in countless thousands—what wiped them out so completely that even the news of the great disaster was carried to their homes, not by a messenger, but only by rumour, except that they substituted anger for valour? Anger, although it will sometimes overthrow and lay low whatever gets in its way, yet more often brings destruction on itself. Who are more courageous than the Germans? Who are bolder in a charge? Who have more love of arms to which they are born and bred, which to the exclusion of all else become their only care?" [95] Seneca would surely have censured the anger that made Charlemagne abuse Ganelon's lenient judges and call them *felun* (3814). He wrote: "For the one who administers punishment nothing is so unfitting as anger, since punishment is all the better able to work reform if it is bestowed with judgment." [96] Today a just judge should render impartial justice rather than appease his anger as Charlemagne did (3989).

The literary influence of the classic writers, particularly Virgil, is evident in many passages of the *SR*. Why should France consistently be called "sweet" (*dulce*)? Why should a single adjective suit both honey and fatherland? Naturally, it is because the Roman writers like Virgil used the word in this transferred nonsensuous sense and because many medieval writers followed them in this usage.[97] There is no reason for a fatherland to be sweet. It could just as well be spicy, succulent, or sharp; and it could appeal to the eye, ear, or fingertips as well as to the tastebuds. According to Hans-Friedrich Rosenfeld (p. 386), the earliest example of

---

[95] *De Ira,* I, xl, 2–3.

[96] Nil minus quam irasci punientiem decet, cum eo magis ad emendationem poena proficiat, si iudicio lata est (*De Ira,* I, xv, 3).

[97] Roland's dying thoughts of *dulce France* (2379) are reminiscent of those of Antores in the *Aeneid* (X, 781), who thinks of sweet Argos (*dulces moriens reminiscitur Argos*). In the *Waltharius* (v. 60), King Heriric doubts that he can save his "sweet fatherland" (*patria dulcis*) from Attila. Later, Walter yearns to see his *patriam dulcemque gentem* again (v. 600).

this expression in German literature (*süsses Vaterland*) is found in the works of the humanist Eberlin von Günzburg.

Also of classic origin are the olive branches carried as symbols of supplication or surrender, since this custom was not practiced in medieval Europe but was merely a literary motif lifted from the Latin classics.[98] When Marsilie tells his messengers that their olive branches will signify *pais e humilitet* (73), it is really Turold informing his own public. If olive branches had had this significance in Marsilie's day, he would not have had to explain it to his men. Whereas "sweet France" and the olive branches clearly betray their classic origin, the bristles on the swine's back in v. 3223 do not, yet they too were a Latin commonplace stressed by Virgil and others. In fact bristles appear on the backs of swine in Western literature from Meleager's boar to Colkelbie's sow. In some other culture people might tend to refer to a boar's curved tusks or corkscrew tail. The ancient Hebrews, on the other hand, were more concerned with the swine's cloven hoof, which made it unclean.

Classical influence appears in the ethos of the *SR*, or at least in the expression of that ethos, when Turpin and his comrades declare that it is better to die with honor than to live with dishonor. In stating that Germanic warriors disgraced in battle would sometimes hang themselves to escape a life of shame,[99] Tacitus implied that they preferred death to dishonor. He did not formulate this thought with one of his usual succinct aphorisms in his *Germania*, but he did do so in his biography of his father-in-law Agricola, who exhorted his troops with the harangue: "An honor-

---

[98] Mentioned by Virgil in *Aeneid* (vii, 154; vii, 116; xi, 101, 332). The fact that this literary commonplace was not familiar to the general public in twelfth-century France is indicated in the *Eneas* (6009–6010), when the author explains it: ce estoit signe a icel jor de pais, d'acorde e d'amor. On the other hand, *Renaus de Montalban* mentions this custom without indicating that it is obsolete: Portèrent rains d'olive; c'est senefiement De pais, d'umilité, que il la vont querrant (*Renaus*, p. 37, vv. 6–7).

[99] multique superstites bellorum infamiam laqueo finierunt (*Germania*, #6).

able death is better than a life of shame" (*honesta mors turpi vita potior*).[100] This thought became a commonplace in medieval Latin literature. It appears, for example, in *Beowulf* when Wiglaf reminds the hero's faithless followers that "for a noble man, death is better than a shameful life." [101]

The Franks' desire to die for their leader echoes another sentiment dear to literature. In the *Heliand*, a ninth-century Low Saxon epic about Christ, Saint Thomas says to his fellow disciples: "It is a hero's choice to stand steadfast with his lord and to die with him on the day of decision. Let us all do so, let us follow him on his journey, nor let us consider our lives of any value, if only we die with our lord in the host. Then at least our fame will live with us afterward as good words before men." [102] Although this well expresses the Germanic ideal of loyalty, Saint Thomas's decision to die with his lord is based directly on the biblical account.[103] On the other hand, it must have been pagan reasoning that made him favor such devotion as a means to achieve posthumous fame. As we have seen, this worldly incentive is included whenever the SR praises such devotion unto death.

Classical sources, or at least parallels, can be found for many of the sentiments expressed in early Northern poetry, even for sentiments frequently cited as examples of Germanic spirit. In consoling Hrothgar for the loss of one of his dearest retainers, Beowulf says: "It is better for each of us to avenge his friend rather than

[100] *Cornelii Taciti de Vita Agricolae*, Oxford, 1922, cap. 33.

[101] Deað bið sêlla eorla gehwylcum þonne edwîtlîf (*Beowulf*, 2891). An early example of this topos is found in the Spanish ballad *Fuga del rey Marsin* (v. 36) when Turpin says: "Más vale morir con honrra que con desonrra vivir". This slogan still lives. The motto of the Gurka regiments in the British army is *Kafar Hone Bhanda Morne Ramro* (Better to die than to live a coward).

[102] that ist thegnes cust, that hie mid is frâhon samad fasto gistande, dôie mid im thar an duom. Duan ûs alla sô, folgon im te thero ferdi: ni lâtan ûse fera uuið thiu uuihtes uuirðig, neba uui an them uuerode mid im, dôian mid ûson drohtine. Than lêbot ûs thoh duom after, guod uuord for gumon (Heliand, 3996–4002).

[103] Eamus et nos, ut moriamur cum eo (*John*, 11, 16).

mourn greatly for him. Each of us will see the end of his life in this world. Let him, who can, win renown before his death. That is the greatest joy for the deceased warrior." [104] This is genuinely Germanic, yet it resembles Jupiter's words in the *Aeneid* when Hercules intercedes for Pallas: "Everyone has an appointed day. The span of life is short and irretrievable for everyone; but the task of virtue is to lengthen one's fame by deeds." [105] Two of Beowulf's ideas are anticipated here: our death is certain, and we should win lasting fame before we die. Beowulf's only addition was the notion that it is better to avenge a friend than to mourn him, a sentiment which, as we shall see, is shared by Naimes in the *SR*.

In wishing to die for their country, the heroes of the *SR* are following another ancient Roman precept popular throughout the Middle Ages. In a hagiography written near the end of the tenth century by Abbo of Fleury, an Anglo-Saxon king named Edmund says: "It would be honorable for me to die for my country." [106] The *Gesta Romanorum* tells of a king who says, "It is sweet and proper to die for the fatherland" (*decorum est et dulce, mori pro patria*).[107] This thought, which comes from Horace,[108] may be reflected when the Franks in the *SR* wish to die for "sweet" France. These patriotic sentiments must have originated in Rome, since the Germanic peoples, particularly during their migratory

---

[104] Ne sorga, snotor guma! Sêlre bið æghwæm, þaet hê his frêond wrece, þonne hê fela murne. Ure æghwylc sceal ende gebîdan worolde lîfes, wyrce sê þe môte dômes ær dêaþe; pæt bið drihtguman unlifgendum æfter sêlest (*Beowulf*, vv. 1384–89).

[105] See note III, 74.

[106] Et quid suggeris? ut in extremis vitae, desolatus meo satellite, fugiendo inferam crimen nostrae gloriae! Semper delatoriae accusationis calumniam evitavi, numquam relictae militiae probra sustinui, eo quod honestum mihi esset pro patria mori (*Vita s. Eamundi*, Migne, *Patrologia Latina*, 139, col. 512). The *Vita Oswaldi*, which was written between 997 and 1005, says that Byrhtnoth fought for his fatherland (*pro patria*, cited in *The Battle of Maldon*, ed. E. V. Gordon, London, 1937, p. 6).

[107] *Gesta Romanorum*, no. 124.

[108] Dulce et decorum est pro patria mori (*Odes*, III, ii, 13).

period, had attached their loyalty to their leaders or their tribe rather than to the soil they occupied. Later, as they became more deeply rooted, they learned to love their soil, as did Byrhtnoth, who died at Maldon "for folk and land" (folc, foldan).[109] As C. E. Stevens (p. 34) observes, the Romanized Gauls felt pride in their country; and this seems to have been transmitted to the Franks, for in the *Waltharius* the Frankish king Gunther fears that France will never overcome her disgrace if his forces are defeated by one man.[110] Perhaps the most patriotic Frankish encomium was one written by the ninth-century Alsatian monk Otfried of Weissenburg in the introduction to his *Gospel Harmony*.[111] Because his pride is still more tribal than territorial, he praises his countrymen more than his country; in fact, all he can say for the Frankish land is that it is rich in gold and silver and other metals. He explains that he has written his *Gospel Harmony* in the Frankish vernacular because the Franks are just as brave as the Romans and Greeks, who wrote in their own tongues. Although he is a churchman telling the story of Jesus, he praises his people for their wealth, power, and warlike virtues rather than for their humility and meekness.[112]

Besides detecting classical literary influences in the *SR*, Wilhelm Tavernier, Maurice Wilmotte, and others believed it the heir to a long Latin literary tradition handed down unbroken since Virgil; [113] and as evidence they found similarities between passages in the *SR* and passages in various medieval Latin poems, including the *Waltharius*. On the other hand, Francesco Torraca

[109] *The Battle of Maldon*, v. 54.
[110] Dedecus et tantum superabit Francia numquam (*Waltharius*, v. 1085).
[111] *Otfrids Evangelienbuch*, ed. E. Schröder, Halle, 1934, I, 1. Also found in Braune, XXXII, 4. Although Otfrid wrote in his vernacular, his sources were all in Latin, as are his elaborate acrostics.
[112] See particularly vv. 59–91.
[113] Wilhelm Tavernier, *Zeitschrift für französische Sprache und Literatur*, 42, 1914, pp. 41–81. Maurice Wilmotte, "Une source Latine de la *Chanson de Roland*" (*Mélanges* . . . *Gustav Lanson*, Paris, Hachette, 1922, pp. 77–84), *L'Épopée française*, Paris, 1939.

wrote a scathing criticism of their efforts and claimed that the parallels prove nothing because even closer parallels appear in the Indian epic *The Ramayana*, a work unknown in Western Europe until the eighteenth century.[114] Despite Torraca's devastating ridicule, Giuseppe Chiri still accepted the *SR*'s dependence on medieval Latin literary tradition; and Curtius and others have subsequently proved it beyond any doubt.[115]

The ethos of the *Waltharius* has much in common with that of the *SR*, even though it makes little reference to Christianity. Similarities could have resulted from direct influence, for Turold may have read the Latin poem.[116] On the other hand, they may just reflect the ethos of the societies they represented, societies that were somewhat similar in ethos. Christianity made amazingly little impression on the *Waltharius* despite its clerical author,[117] and it also had little effect upon the basic ideals and attitudes of the *SR*. To understand this contradiction, we must remember that the Germanic invaders of Gaul were first converted by missionaries who were themselves only partially converted.

Nora Chadwick (p. 275) argues that the fifth-century Gallo-Roman churchmen still belonged at heart to the classical world.

---

[114] Francesco Torraca, "Alla ricerca di Turoldo", *Nuova Antologia*, 244, 1925, 289–310.

[115] Giuseppe Chiri, *L'Epica Latina Medioevale e la Chanson de Roland*, Genova, 1936; Ernst Curtius, "Über die altfr. Epik", *Zeitschrift für romanische Philologie*, 64, 1944, pp. 232–320.

[116] Several manuscripts of the *Waltharius* existed in France during Turold's life-time. It is reasonable to think that his choice of the name Gualter de Hums (2067) was a courtesy to the author of the older epic. Since Walter was long a vassal of Attila, the name Walter of the Huns would be meaningful (Note that *Hums* in v. 3254 means Huns). Like Walter, Gualter holds a mountain pass against great odds. Whereas similarities between the two works do not prove borrowing, they certainly suggest it.

[117] Both Ekkehard and Gerald were clergymen. For their relative claims, see Edwin H. Zeydel, *Festschrift for John G. Kunstmann*, Chapel Hill, 1959, pp. 21–38; Karl Hauk, "Das Walthariusepos des Bruders Gerald v. Eichstatt," *Germanisch-romanische Monatsschrift*, Neue Folge, 4, 1954, pp. 1–27; Hans Walther, "Noch einmal zum Waltharius," *Zeitschrift für deutsches Altertum*, 90, 1960, pp. 269 ff.

"Christianity was," she states, "a new and important spiritual concern; but one feels that for these men it was almost more a profession than a vocation, certainly not an all-pervading spiritual revolution. There is no sign of spiritual clash or conflict, or readjustment. The new religion was blended and harmonized with the standards already set by a classical training, and a balance was maintained." Stevens also notes the superficiality of Christian ethics among Gallo-Roman churchmen. In discussing Sidonius Apollinaris, the most eminent clergyman of his age, he says (p. 133): "When we find Sidonius supporting such a savagely retributive theory of punishment as leads him to say that the death of a murderer at least affords the satisfaction of revenge to the survivors of the murdered, one begins to wonder whether he understood the lessons of the New Testament at all: such language becomes an old Roman rather than a Christian bishop." Such language would also have become the Germanic barbarians who were then overrunning Sidonius's country. Gregory of Tours, also a Gallo-Roman Churchman, likewise showed little understanding of Christian ethics. After relating the details of Clovis's greed, treachery, cruelty, and parricide, Gregory naïvely adds: "God daily cast down his enemies under his hand and increased his kingdom, because he walked before Him with an upright heart and did those things that were pleasing in His eyes." [118] The pleasing thing that Clovis did was to choose the Roman rather than the Arian faith, and God seems to have overlooked his lack of charity, morality, or regard for the Ten Commandments.

The SR portrays Charlemagne as punctilious in observing mass, generous in endowing religious foundations, and brave in fighting for the Church of Rome. This suffices to make him a good Christian, even though he fails to practice Christian love, humility, or forgiveness. He massacres all Mohammedans and Jews at Sara-

[118] Prosternebat enim cotidie Deus hostes eius sub manu ipsius et augebat regnum eius, eo quod ambularet recto corde coram eo et facerit quae placita erant in oculis eius (*Historiarum Libri Decem*, II, 41).

gossa except the hundred thousand who accept Christianity; and we may assume that he massacres more of them than he converts, in view of their traditional obstinacy in refusing the blessings of Christianity. And no exceptions seem to be made for women and children save for Queen Bramimunde, who eventually realizes the value of becoming a Christian.[118a] Even the mercy shown to Bramimunde does not necessarily depend upon Christian tradition, since the pagan Greeks and Romans had also advised showing mercy to the suppliant.[119] It is to be remembered that the Christian fervor shown at Saragossa was matched by that of the Christians who butchered the inhabitants of Jerusalem during the First Crusade.

Considering the previous state of Christianity in Gaul, it is understandable that the Frankish invaders were converted only superficially. Moreover, in trying to win the heathens to their faith, the missionaries appealed primarily to their practical and utilitarian instincts. According to legend, Clovis accepted Christianity only because the Christian God proved more effective than the pagan gods had been. Moreover, his conversion had been prepared by his Christian wife Clotilda, who had married him in hope of persuading him to kill her uncle and thus avenge her father. Thranbrand, the Saxon missionary to Iceland, proved the superiority of Christianity by challenging and defeating the champions of the old faith in trials by combat; and in this way he won many converts to the new faith, even though his duels sometimes resulted from questionable involvements with women.[120] The *SR* was by no means old-fashioned in recognizing victory as

[118a] Whereas most modern readers would assume that women and children were spared, this is nowhere implied, not even in Conrad's *Rolandslied,* which says that men were killed by the sword while women and children were killed by fire (*Mit swerten cholten si die man, mit fûre kint und wîb,* 888–889). Stricker merely says that the Christians killed men, women, and children (*die kristen sluogen zetal beidiu man kint und wîp,* 1506).

[119] See Jones, "Grim to your Foes . . .", pp. 98–101.

[120] *Brennu-Njálssaga,* C–CV.

proof of Christian superiority. Some six centuries later Luis Vaz de Camões could still write that King João of Portugal was "the first monarch to go forth from his native land and compel the African to recognize by ordeal of battle how superior is the Christian faith to that of Mahomet." [121]

Even Sidonius Apollinaris had taught a *do ut des* religion. In soliciting donations for the church he promised that "whatever you give to the church is really gathered in for yourself." [122] It was natural for the Germanic converts to accept and emphasize the practical value of Christianity, since they had supported a culture based on service and reward. The Venerable Bede stated that Edwin of Northumbria's conversion had gained him the kingdom of heaven as well as an increase of his kingdom on earth; [123] and Boniface, the Anglo-Saxon missionary to the Germans, advised his confreres to win the heathens by reminding them that the Christians possessed all the provinces that abound in fertile fields and vineyards and had left only cold and barren lands to the pagans and their Gods.[124] Such arguments appealed to calculating souls more than to selfless ones, nor did they inform the converts that any change of heart was required.

The stories recorded by Gregory of Tours disclose that most charitable donations of his day were frankly business transactions with God, a strictly materialistic bartering of earthly wealth for heavenly reward (*terrena pro caelestibus*). This attitude still prevails in the *SR*, which notes no undue calculation when Pinabel and Thierry give large offerings to the cloisters just before submitting to God's judgment.[125] Such last-minute

[121] *The Lusiads, Canto IV*, p. 111.
[122] Cited by Stevens, p. 121.
[123] *Baedae Opera Historica*, ed. J. K. King, Cambridge, Mass., 1954, cap. XII, p. 281.
[124] Et cum ipsi, id est christiani, fertiles terras vinique et olei feraces ceterisque opibus habundantes possident provincias, ipsis autem, id est paganis, frigore semper rigentes terras cum eorum diis relinquerunt (*Die Briefe des heiligen Bonifatius und Lullius*, ed. M. Tangl, 1916, p. 40).
[125] Mult granz offrendes metent par cez mestiers (3861).

donations would now be viewed as bribery. The utilitarian purpose of good works is everywhere apparent in the *SR*, but it is
nowhere so clearly revealed as it is in the *Rolandslied* when
Conrad frankly states that the Christians hurry to their death in
battle and thus buy God's kingdom.[125a]

Considering the lapse of some six centuries between the conversion of Clovis and the composition of the *SR*, one might
marvel that so much pagan-Germanic ethos remains in the song.
This ethos may have received a new lease on life from the Northmen, who devastated so much of northwestern Europe during the
centuries just before Turold wrote. In order to defend themselves
from the heathen Vikings, the recently converted Christians had
to retain or recover the martial virtues of their pagan ancestors.
Primitive Christianity had taught pacificism, but such an outlook
would have spelled doom for the Church in areas subject to
Viking raids.

Warlike reaction to outside pressure is well illustrated in the
Lay of Louis, a vernacular song in honor of a Westfrankish king,
Louis III, who defeated the Northmen at Saucourt in 881. Written
within a year after the victory, this song explains the battle in
terms borrowed from the Old Testament. After serving as
guardian to the orphaned young king, God decides to send the
Northmen to test him and to admonish the Franks of their sins.
As soon as the wicked have repented their misdeeds, God takes
mercy on them and calls upon the young ruler to save His
people. Promising to do so, Louis raises his banner and hastens
to Franconia, where his subjects thank God for his arrival. Louis
announces that God has sent him to save His people and promises
that he will not spare himself, if they think he should fight there.
Calling upon all of God's faithful to follow him, he reminds
them that their sojourn on earth will last only as long as Christ

[125a] Ze dem tôde begonden si harte gâhen. Si chouften daz gotes rîche (*RL*
3448–3449).

wishes. If they do God's will in battle, he will reward the survivors and the families of the slain. Setting out to wreak vengeance on his opponents, he begins a *kyrie eleison* and then surpasses all his vassals in valor, as becomes his birth. Thanks to God's power and to all the saints, Louis is victorious! May God in His mercy keep him! [126]

This song expresses an ethos much like that in the *SR*. God is a God of Hosts, and Louis and his men are His vassals on earth. Although Louis mentions God's will, he appeals primarily to his men's practical sense by promising earthly reward to them or their families; and the immediate goal of his attack is revenge. His reminder that man's sojourn on earth lasts only as long as God wills it accords with the traditional Germanic belief in the inevitability of fate. There is no reference to heavenly reward, and the Franks wish to kill rather than convert the invaders. Although this blood-lust resembled the attitudes of the Franks' pagan ancestors, it also agreed with the teachings of certain Christian clergymen. In his *Memorialis sanctorum* of 851 the Spanish cleric Eulogius called for a holy war against the Saracens in Spain; and three years later his friend Alvaro advanced his ideas even further in his *Indiculus luminosus*. Alvaro demanded "holy cruelty" (*crudelitas sancta*) in avenging contempt toward God; and he justified his bloody purpose by citing passages from the Old Testament.[127]

Not only did the Northmen's incursions intensify the Franks' warlike ethos, but their permanent settlement in Normandy did so even more. To be sure, Rollo and his followers professed Christianity when they received their dukedom in 912, but they were scarcely more Christian than Clovis after his conversion four centuries earlier. In speaking of the Scandinavian converts, Jan de Vries says: "During the first centuries after the conversion,

---

[126] Braune, XXXVI.
[127] Heisig, p. 17.

customs were not essentially changed and the new Christian faith had scarcely exerted any influence on the Germanic soul." [128] This was almost as true of the Northmen who settled in Normandy. To be sure, they settled among a more numerous Christian population, and they embraced and protected the Church and eagerly adopted its doctrines. Yet, since its ethos was diametrically opposed to their own, the ruling classes could not or would not adopt its ethos along with its dogma and ceremonies. In speaking of the Norman adventurers in Sicily during the century preceding the *SR*, Carl Erdmann comments on the unusual way in which their love of fighting was mixed with devotion to the Church,[129] and this paradox seems to hold for the heroes of the *SR* as well.

It is significant that Turold had a Norman name. Whether derived from Thorvaldr or Thorolf, it was clearly of Scandinavian origin; [130] and one can safely assume that Turold inherited more than just his name from the Norse invaders. In a meticulous attempt to identify the various heroes of the *SR*, Boissonnade found more similarities with Norman personages than with those of any other area. This may only prove that he sifted his Norman sources more carefully in order to prove his point, but it may indicate that the author was of Norman descent, despite the French (Île de France) bias of his poem.[131] The name Roland was particularly popular in Normandy, as were several other names found in

[128] . . . die Sitten haben sich in den ersten Jahrhunderten nach der Bekehrung nicht wesentlich geändert, und der neue christliche Glaube hatte auf die germanische Seele noch kaum Einfluss ausgeübt (Vries, p. 5). Cf. Den Kern der heidnischen Sittenlehre tastete man nicht an: das Ehrgefühl des auf Selbsthilfe gestellten, kriegerisch erzogenen Mannes; die Hochschätzung des Besitzes, der Macht, der Rache (Heusler, *Germanentum,* p. 128).

[129] Wilde Rauflust und devote Kirchlichkeit scheinen sich in ihnen auf das sonderbarste gemischt zu haben . . . (Erdmann, p. 113).

[130] Jenkins (p. 374) says Thorvaldr. Boissonnade (p. 478) says Thorolf.

[131] The Île de France bias is particularly strong in the first part of the song, since Roland and his peers are all *Francs de France* (177). Representatives from other areas of Charlemagne's empire play a larger role later on.

the SR.[132] Becker believes the poem to have been written in the eastern portion of the Île de France, perhaps at Reims; [133] yet, even if this is so, Norman influence would still be significant, since Normandy was not far away. Moreover, Normans were prominent in most military ventures of the age and took the initiative in the eleventh-century crusades in Spain.[134]

In discussing the early Icelanders, Stefán Einarsson (p. 9) says that their heroic code "demanded not only generosity toward kinsmen, friends, and guests, but also scrupulous watchfulness against all infringements on one's personal rights or those of one's kinsmen. If such offenses were not avenged, one lost face and his honor was forever tarnished. Death was always preferable to a life of shame." It is apparent that this heathen Viking code resembled that of the SR. A careful reading of the SR tempts one to agree with Hans Rheinfelder that its author was racially Germanic, perhaps Norman, and that his public was still basically Frankish despite its Romanic language.[135]

As we have seen, the bond of *amistiet* was an important institution in the SR. In his study of this custom, William Stowell (p. 399) found most of his examples in Normandy and thinks they "might indicate that locality as the place of origin and chief development of the institution." In praising Archbishop Turpin, whose brand of Christianity he seems to endorse, O'Hagan (p. 18)

---

[132] See Boissonnade, p. 319 *et passim*, and Bédier, *Commentaires*, pp. 37–40.

[133] Becker, pp. 142–45. A. Fuchs also argues that the SR belongs to France proper and expresses an exclusively French political loyalty (pp. 191–93).

[134] See Becker, p. 133.

[135] Wenn wir auch den Verfasser nicht kennen, spricht denn nicht alles dafür, dass er rassisch zu den Germanen, zu den Normannen gehörte? Sind die Recken, die er zum Gegenstand seiner Dichtung nimmt, nicht samt und sonders blutsmässig Germanen, *franceis,* eher noch Franken als schon Franzosen? Hat er uns die Charaktere und ihr Wirken nicht auffällig germanisch dargestellt? War nicht das Publikum, an das er und die Spielleute sich wandten, noch grossenteils fränkisch, also blutsmässig germanisch, trotz der romanischen Sprache? (Hans Rheinfelder, in a review in *Zeitschrift für rom. Phil.* 59, 1939, p. 113).

writes: "When we read the account of his death, and those of Olivier and Roland, it is impossible not to feel what beauty and tenderness Christianity has conferred upon poetry." O'Hagan gives no evidence that Christianity was responsible for this tenderness. To the contrary, the tenderest friendships seem to grow out of the custom of *compagnonage,* which in turn probably developed from the Germanic institution of oath-brotherhood (*Schwurbruderschaft*).[136] This institution may be echoed, for example, when Roland calls Oliver *frere* (1866).

By the very nature of its in-group morality, Germanic society encouraged the formation of close personal alliances, which often induced personal affection. Christianity, on the other hand, taught love for all men and discouraged the individual from loving one man to the exclusion of all others, especially if such friendship required him to accept the hates and feuds of his friend. Realizing this danger, the author of the *Heliand* warned that a man should not follow a *friund* who beckons him to sin.[137] Loving one's friends is not a peculiarly Christian virtue. As Jesus asked, "do not even the publicans the same?" (Matt. 5:46).

In one matter of behavior the heroes of the *SR* differ widely from their Germanic forebears, and perhaps from their contemporaries in real life as well. Tacitus relates that the ancient Germans soon stopped weeping for their dead friends, even though their sorrow continued. It was honorable for women to express their grief in public (*lugere*), but it was honorable for men to

---

[136] Eine besonders strenge Form der Freundschaft war die Schwurbruderschaft. Sie wurde in feierlicher Form geschlossen. Im Norden traten die Freunde unter einen Rasenstreifen, der an beiden Enden noch fest war, und schwuren, wie Brüder zu sein. Das heisst, sie übernahmen gegenüber dem Freunde alle Pflichten des Bruders, vor allen Dingen die Pflicht zur Rache, wenn der andere durch die Waffe fiel . . . (Hans Kuhn, in *Germanische Altertumskunde*, p. 195).

[137] that ênig liudeo ni scal farfolgan is friunde, ef he ina an firina spanit (*Heliand*, vv. 1492–93). Such advice was already pre-Christian. Cf. "Nulla est igitur excusatio peccati, si amici causa peccaveris . . ." (Cicero, *de Amicitia*, xi, 38).

remember theirs privately.[138] This seems to have remained the general rule in Northern Europe up to the present, the men's restraint being later reinforced by Stoic ideas of manly self-control. The heroes of the *SR*, on the other hand, mourn piteously and weep copiously just as the heroes of the *Iliad* do. Many knights weep when Ganelon sets out on his dangerous mission (349), Roland weeps like a wellborn knight at the sight of his dead friends at Roncevaux (1853), and all Charlemagne's men weep for their dead friends and kinsmen (2419–2420).

Nevertheless, the frequent use of the expression *ne puet muër* (he could not help but) in connection with weeping would suggest that men were supposed to try to restrain their tears and sobs. Failure to do so did not betray their weakness as much as it showed the superhuman power of their grief. Ruth Hoppe is certainly right in believing that the violent outbursts of sorrow in the *SR* should be judged merely as artistic expression of abstract emotions rather than as actual characterizations of the heroes.[139] While mourning is important, vengeance is even more so. Just as Beowulf tells Hrothgar that it is better to avenge a friend than to mourn him, Naimes advises Charlemagne to interrupt his mourning and pursue the Saracens to avenge his fallen men.[140] This attitude prevailed throughout the Middle Ages and well beyond, as Shakespeare so well attests in Act IV, Scene 3, of *Macbeth*. When Macduff laments the murder of his family, Malcolm advises him: "Be this the whetstone of your sword. Let grief convert to anger: blunt not the heart, enrage it." As we have seen, the

---

[138] lamenta ac lacrimas cito, dolorem et tristitiam tarde ponunt. feminis lugere honestum est, viris meminisse (*Germania*, #27).

[139] Dagegen lässt sich sagen, dass die Gesten des Schmerzes wohl eher als künstlerisches Ausdrucksmittel zur Darstellung abstrakter Regungen zu werten sind, als dass sie zur tatsächlichen Charakterisierung der Helden dienen (Hoppe, p. 39).

[140] Car chevalchez! Vengez ceste dulor! (2428). In the *Iliad* (XIX) Odysseus advises Achilles to avenge Patrocles first rather than fast in his memory.

heroes of the SR scarcely had to convert their grief to anger, since they hardly distinguished between the two emotions.

The tears in the SR probably flow from literary sources, since copious tears were frequent in the Bible and also in classic literature. Charlemagne seems to weep most of all. He cannot refrain from weeping when Ganelon nominates Roland to lead the rear guard (773), he weeps for the slain at Roncevaux (2415), and he is weeping in the last verse of the song. Turold may have taken his lacrimose emperor directly from Einhard's *vita,* which specifically mentions that Charlemagne's family affection forced him to shed tears at the death of his children and that he even wept at the death of Pope Hadrian.[141] On the other hand, Charlemagne's many tears may just corroborate L. Beszard's observation that kings are the greatest weepers in primitive epics,[141a] or else they may reflect the Christian sentiment that they who mourn are blessed.

Karl Heisig (51) believes that Roland's tears at Roncevaux are a sign of his remorse, but this would not explain why Charlemagne weeps even more. Moreover, Roland weeps "as a wellborn knight" (*cum chevaler gentill,* 1853), and this suggests that his weeping was considered courtly rather than Christian. Even though heroes were expected to constrain their tears, it seems that weeping was commendable; and it will be seen that the villain Ganelon does not weep even when his champion and kinsman Pinabel is killed in the trial. Tears abound in other *chansons de geste* and also in Middle High German romances. Therefore, unless the knights of the twelfth and thirteenth centuries really wept demonstratively, the weeping heroes of their romances

[141] Mortes filiorum ac filiae pro magnanimitate, qua excellebat, minus patienter tulit, pietate uidelicet, qua non minus insignis erat, conpulsus ad lacrimas. Nuntiato etiam sibi Adriani Romani pontificis obitu, quem in amicis praecipuum habebat, sic fleuit, ac si fratrem aut filium amisisset carissimum (*Vita Karoli,* #19).

[141a] Beszard, pp. 389–410.

would contradict the general rule that literary heroes must behave in a manner admired and imitated by their public. The
same is true of fainting from grief or other emotion. Although
Roland and his colleagues swoon as often as heroines in nine-
teenth-century novels, it is improbable that fighting men in
Turold's day actually did so.

Like many other scholars, Beszard (400) assumes that the
Northern peoples exhibited fewer tears than their Southern contemporaries, and he notes that tears scarcely appear in the
Karlamagnús saga even though it was written at the same time
as the later and more lacrimose redactions of the *SR*. The his-
trionic expression of emotion in the *Rolandslied* may result
from Conrad's fidelity to his source, since most early Middle
High German songs were less effusive. Accepting the theory that
the *SR* was composed gradually over many generations, Beszard
(396) conjectures that there had been fewer tears in the "proto-
type" of the song, since the Oxford manuscript itself had fewer
than later versions.

It is tempting to blame Turold for the primitive and warped
concept of Christianity expressed by the *SR*, but this is quite un-
fair, since he was merely echoing the views preached from the
pulpits by leading churchmen. Like Turold, the popes of his day
made no clear distinction between monetary and spiritual rewards
for service against the pagans. Like Charlemagne, they employed
mercenaries; and they did not hesitate to recruit troops by
promising plunder. Pope Gregory VII authorized the French
knights to keep the lands they seized from the Mohammedans in
Spain, and Urban II made the same offer to the adventurers who
went to the Holy Land.[142]

Just as Turold promised both fee and fame to those who fought
the pagans, the popes too appealed to the crusaders' greed for
glory as well as to their greed for gold. According to Fulcher of

[142] Boissonnade, p. 17; Faral, p. 41; Heisig, p. 27.

Chartres, Alexander II promised double glory to those who fought against the pagans.[143] After first promising material rewards, Pope Urban II added that those who died covered with blood would win eternal glory.[144] It might be argued that these holy men were referring to eternal glory in heaven, but they must have known that laymen would understand the promise to refer to worldly fame as well.

The Church recruited volunteers for the crusades by promising them remission of sins. In making this promise in the *SR*, Turpin is following the example of Pope Alexander II, who promised remission of sins to all those who departed to fight the Spanish Saracens in 1064.[145] Turpin is also following the example of Urban II, who assured the troops leaving for the Holy Land: "Confident in the mercy of God and in the authority of the apostles Peter and Paul, we accord the total remission of sins to all those Christians who take arms against the infidels and associate themselves with this holy expedition. As for those who succumb, full of true penitence, let them know that they shall obtain pardon for their faults and eternal recompense." [146] Here we find the reservation that pardon requires true penitence; but Turpin, like most recruiters, does not stress this point. The Council of Clermont declared that those who fought for the cause were free from the necessity of doing penance. This was merely a pardon from doing penance, yet people generally understood it to be a remission of sins.[147] As we have seen, Turpin considers sword-play a sufficient penance and does not emphasize penitence. Even Priest Conrad's Turpin assigns his men the penance of killing as many

---

[143] pro honore duplici laborent (*Fulcheri Carnotensis Historia Hierosolymitana*, ed. H. Hagenmeyer, Heidelberg, 1913, Book I, cap. III, 3, 7, p. 136).

[144] Faral, p. 41.

[145] Faral, p. 33; see also Heisig, p. 27. Nearly two centuries earlier, in 878, Pope John VIII had promised remission of sins to all who died fighting for the faith (Heisig, p. 9).

[146] Faral, 41.

[147] Erdmann, 316.

heathens as they can. After his sweet speech they fall to the ground and receive indulgence.[148]

Although Christianity began as a religion of peace, the Roman Church had already accepted war as an instrument of policy before Turold wrote his poem; and the Church Militant gradually became a church militaristic. Archbishop Turpin shows more prowess than any other cleric,[149] but even Turpin could not compare in military might with Pope Gregory VII, who humiliated Henry IV at Canossa. To be sure, there were still some pacificists like Petrus Damiani who cried out against the idea of holy war; [150] yet most church officials favored a church militant. The *SR* well illustrates what Helen Adolf (p. 46) has termed the "three fallacies", namely the three premises upon which the crusaders based their undertakings. These were the "prophetic" fallacy (It is God's will), the "feudal" fallacy (God is the supreme liege lord for whom all Christian knights are duty-bound to fight), and the "magical" fallacy (He will protect them and give them victory by means of miracles). To explain the origin of these fallacies, she continues: "Again and again Christianity, the 'fine fleur' or quintessence of Judaism plus an extra share of graces from above, has been forced to make strange alliances—with Greek philosophy and sophistry—with Roman and Byzantine imperialism—and, in the early Middle Ages, with the barbarous way of life of the Teutonic tribes. From this last was derived the barbarous piety of the Crusaders. Cruel to the point of brutality, they did not spare themselves either; acting on their three fallacious premises, they went all out, taking the consequences, and

[148] "Swaz ir der haiden hiute muget erslân, daz setze ich iu ce buze." Nâch dirre rede suze vielen si alle zû der erde. Dô segenôt si der herre; er sprach in indulgentiam: der antlâz was vor gote ze himile getân (*RL,* 3934–3939).

[149] Tel coronet ne chantat unches messe Ki de sun cors feist tantes proecces (1606).

[150] Despite the general fervor for the Spanish crusade of 1064, Petrus Damiani still opposed the idea of holy war (Erdmann, p. 131).

thus unwittingly testing their premises: they were worthy of being given an answer."

Carl Erdmann also notes the influence of the Germanic way of life upon the crusading spirit. Concerning the martial attitudes of the eleventh-century Church, he states: "In comparing them with the church teachings of late antiquity, one can see a retrogression in such attitudes. But one thing should not be forgotten: an entirely new situation had been created by the entrance of the Germanic peoples into Christian history. War was the vital element of the Germanic peoples, who were beginning more and more to form the most important part of the clergy. The ethos (*sittliche Vorstellungen*) that they brought with them out of their heathen past was entirely geared to struggle. Its main point was heroism: famous deeds on the part of the military leader, loyalty on the part of his followers, revenge for the slain, courage in the face of death, scorn for a comfortable life at home." [151]

These are precisely the virtues glorified in the *SR*. Having come from fighting families, most of the higher Frankish clergy had absorbed warlike attitudes in early childhood; and even those four-penny monks who prayed in the cloisters usually prayed for victory rather than for peace, just as Charlemagne does in the *SR* (3100–3109). The twelfth century must have accepted bellicose clergymen like Turpin, if we can accept the historical account of Archbishop Rainald of Dassel, Frederick Barbarossa's chancellor. According to Otto Morena or his continuators, this church dignitary seized a banner and advanced with the German troops against the Romans on Barbarossa's campaign in Lombardy.[152]

---

[151] Erdmann, p. 16.

[152] Ipsi scientes et videntes se aliter evadere non posse, nisi iter ferro aperirent, ipsimet archiepiscopus et cancellarius vexillum in manu accipiens signoque dato maximis vocibus cantum Teutonicum, quem in bello Teutonici dicunt, videlicet 'Christus qui natus' et cetera, omnes levantes acriter super omnes Romanos irruerunt (*Das Geschichtswerk des Otto Morena*, ed. F. Güterbock, Berlin, 1930, p. 198).

The martial attitude of the Church was without doubt intensified by the spread of Islam and the need to counter force with force.[153] Violence was easily justified by the Old Testament. The brutality toward the inhabitants of Cordres and Saragossa is less extreme than God's command to Saul to "go and smite Amalek, and utterly destroy all that they have, and spare them not; but slay both man and woman, infant and suckling, ox and sheep, camel and ass" (I Samuel, 15:3). We can at least rest assured that the Franks spared the camels and asses.

To discover which appeals were most effective in attracting men to the crusades, we might well examine the popular "crusade songs" composed to arouse enthusiasm for religious expeditions. Although many in number, these songs are limited in scope and revolve around a few themes belabored in myriad variations. Typical of these is a song composed by Conon de Béthune to recruit volunteers for the crusade of 1189. In a song of farewell the poet assures his ladylove that, although his body is going off to serve the Lord, his heart will remain entirely in her service. Reluctant to leave, he is going to Syria through fear that God will fail him in his hour of need if he does not go. All men should fight there, because there they can win paradise, honor, fame, and the love of their ladies. Now we can show who is really courageous by avenging the grievous shame (*honte dolereuse*) about which we should feel angry and disgraced (*iriez et honteus*) because the Holy Land has been lost in our time. If we leave the enemy there, we will be shamed the rest of our lives. . . .[154]

[153] Heisig (p. 19) insists that the Mohammedans developed the idea of holy war before the Christians and must have influenced Eulogius, Alvaro, and other militant Christians who lived in their midst. Naturally, the ultimate source of the idea was in the Old Testament.

[154] Se li cors vait servir Nostre Seignour, Li cuers remaint du tout en sa baillie. Pour li m'en vois souspirant en Surie, Quar nus ne doit faillir son Creatour. Qui li faudra a cest besoing d'aïe, Sachiez, que il li faudra a greignour; Et sachiez bien, li grant et li menour, Que la doit on faire chevalrie, Qu'on i conquiert paradis et honor Et pris et los et l'amour de s'amie. Dex! tant avom esté preu par huiseuse! Or i parra qui a certes iert preus, S'irom vengier

Here, nearly a century after the *SR*, we find most of the old incentives still in force. Although Conon also promises a glorious
life in paradise to those who die on the crusade,[155] he still appeals
chiefly to concern for worldly honor and shame. The same holds
true of most German crusade songs. In mentioning the two chief
incentives for going on a crusade, Hartmann of Aue lists the
world's honor (*der werlte lop*) before the soul's salvation (*der
sêle heil*).[156]

People tend to consider the Middle Ages an especially religious
age; in fact a popular anthology of medieval writings is named
the *Age of Belief*.[157] It was, to be sure, an age of belief, if belief
means uncritical acceptance of all information, including superstition and old wives' tales. Turold's ideas about the Moslems and
their idols illustrates the inability or unwillingness of his age to
question its traditional or popular beliefs. His contemporaries
seldom questioned the dogmas of the Church, even when failing
to comply with the ethics it preached. And despite their avowed
obedience to the Christian faith, they seem to have retained a
large part of their pagan ethos, often in conscious defiance of
Christian dogma. In other words, in embracing Christianity, they
had accepted its mythos but not its ethos.

---

la honte dolereuse Dont chascuns doit estre iriez et honteus, Car a no tanz est
perduz li sains lieus U Dieuss soufri pour nous mort angoisseuse; S'or i laissom
nos anemis morteus, A touz jours mais iert no vie honteuse. . . . Qui
revendra mout sera eüreus: A touz jours maiz en iert Honors s'espeuse . . .
Sachiez cil sunt trop honi qui n'iront . . . Ne pueent pas demorer sanz
hontage (*Chansons de Croisade*, pp. 32–34, vv. 7–24, 31–32, 45–48). The
idea that the crusader's body wishes to fight against the heathens while his
heart wishes to remain with his lady-love is also expressed by the German
poet Friedrich of Husen in his song which begins: Mîn herze und mîn lîp
diu wellent scheiden (*Des Minnesangs Frühling*, IX, 47, 9–48, 2).

[155] Qui ci ne veut avoir vie anuieuse, Si voist pour Dieu morir liez et
joieus, Que cele mors est douce et savereuse Dont on conquiert le regne
precieus; Ne ja de mort nen i morra uns seus, Ainz naistront tuit en vie
glorieuse (*Ibid.*, vv. 25–30).

[156] wan swem daz ist beschert daz er dâ wol gevert, daz giltet beidiu teil,
der werlte lop, der sêle heil (*Des Minnesangs Frühling*, XXI, 210, 7–10).

[157] by Anne Fremantle, *Mentor Books*, 1954.

The way in which men can accept a mythos without the corresponding ethos is well illustrated in an anecdote about a caravan that was captured by bandits while crossing the Gobi Desert. Knowing the reputation of their captors, all the members of the caravan lost hope, except for one young American missionary still new to the area. Convinced that the poor benighted heathens would see the light if only it were shown to them, he announced to the bandits that he had a tale to tell them. Then, with the aid of an interpreter, he began his story of the creation of heaven and earth, the fall of man, and the trials and tribulations of the children of Israel. Hastening through the birth and miracles of Christ, he stressed His passion, death, and resurrection. Observing the attentive faces of his audience, the young missionary could see that the seed had fallen upon good ground; and, sure enough, the next morning he and his companions were allowed to proceed on their way unmolested. However, the next caravan that attempted to cross the desert was also captured, and its members were crucified, while their captors cast lots for their garments.

A century or so after Turold composed his song, the German poet, Walther von der Vogelweide, jocularly stated that he was unwilling to love those who hated him even if it meant renouncing God's forgiveness,[158] and it takes no psychiatrist to know that such jocular remarks often reveal much truth. Similar defiance was expressed very seriously by William Marshal, an English contemporary of Walther's. Advised that he would not be saved unless he returned all the booty he had won, William answered: "The clerks are too hard on us. They shave us too closely. I have captured five hundred knights and have appropriated their arms, horses, and their entire equipment. If for this reason the kingdom of God is closed to me, I can do nothing about it, for I cannot return my booty. I can do no more for God than to give

---

[158] Wie solt ich den geminnen der mir übele tuot? mir muoz der iemer lieber sîn der mir ist guot. vergib mir anders mîne schulde, ich wil noch haben den muot (Walther 26, 10–12).

myself to him, repenting all my sins. Unless the clergy desire my damnation, they must ask no more. But their teaching is false— else no one could be saved." [159] Turold must have been quite unaware that the Church opposed the taking of plunder, for his Archbishop has no qualms about riding the horse he took from the king he killed in Denmark. Nor would he be any less reluctant than William Marshal to give up his booty or to repent for having taken it.

It is true that medieval men devoted much ink, parchment, and man-hours to theological disputations and scholastic speculation; yet the fact that most documents surviving from the Middle Ages contain religious matter does not prove that the general public preferred it to oral tales of martial prowess. It only proves that parchment is more durable than men's memories. Should World War III destroy all libraries except one in a theological seminary, post-atomic scholars would conclude that men of our era were more concerned with sin and salvation than with sports and social status. In judging the acts of medieval rulers, we must remember that their biographers were invariably clergymen, who naturally exaggerated their rulers' religious faith and pious deeds in order to edify their readers. It is not surprising that Charlemagne passed as a saint for many centuries, even though his actual conduct was anything but saintly.

There were many theologians in twelfth-century France, but they were outnumbered by their military counterparts; and even their writings often suggest more casuistry than conviction. As the only intellectual pursuit available, theology attracted many minds driven by intellectual curiosity rather than by religious fervor. Twelfth-century clerics parodied holy things in a way which would shock even the most irreverent minds today.[160]

[159] Quoted from *William Marshal,* by Sidney Painter, Baltimore, 1933, pp. 285–86.
[160] For a good anthology of such parody, see Paul Lehmann, *Die Parodie im Mittelalter,* Munich, 1922.

Although political and military leaders frequently claimed religious motivation, their actions most often betray purely secular considerations. The twelfth century is usually judged an especially religious age, but we should remember that during it four Christian gentlemen saw fit to murder an archbishop at his altar while a Christian emperor welcomed the opportunity to seize a fellow Christian ruler returning from a crusade and to hold him for ransom. It was also an age in which a high church dignitary could castrate a colleague to punish him for his sexual transgressions. A Romanesque cathedral may reveal the religious aspirations of its architect and builders, or it may just reveal their worldly pride as artists and artisans. The donor may have wished to buy his way to heaven, but he may also have been trying to surpass the magnificence of a rival ruler.

Scholars often compare the religious Middle Ages with the irreligious Renaissance, as if it were a comparison of black and white. In an excellent study of the Renaissance concept of honor, Curtis Brown Watson convincingly demonstrates that Shakespeare's ethos was basically secular and was expressed largely in commonplaces ultimately derived from Aristotle, Cicero, Seneca, and the Stoics.[161] But then he draws a conclusion which would have delighted the heart of Jacob Burckhardt, whose views he has defended earlier in his study. He states (p. 208): "In the Renaissance merging of Christian and classical values, Christian values have not maintained the dominant position they held in the Middle Ages." He then justifies this contrast by continuing: "A great and fundamental shift of attitude is evident here if we consider the extent to which Aquinas and Shakespeare differ in their attitudes toward the permanence of honor." But this is a false comparison. It is like saying that animals must be getting fiercer, because Renaissance lions were more predatory than medieval lambs. If we must compare, then let us compare lions with lions

[161] *Shakespeare and the Renaissance Concept of Honor*, Princeton, 1960.

and lambs with lambs—laymen with laymen and clergymen with clergymen.

The fact that Renaissance drama was more secular than medieval scholasticism does not prove that religion lost ground during the interim. It merely proves that dramatists are less clerical than clerics. Shakespeare's attitude toward the permanence of honor differs no more from that of Aquinas than it does from that of Bossuet.[162] Instead of comparing the views on honor expressed by Aquinas and Shakespeare, we might just as fairly compare those expressed by Turold with those expressed by Calvin. Then we would draw the amazing conclusion that twelfth-century men still had a pagan code of honor, which sixteenth-century men at last succeeded in overcoming. It is not a case of age versus age, but of court versus cloister. Many sixteenth-century men expressed un- and even anti-religious sentiments, but many others burned rather than renounce their faith.

Siciliano denies that the religious elements in the *chansons de geste* can be distinguished from the heroic; and he doubts that anyone will know whether the poets "first conceived the warrior and then the Christian, because the hero is a Christian warrior. No one will know whether it is the Christian spirit which penetrates the heroic spirit, or vice versa; because it is a question of deep and impenetrable synthesis." [163] The civilization of the twelfth century is often explained as an amalgam or synthesis of pagan and Christian elements, which were best harmonized in the crusades. But can such disparate and conflicting values be harmonized? Can a theocentric guilt-culture be harmonized with an anthropocentric shame-culture? To be sure, Christian forms and ritual, and even much Christian dogma, can be adapted to

[162] See note 86 above.

[163] C'est ainsi que les poètes ont conçu leurs poèmes et les drames de leurs héros et personne ne saura s'ils ont d'abord conçu le combattant et puis le chrétien, parce que le héros est un combattant chrétien. Personne ne saura si c'est l'esprit religieux qui influe sur l'esprit héroïque ou vice-versa, parce qu'il s'agit d'une synthèse profonde et impénétrable (Siciliano, p. 218).

serve a completely alien ethos; but the contradictory elements can only be juxtaposed, not synthesized. They do not blend like water and wine, but rather they intermingle like water and oil, and one might well say that the Christian ingredients in the SR are in suspension rather than in solution. As is so abundantly evident in the song, appeals to greed and pride are juxtaposed with appeals to religious duty and hope of heavenly reward; but nowhere are they truly harmonized. When Charlemagne prays to God to help him gain vengeance, he is not harmonizing pagan and Christian ethics. He is using a Christian form, but he is using it to express a sentiment diametrically opposed to Christian ethics.

When Siciliano says that the Christian spirit in the SR forms an impenetrable synthesis with the heroic, he is correct, provided the word "Christian" is understood as it was understood by the fighting classes of Western Europe in the twelfth century. But it must be remembered that, when Christianity accommodated itself to the tastes of the heathen converts, the Christian God had to adapt Himself to their previous ideals. In urging his men to stand firm lest brave men sing shameful songs about them, Turpin asks it of them "for God's sake" (pur Deu, 1516).[163a] Such a proud God was quite in keeping with the jealous Jehovah of the Old Testament, who saved his people "for his name's sake, that he might make his mighty power to be known".[164]

Judged by their own lights, the barons of the SR are surely "true Christians", just as truly Christian as the hundred thousand Mohammedan apostates who accept baptism and thus become "true Christians" (veir chrestien, 3672) rather than suffer the Christians' sword, noose, or stake. The conquerors seem little concerned with the inner conversion of the conquered, nor do

[163a] Possibly pur Deu is merely an exclamation, like the frequently used Deus!

[164] Psalms, 106:8. This motivation also appears in the well-known 23rd Psalm. Cf. "I am the Lord: that is my name: and my glory will I not give to another, neither my praise to graven images" (Isaiah, 42, 8). See notes II, 136, 137, 139, 141.

they give much evidence that they themselves have a very lucid idea of the religion they are propagating. In any case, they would have found it hard to convince their captives that they were spreading a religion of peace and brotherly love. Albert Fuchs pronounces a masterful understatement in saying that the notion of Christianity (*pensée chrétienne*) in the *SR* "remains free of any ideological nuance".[165] Since ideology is the quintessence of an ethos, there can be little Christian ethos in the *pensée chrétienne* of the *SR*. It is abundantly evident that honor and shame are stronger sanctions than religious duty and that Roland and his men accept Christian dogma without Christian ethics. They believe in the forgiveness of sins, but not in the forgiveness of insults.

After weighing the evidence of the preceding three chapters, it is easy to agree with most of the following statements: "There is something . . . more valuable to Roland than life itself—his honor and reputation. It is not the glory of the cause nor the help he might be to others that galvanizes him into action but the fear of having his own reputation besmirched with the accusation of cowardice. . . . To many modern readers, Roland may appear to be proud, selfish, egotistical, and unbelievably stubborn, and therefore deserving of neither admiration nor sympathy. To some modern critics, on the other hand, he seems to be essentially a tragic character, who, by excess of . . . pride, brings about the death of his dearest friend and dozens of his fellow Franks. If we look carefully, it becomes apparent that every detail of the story, as it touches Roland, gyrates around his quest for and insistence on his own personal honor and fame above all other values. . . . Roland's personal honor, in fact, was behind almost every move, great and small, that he made throughout the whole *SR*. . . . Roland had at last attained his greatest wish,

---

[165] . . . cette pensée chrétienne reste libre de toute nuance idéologique (Fuchs, p. 191).

even if he had paid for it with the death of so many Franks, including that of his dearest friend. . . . We get, in all this attention to the gory, anatomical details of the battlefield, a fleeting glimpse of an ideal that is not too far removed from savagery. . . . There is no possible doubt that personal glory was the dominant element in the primitive Frankish heroic ideal, and for Roland it was definitely glory won on the battlefield. . . . It is also important to notice that Roland is not criticized in the *SR* for his stand in the matter of personal honor. . . . He had lived gloriously; he had fought gloriously; he died gloriously and was gloriously honored after his death; and he had the assurance that his glorious reputation would live on in the ears of men forever. . . . The poem ends with Roland triumphant; he has gained all that he set out to get."

Although these remarks are largely true of Roland and his comrades, it is to be noted that they were not originally made about Turold's Christian epic. If we change the words *Roland, Franks,* and *SR* to read *Achilles, Greeks,* and *Iliad,* we find that they were actually made about Homer's *Iliad,* in a chapter in which Father Maurice McNamee attempts to define a pagan concept of honor.[166] As we can see, these criteria of paganism hold, to a large extent, of the *SR*, despite its Christian apologists.

[166] McNamee, pp. 3, 8, 11, 14, 18, 24, 24, 24, 32, 33.

CHAPTER IV

ETHICAL CONSISTENCY
IN THE *SONG*
OF ROLAND

As MENTIONED IN THE INTRODUCTION, this study has dealt with
the ethos of the *SR* without reference to its literary merits. In
contrast, this chapter will try to observe whether the song's ethos
throws any light upon its composition or artistic intent. Scholars
have sometimes viewed the relative importance of religion in the
various parts of the *SR* as evidence of the song's literary unity or
disunity. Those who considered the *SR* a compilation of independent *cantilènes* generally questioned whether the "Baligant
episode" was really an integral part of the work, and some decided
that it had been added subsequently by another poet. By the
"Baligant episode" is meant the section of the song in which
Baligant, the Emir of Babylon, comes to Spain with all the forces
of heathendom to assist his hard-pressed vassal Marsilie and is in
turn defeated by Charlemagne and all the forces of Christendom.

This entire action, comprising more than a fourth of the epic
(2476–2844, 2974–3632), can be deleted without serious damage
to the plot. Certain editors even think the epic better without it.

Some scholars consider it a later and inorganic interpolation because it is omitted from the *Carmen* and the *Karlamagnús saga*. On the other hand, although Jules Horrent considers the Baligant episode an addition (258), he nevertheless believes that it had appeared in the original version on which the *Carmen* and the *saga* were based (125–129). This would seem likely, since the Baligant episode appears in the *Rolandslied,* which was written before the *Carmen* and the *saga,* even if not as early as previously believed.[1] If it is true that the authors of the *Carmen* and the *saga* both deleted the Baligant episode intentionally, this would suggest that they considered the Roncevaux episode sufficient in itself and in no need of a sequel.

In 1950 W. S. Woods (p. 1256) argued that the Baligant episode must have been written by a different author not only because it has no *laisses similaires,* but also because it is not divided, as the rest of the song is, into triads of closely related but dissimilar strophes. Nine years later Robert A. Hall, Jr. still argued for multiple authorship on the grounds of varying linguistic strata in the song,[2] for which purpose he reverted to arguments presented by Wendelin Foerster three quarters of a century earlier. These arguments have been known all this time, yet most critics, including Bédier, Becker, Pauphilet, and Curtius, have ignored them and insist that the poem is the work of a single author.[3]

---

[1] The *RL* was formerly dated ca. 1130 and thus served as an early *terminus ante quo* for the *SR*. Now it is more generally dated ca. 1170.

[2] "If we accept the evidence of the assonances, there can no longer be any question of the Roland being the work of a single author, even in a large part" (Hall, "Linguistic Strata . . .", p. 158).

[3] Bédier (*Légendes,* III, p. 399, footnote 1) refutes arguments based on vocalism. Becker (p. 3) denies an earlier version on stylistic and literary grounds: "Jede Untersuchung über das Rolandslied muss bei dieser Sachlage von der Oxforder Fassung ausgehen, und sie darf es mit gutem Gewissen tun; denn bisher ist es trotz aller Anstrengung nicht gelungen, die dichterische Ursprünglichkeit unseres Rolandslieds mit Erfolg anzufechten und das Vorhandensein einer älteren Rolanddichtung als Vorstufe der unseren wahrscheinlich zu machen. Alle darauf gerichteten Versuche kommen gegen die feste Geschlossenheit und die geniale Einheitlichkeit der Dichtung, wie sie

Hall has recently entered the lists again to champion multiple authorship. This time he bases his arguments on the marked differences between the *laisses* with earlier-type assonance and those with later-type assonance. In the former he sees a naïve story of a pure and saint-like hero who has far less dramatic value than the cocky, over-sure, insensitive young man of the later-type *laisses,* whose downfall is caused by his own pride.[4]

Similarities in style and vocabulary do not prove a single author, because a continuator could have purposely imitated or borrowed verses from the older sections. On the other hand, even if the Baligant episode was a later interpolation, it could still have been written by the same author. Turold may have first written his song for a secular patron and later rewritten it for an ecclesiastical patron to popularize a crusade. Possibly the authors of the *Carmen* and the *saga* followed copies of the song made before Turold added the Baligant episode, whereas Conrad, although earlier, followed a later copy that included it. Or else Conrad may have retained it because of his religious intent, while the two later poets dropped it as unnecessary to the plot and detrimental to the main action, which is the battle of Roncevaux.

The episodes relating Ganelon's mission to the Saracens and his eventual punishment complement the Roncevaux story; and these three together form a complete and self-sufficient whole. On the other hand, the Baligant episode is superfluous to the basic plot of the song, notwithstanding Curtius's insistence that it grew out of "inner necessity" (p. 285). Charlemagne needs no satisfaction from the Saracens for slaying Roland, who has already defeated them, maimed their king, and killed his son. At most, he must pursue the defeated king and destroy him and his city of Saragossa and thus complete his seven years' war, for

---

vorliegt, nicht auf." In brief: "Wer behaupten kann, das Werk sei nicht aus einem Guss, hat es eben nicht verstanden" (*Ibid.,* p. 7).

[4] Hall, "On Individual Authorship . . ."

vengeance on Ganelon alone would provide both poetic justice and literary balance. Yet, even if the Baligant episode were an infelicitous addition, this would not prove that a talented and inspired poet like Turold could not have added it. Critics generally agree that the *Walpurgisnachtstraum* detracts from Goethe's *Faust*, yet few doubt that Goethe wrote it or that Goethe was a literary genius. The best poets are not always the best critics, especially of their own works.

Crusading fervor dominates the Baligant episode. No longer do Roland and the Franks of France hold the stage, but rather Charlemagne and all the various peoples of his empire, including Saxons, Bavarians, Alemanni, Frisians, Bretons, Burgundians, and many more. Instead of a punitive expedition against the violators of Charlemagne's envoys, it is a holy war against the combined forces of heathendom. Charlemagne defeats not only the Mohammedans, but also the heathens from the Baltic lands as well as heretics and schismatics from elsewhere.

If the Baligant episode is accepted as an integral part of the *SR*, then the *SR* appears at first glance to be inconsistent in both plot and ethos. Throughout the song the poet assures us that Charlemagne can do nothing without Roland's aid. Ganelon tells Marsilie that Charlemagne will be safe as long as Roland and his twelve peers live but will lose his right arm and have to discontinue his campaign if Roland dies.[5] The pagans later repeat this thought by saying that the war will be resumed and Spain will be lost if Roland survives (2118–2119). Roland tells his sword that he has won most of Charlemagne's lands for him; and Charlemagne subsequently regrets that his own power will wane after Roland's death and that he will have no one to defend his honor.[6]

---

[5] *SR*, 544–549, 596–600. Stricker too maintains that Charlemagne can do nothing without Roland's aid (da ist sîn stiefsun Ruolant, der ist ein sô gewaltec man, daz Karl enmac noch enkan niht getuon wan alse er wil, 2696–2699).

[6] *SR*, 2306–2308, 2322–2334, 2902–2903. Stricker lets Charlemagne re-

Baligant too believes that he will easily win now that Charlemagne's nephew is dead, for he would not give a glove for all the
rest of Charlemagne's men.[7] In like manner the *Carmen* states
that Rollandus is the only hope, fame, and honor of the Gauls,
without whom Gaul will fall. He alone is the glory of the Frankish nation: with him it was the honor of the world, without him
it is absolutely nothing.[8]

Misled by such statements, Siciliano considers Roland the hero
of the whole poem. Of Charlemagne he says: "Without Roland,
he is nothing and he can do nothing. That is what is clearly said
by the poet, what is said by Ganelon, what is said by the pagans,
what is said by Baligant, what is said by Roland, what is said by
Charlemagne himself." [9] But the Baligant episode shows that
Turold, Ganelon, the pagans, Baligant, Roland, Charlemagne, and
Siciliano were all mistaken. Although deprived of Roland's help,
Charlemagne promptly attacks and quickly destroys Baligant's
huge army, which is many times greater than that which caused
Roland's death. It is not enough for a poet to tell how indispen-
sable one of his characters is: he must let the character prove it
through his actions.

Those who accept the Baligant episode as an integral part of
the *SR* must agree with Pauphilet that Charlemagne is the true
hero of the song, no matter how much scholarly attention has
been attracted to Roland.[10] On the other hand, Faral maintains

---

proach Ganelon for causing the death of all those upon whom his honor depended (Du hâst mir alle die verlorn, an den mîn êre elliu lac, 7140–7141).

[7] *SR*, 3182–3183, 3189.

[8] Gallorum tu spes, tu fama fuisti, Et probitas et dux et decus omne simul!
Gallia te nudata jacet, quia te prius ente Quid fuit? orbis honor; quid modo?
tota nihil (*Carmen*, 465–469). Francigene gentis gloria solus erat (v. 472).

[9] Sans Roland, il n'est rien, il ne peut rien, et c'est cela que dit clairement
le poète, ce que dit Ganelon, ce que disent les païens, ce que dit Baligant,
ce que dit Roland, ce que dit Charles lui-même (Siciliano, p. 117).

[10] Que le relief extraordinaire du caractère de Roland, que la force drama-
tique de ces aventures aient attiré sur lui toute l'intention des érudits, il n'en
est pas moins vrai que le véritable héros du poème, aux yeux du poète,

that the *SR* should be named for Roland because he is always present, "present in his living person or, after his death, present in memory"; and Paul Aebischer seconds him in this view.[11] Using the same reasoning, we could say that the *Lay of the Nibelungs* should be called the *Lay of Siegfried,* since Siegfried dominates the first half and the vengeance of his murder dominates the second half. Thomas Greene (p. 200) maintains that "it might be said that the whole poem belongs essentially to Roland, even though a considerable part of the action occurs after his death; Charlemagne's victory would thus be read as a response to Roland's defeat. This is a defensible reading but so is the contrary—that the poem belongs essentially to Charlemagne, with whom it begins and ends, and that Roland's defeat should be seen as a peripety in his liege's larger, circumscribing career. Both readings are legitimate; to the degree that they conflict, the poem could be called complex."

If Roland is the true hero of the song, then the song cannot be considered a religious epic, because Roland's motivation is almost entirely secular. Religion plays almost no part until Roland is about to die: he never once refers to the Spanish campaign as a holy war, nor does he ask God for aid.[12] As we have seen, he appeals almost exclusively to his men's greed and vainglory by promising plunder and fame, and he never reminds them of their

---

c'était Charlemagne (Pauphilet, p. 191). Cf. La *Chanson de Roland* est bien la chanson de Roland, un poème épique dont le personnage central est le neveu de Charlemagne (Aebischer, p. 179).

[11] Il (the title *Chanson de Roland*) lui convient parfaitement, puisque aussi bien, depuis le commencement jusqu'à la fin, le personnage de Roland y est présent, présent de sa personne vivante ou, après sa mort, présent par le souvenir (Faral, p. 241). Et Roland est toujours là, sinon personnellement, du moins idéalement . . . (Aebischer, p. 180).

[12] When Oliver sees the Saracens and announces the impending battle, Roland exclaims: *E! Deus la nus otreit!* (1008). This is purely heroic pleasure in anticipating a good fight: he asks God to grant the battle, but he relies on his own ability to win it. He then explains that the rear guard is there to fight for the king: *Ben devuns ci estre pur nostre rei.*

religious duty. He prays only when about to die, and even then his three prayers total fewer verses than his vainglorious apostrophe to his sword.[13] Not once does God act on his behalf, until He sends His angels to fetch his soul. To borrow a term from Greene (p. 198), Roland's heroism may be said to evoke "epic awe", as distinguished from the religious or mythical awe inspired by the miracles God performs for Charlemagne. The final combat between Charlemagne and Baligant, those white-bearded patriarchs, hovers between the sublime and the ridiculous, depending upon the emotional participation of the audience. Deprived of its mystique, this scene runs the risk of appearing grotesque, whereas the battle at Roncevaux has continued to move all audiences right down to our own skeptical age.

Charlemagne dominates both the first and the last strophe of the song, whereas Roland makes his first appearance in v. 104 and his last living appearance in v. 2396, which is only slightly past the middle of the work. In fact Charlemagne is named in the very first verse and is the subject of the very last verse, if one excepts Turold's controversial colophon. Priest Conrad, who retains the Baligant episode, is quite correct in saying that he is going to write about Emperor Charles (*RL*, 1–16).

It has been stated that the "religious theme" is more prominent in the Baligant episode than elsewhere in the *SR*, but it might be argued that the religious element in the Baligant episode sometimes seems extraneous and not entirely assimilated into the literary style of the rest of the song. The various classical and

---

[13] His first prayer is immediately followed by the verse *Ço sent Rollant que la mort li est près* (2259). In other words, as long as it is possible, he relies on self-help, like the heroes of the pagan sagas. His three prayers (2252–2258, 2369–2372, 2384–2389) total 16 verses, as compared with 33 in his apostrophe to his sword (2316–2337, 2344–2354). The same situation holds in the *Carmen*, in which Rollandus becomes religious in verse 458 of 483 verses, and only when dying (*Dum moriens . . . supplex veniam supplice voce rogat*). He even interrupts this prayer to kill the pagans who try to steal his horn.

biblical reminiscences in the earlier portions of the song are so well-digested and blended into the poet's idiom that scholars have been unable to prove a single literary borrowing.[14] In general Turold seems to have expressed his ideas and sentiments spontaneously, unaware that he has found some of his thoughts, or at least his means of expressing them, already formulated in Latin literature and oral tradition.

Turold adapted most of his literary sources so thoroughly that they reappeared as completely original creations when transformed by his genius. Numerous passages of his song suggest verses in Scripture, yet they are too elusive to identify and too vague to classify as borrowings. A good example of these literary will-o'-the-wisps appears when the pagans flee before Roland while the Franks are as fierce as lions,[15] for this situation recalls the proverb that "the wicked flee where no man pursueth; but the righteous are as bold as a lion."[16] Despite the apparent similarity, no borrowing can be proved; at best one could claim that Turold used some half-forgotten recollection stored away in a dark corner of his subconscious.

Nevertheless, this rule does not hold for some of the prayers in, and just before, the Baligant episode. Tavernier observed that Charlemagne's prayer before the final battle was based on the *Ordo commendationis animae,* and it is evident that this prayer follows its source more closely than any of Turold's other literary borrowings. Charlemagne alludes to Jonah and the whale,

[14] Et pourtant il faut convenir qu'on ne peut mettre un seul vers de la Chanson de Roland en regard d'un vers de Virgile, de Stace ou de Lucain et conclure que notre poète a consciemment emprunté, imité (Bédier, *Commentaires,* p. 60). Entre les deux poèmes (*Aeneid* and *SR*), combien d'analogies, de concordances, d'harmonies! Mais, chose très digne de remarque! jamais le rapprochement n'est assez précis pour qu'on puisse affirmer que notre auteur a directement, consciemment imité (*Ibid.,* p. 316).

[15] Devant Rollant si s'en fuient paiens (1875); Pur ço sunt Francs si fiers cume leuns (1888).

[16] Fugit impius, nemine persequente; iustus autem quasi leo confidens absque terrore erit (*Proverbs,* 28, 1).

the King of Nineveh, Daniel in the lion's den, and the three men
in the fiery furnace (3100–3109); and these allusions suggest
more pedantry and virtuosity on Turold's part than literary or
even religious inspiration. Structurally, Charlemagne's prayer resembles the much shorter prayer said by Roland just before his
death.[17] If Turold or some other continuator added the Baligant
episode subsequently, he could also have interpolated Roland's
prayer and various other religious passages into the Roncevaux
episode, which had until then been predominantly secular in
tone. This could account for all angelic intervention, as when
Gabriel receives Roland's glove and when Saint Cherubim and
Saint Michael take his soul to paradise (2390–2395).

In comparison with the *Rolandslied,* the *SR* shows a very superficial understanding of Christian ethics. Whereas religion is immediately important in the *RL,* it is of little significance in the *SR*
until shortly before Roland's death. To be sure, the Baligant
episode is relatively longer in the *SR* than in the *RL;* but that is
of little consequence, since the entire *RL* resembles the Baligant
episode in that it depicts a holy war from the very first verse of
the song. Conrad's opening verses declare that he is writing
about Charlemagne, who has conquered and converted so many
heathens and has thereby won the kingdom of heaven. As God's
vassal, the emperor is distressed to see the Spaniards living
wickedly and worshiping idols, and he sets out at God's command to convert them and to seek a martyr's death.

To be sure, Conrad retains some of the heroic values of his
source. He prolongs the battles as if they are to be enjoyed for
their own sake, and he even lets Turpin shout that anyone who
does not wield his sword is unworthy of being a man and should
be a monk (6297). Charlemagne expresses indignation because
his envoys have been violated (818), and his men wish to avenge

[17] *SR,* 2384–2388. Both prayers begin with the words V*eire Patene;* and
both name certain people whom God has previously aided in time of trouble,
among these being Daniel.

their fallen friends (5882). But these are rare exceptions, for
Conrad more often emphasizes the value of winning salvation.
Unlike Turold, he also warns against hell's fire, which Turold
reserves for pagans only.

Conrad exploits two motifs popular in epic literature, namely
the assertions that a man should avenge rather than mourn his
friend and that a man cannot avoid his fate; but because of his
Christian ethos he puts both these assertions into pagan mouths.
When one of Marsilie's men tells him that it is not fitting for him
to wear the crown if he fails to avenge his men, he is paraphrasing
the words spoken by Oger to Charlemagne in the SR; [17a] and
this suggests that much of what is spoken by Turold's Christians
would suit only Conrad's pagans. Joleun urges Paligan to attack
the Franks despite their ferocity because "none but the doomed
will die".[17b] Had one of Conrad's Christians been speaking, he
would probably have said that none will die but those chosen by
God. Conrad praises the virtues of modesty, chastity, obedience,
patience, and humility; and he extolls peace by letting Charlemagne promise Marsilie peace "for God's sake" (834). Charlemagne also spares women and children (890) and promises to
protect the new converts from robbery just like the other Christians (3164). Charlemagne realizes the vanity of life on earth,[18]
in fact *memento mori* and *vanitas vanitatum* largely replace the
heroic affirmation of life found in the SR. There can be no tragedy, since Charlemagne and his men yearn to die the martyr's
death.[19]

Whereas the SR endorses wealth and fame as worthy incentives,
the RL denounces them as suitable only for the infidels. While

---

[17a] Herre, chunc ûz Yspanie, diu chrône gezimet (dir) nîmêre ze tragene,
dune rechest dîne tôten (RL, 5195–5197). Cf. Ja Deu ne placet qu'el chef
portez corone, S'or n'i ferez pur venger vostre hunte (SR, 3538–3539).

[17b] Hî nesterbit nîmen wan di vaigen (RL, 8402). Cf. dâ sterben wan die
veigen (NL, 150, 2).

[18] RL, 3421–3423; 3508; 3008–3011.

[19] RL, 3252–3254, 3878–3888.

the Saracens goad their men forward by warning that no fiefs will be given to those who flee (329, 8115), the Christian leaders promise only the kingdom of heaven. The pagans seek plunder whereas Charlemagne's men constantly refuse it. Instead of Marsilie's gifts, Charlemagne wishes only salvation; and Roland's men disregard wealth and tread on their captured treasures.[19a] In like manner, only the pagans desire worldly glory. Marsilie asks his men to advise him "for the sake of their own honor", whereas Charlemagne is more concerned with God's honor.[20] In his final prayer, Conrad's emperor requests victory, not to avenge Roland as Turold's does, but for the future of the Holy Spirit (7927). Whereas Turold's Roland is afraid that some coward might get his sword and thus bring ill repute upon his memory, Conrad's Roland is afraid that it will fall into heathen hands and thus be used to harm the Christians (6816–6820). Nowhere is there any reference to scurrilous songs, nor does Roland die with his head turned toward the enemy.

Both Alterot and Targis wish to kill Roland in order to win fame, and Cursabile swears he will kill Turpin so that people will sing his praises.[21] Even pride of family is restricted to the heathens, instead of being exalted as it is in the SR. Marsilie declares that Alterot will honor all his kindred by killing Roland; and Cursabile wishes to kill Turpin to honor Mohammed, his own kinsmen, and himself.[22] The pagans and Christians are skillfully contrasted in a few words: "Targis fought for honor, Anseis for his soul, Targis for earthly kingdoms, Anseis for the kingdom of heaven."[23] This implies that Conrad rejected two of Turold's strongest motivations.

[19a] *RL*, 908–910, 3257–3258, 4212–4215.

[20] durch ûwer selber êre (423); dînen heiligen namen an uns êre! (7908), man nimt iz âne gotes êre (1152), Tut iz durch gotes êre (1161), etc.

[21] *RL*, 3560, 3685; 4400.

[22] *RL*, 3572, 4397–4399.

[23] Targis vacht umbe êre, Anseis umbe di sêle, Targis umbe ertrîche, Anseis umbe daz himilrîche (*RL*, 4719–4722).

Compared with Conrad's song, even the Baligant episode in the SR lacks a genuinely Christian ethos. To be sure, Turold presents the battle against the Emir as a holy war, as the decisive conflict between Christianity and Islam. Charlemagne invokes God and Saint Peter and asks God for victory and vengeance, Gabriel guards him in his camp and aids him in his peril,[24] and the Franks destroy the synagogues and mosques in Saragossa, as well as all inhabitants who refuse conversion. Yet, despite all this crusading fervor, the underlying ethos of Turold's song remains predominantly martial and heroic. One of the few truly Christian sentiments is Charlemagne's desire to convert Bramimunde through love rather than through force (3674), and in this case mercy is permissible only because Bramimunde is so obviously in Charlemagne's power that his leniency will not be attributed to fear. As we have seen, such mercy does not necessarily result from Christian teachings, since Charlemagne is clearly obeying the pagan-classic precept that an ideal ruler should spare the suppliant.[25]

Unlike the RL, the Baligant episode in the SR features worldly honor as a worthy incentive. Charlemagne declares that he will make the Arabs pay dearly for Roland's death, he prays to God to help him avenge Roland, and he calls upon his men to avenge their sons, brothers, and heirs. Egging him on, Oger appeals to Charlemagne's pride rather than to his sense of religious duty; and Charlemagne refuses to submit to Baligant, not because it would be a sin, but because it would be a disgrace. Far from advising mercy to the defeated enemy, he tells his troops to take pleasure in their vengeance.[25a] Charlemagne's crusade seems to have occurred without his volition. Finding his beloved and use-

---

[24] SR, 2998, 3100; 2847, 3612.

[25] Many medieval writers paraphrased Virgil's *parcere subiectis et debellare superbos* (*Aeneid*, VI, 853). For example, Lambert of Hersfeld said of Emperor Henry IV: *Supplicibus mitis, contrarius atque superbis* (*Carmen de bello Saxonico*, ed. A. Pannenborg, Göttingen, 1892, II, v. 204). For further examples, see my article "Grim to your Foes."

[25a] SR, 3011, 3100, 3411–3412; 3537, 3595; 3625.

ful nephew dead at Roncevaux, he pursues the enemy as far as the Ebro to avenge himself (2455). There he thanks God at seeing so many of the enemy slain or drowned and at seeing his knights win such great booty (2478); but, instead of pursuing Marsilie to Saragossa, he spends the night beside the Ebro before returning to Roncevaux to care for the dead. Unaware that Baligant has come from Babylon to succor Marsilie, Charlemagne is about to return to France when Baligant's messengers arrive and deliver the Emir's challenge;[26] and this shows that he has not intended to resume the conquest or conversion of Spain. Once he has been challenged, his honor alone suffices to make him stand and fight.

The preceding paragraphs indicate that, despite its greater fervor and crusading spirit, the Baligant episode is hardly more Christian in ethos than the Roncevaux episode and could therefore have been written by the same author, even if at a later date. This conclusion is negative, for it merely shows that an ethical analysis of the two parts of the song does not disqualify Turold as author of both. Nevertheless, this negative evidence is of some value, since it offers a fairly persuasive argument that one author did write both. In the case of most continuations of medieval works, the continuator is more successful in imitating the language and style of the original than in comprehending or reproducing its ethos. One need only imagine what ethical values the Baligant episode would express if Priest Conrad had added it.

An unbiased evaluation of the *SR*'s ethos may also discredit certain literary interpretations based on the commonly accepted idea that the song is essentially Christian.[26a] As an example of

[26] When Turold says: Venir s'en volt li emperere Carles, Quant de paiens li surdent les enguardes (2974–2976), he seems to mean that Charlemagne wanted to return to France, as most translators have assumed. This is what Baligant's envoys assume too, for they say: "Reis orguillos, nen est fins que t'en alges!"

[26a] The following pages incorporate a paper read to the 1961 congress of the Société Rencesvals at Venice and subsequently published as "Roland's Lament—a Divergent Interpretation" in *Romanic Review* (Vol. 53, 1962, pp.

such interpretatons one could cite a recent study of Roland's lament in *Laisse CXL,* in which Alain Renoir stresses Roland's guilt, humility, and penitence.[27] This penetrating literary analysis proves convincingly that *Laisse CXL* "is not only a powerful piece of work; it is the focal point for the tone and structure of the first half of the poem" (p. 583), yet it does not prove that Roland's inner tragedy stems from guilt and remorse. By failing to investigate the song's ethical vocabulary, Renoir has fallen into the common error of attributing alien attitudes to its hero. Thus, like most of his predecessors, Renoir interprets Roland's quandary in terms of sin, remorse, and forgiveness, rather than in terms of humiliation, chagrin, and vindication. In other words, he interprets an heroic epic as if it were a hagiographical legend. For reasons explained later, the *laisse* appears here in three sections, as divided by Renoir (p. 572):

> Rollant requardet es munz e es lariz.
> De cels de France i veit tanz morz gesir,
> E il les pluret cum chevaler gentill:
> "Seignors barons, de vos ait Deus mercit.
>
> v. 1855 Tutes vos anmes otreit il pareis;
> En seintes flurs il les facet gesir.
> Meillors vassals de vos unkes ne vi.
> Si lungement tuz tens m'avez servit,
> A oes Carlon si granz pais cunquis.
>
> v. 1860 Li empereres tant mare vos nurrit!
>
> Tere de France, mult estes dulz pais,
> Oi desertet a tant robustl exill.
> Barons Franceis, pur mei vos vei murir.
> Jo ne vos pois tenser ne guarantir.
>
> v. 1865 Ait vos Deus, ki unkes ne mentit.

3–15). A similar stand is taken by D. D. R. Owen in "The Secular Inspiration of the *Chanson de Roland*" (*Speculum,* 37, 1962), which appeared after this MS was submitted to the press.

[27] "Roland's Lament", *Speculum,* 35, 1960, pp. 576–83.

Oliver, frere, vos ne dei jo faillir.
De doel murra, se altre ne m'i ocit.
Sire Cumpainz, alum i referir!"

Italo Siciliano had previously argued that "the catastrophe of the vanquished baron needs the catharsis of the repentant sinner"; [28] and Ronald Walpole (p. 15) had stated that "penitence follows humility, and then God's pardon, so that Roland's spirit is taken up into heaven to evolve in an immortality which the ancients had not conceived and which he himself had truly apprehended only as, after defeat, he shed the last pagan elements of his nature." Pierre Le Gentil had considered the drama of Roncevaux to be a story of a soul that redeems itself through much suffering and a little humility, and Albert Pauphilet had called Roland "a proud man who remains obstinate for a long time but whom the suffering and death of his men gradually reform, purify, and sanctify." [29] Jessie Crosland (p. 83) was rather exceptional in giving Roland only a "twinge of conscience" instead of the customary pang. In one of the most recent discussions of this problem, W. T. H. Jackson (p. 167) concurs with the consensus in believing that "Roland's defiance and his final realization of his faults grip the reader's interest and at the same time represent the path of the Christian man who sins, repents, and does penance for his sin."

As our preceding chapters have shown, Christian values should not be assumed for the *Chanson de Roland* except where the text clearly warrants. Humility, remorse, and penitence on Roland's part in this episode would clash with his character else-

---

[28] "Que la catastrophe du baron vaincu a besoin de la catharsis du pécheur repenti", *Les Origines des chansons de geste,* Paris, 1951, p. 218.
[29] 'C'est pourquoi le drame de Roncevaux est pour une large part l'histoire d'une âme qui se rachète", "Beaucoup de souffrance et un peu d'humilité étaient nécessaires" (Le Gentil, p. 124); ". . . un orgueilleux qui s'obstine longtemps et que peu à peu la souffrance, et la mort des siens amendent, purifient, sanctifient" (*Romania,* 59, 1933, p. 178).

where in the song; and this is to be avoided because, as Jessie Crosland insists, "Roland's character . . . is all of one piece" (p. 90) and "the poet's psychological instinct never fails him. There is nothing incongruous or inconsistent in any of his characters" (p. 91).

In discussing Roland's "profound humility", Renoir (p. 575) says that, "like a true aristocrat, he knows how to admit the tragic extent of his failure with all the humility—and the concomitant dignity—required for such an admission." But does Turold really attribute humility to Roland? This is unlikely, since he nowhere recognizes humility as a virtue in his haughty fighting men.[29a] As previously mentioned, he lacked a word for "humility" and used the word *humilitet* only in the sense of homage, which suggests humiliation rather than humility. We have also seen that, in letting Roland look *humeles* at his friends, Turold was following the classical literary tradition of praising rulers who are grim to their enemies but kind to their friends. For Turold, Renoir's expression "triumphant in humility" would have been a paradox.

In considering dignity to be concomitant with admission of failure, Renoir reflects attitudes held by Greek Stoics and by some modern men, but not by Turold and his public. As we have seen, Turold branded all failure as shameful, regardless of the circumstances; and it is significant that he used the word *honte* to mean defeat even if the vanquished went down valiantly. Admission of failure would have been especially shameful for "a true aristocrat", for, as connoisseurs of honor from Aristotle to Ashley have agreed, nobles make the best warriers because of their great concern for their good names. Renoir's use of the word "dignity" is also questionable, since Turold did not understand such a concept. Europeans needed many more centuries to discover the innate dignity of man, as independent of rank and condition. When

[29a] According to Frank G. Ryder (p. 3), "The chivalric world was of course not averse to well-founded pride, and verbal humility was not one of its virtues . . .".

Shakespeare made his Montagues and Capulets "alike in dignity", he was referring to rank or social status rather than to excellence of character or innate worth. As we have seen, Turold used the word *deintet* only in its sense of "sovereignty".

Renoir believes that Roland proves his penitence by acknowledging his responsibility for his men's death; and as evidence of this he cites Roland's words *Barons franceis, pur mei vos vei murir* (1863). He agrees with T. A. Jenkins that Roland means "through my fault" rather than "for me", as Bédier and many others believed, because Bédier's solution presupposes "a concept nowhere intimated in this poem: that the French barons have been fighting for Roland personally rather than for their emperor or the honor of France" (p. 574). Here he contradicts what he has said on the previous page, namely that Roland "acknowledged their faithful service to himself and to Charles." Roland's actual words (*Si lungement tuz tens m'avez servit*, v. 1858) prove that he accepted the barons' service as a service to himself as commanding officer. Direct loyalty was then, is now, and ever shall be the essence of military chain-of-command. The subordinate owes personal loyalty to his immediate superior, and only through him to the higher commander.[29b] Although twelve of the barons at Roncevaux are Roland's "peers", they too are under his direct command during the rearguard engagement and must fight for him to their death. Although *pur mei* sometimes means "because of me", it more likely means "for my sake" in this passage, which contrasts the barons' loyal service with Roland's failure to protect them.

Believing that Roland's ordeal at Roncevaux transforms his

[29b] That this principle held in the Middle Ages is attested by William Stowell (*Titles*, p. 159), who states that the followers of a liege considered themselves his *home* but not the *home* of his seigneur. This was the essence of the feudal hierarchy. As evidence that there was no legal relationship between a lord and his vassal's vassal, Ganshof (p. 102) cites a formula current in 13th century France: . . . *queritur utrum homo hominis mei sit meus homo. Et dicendum est quod non.* . . .

character, Renoir considers his behavior to be "the logical outcome of his redemption from the sin of pride" (582). But Renoir
fails to prove that Roland, or even Turold, really considered pride
a sin. As we have seen, all the Christian knights in the song are
fiers and act *fierement*. Roland's deeper motivation is like that of
Shakespeare's Henry V, who says to Westmoreland: "I am not
covetous for gold. . . . But if it be a sin to covet honour, I am
the most offending soul alive." Like Henry, Roland realizes that
"the fewer men, the greater share of honour"; but, unlike Henry,
he does not seem to realize that it is "a sin to covet honour".
When Oliver scolds him for having destroyed the rear guard
through his pride, Roland innocently asks him why he is angry
(*Por quei me portez ire?*, 1722). Apparently even Oliver's de-
tailed answer does not make him contrite, because Turpin must
come to stop their quarrel. Yet, because he is unaware that his
pride has caused the havoc, it is easy to imagine that he will join
the Innocents in heaven, as Turpin has promised (1523).

Assuming that vainglory was judged blameworthy, Renoir censures Roland's braggadocio before Charlemagne early in the
song and says that "not only is the outburst utterly uncouth, but
Roland's uncalled-for recital of his own accomplishments con-
stitutes an embarrassing display of the most outrageous pride"
(576). But nowhere does Turold share this aversion. Like his contemporaries, he admired the warrior who could vaunt eloquently
of both his past and his future deeds; and he let Charlemagne
fondly remember Roland's boast that he would advance further
into the enemy territory than any of his men and that he would
die as a conqueror. As we have seen, Roland lists even more accomplishments in his final and longest self-adulation, which occurs after his putative remorse for having let his pride destroy
his men.

If Roland's "redemption from the sin of pride" has caused a
transformation in his character, then his redemption is not very

permanent and Turold has failed to create a consistent character. Renoir states that "Roland's humility in the *laisse* reveals its full import only when considered in contrast to his behavior in earlier scenes, where he appears as a rash, proud, and inconsiderate warrior" (575); and this indicates that Renoir has failed to note that Roland is vainglorious not only in earlier but also in later scenes. To prove Roland's subsequent vainglory, we must merely repeat a few facts mentioned and documented earlier in this study. After Oliver's death, Roland boasts that he will never desert Turpin because of any living man, and then he brags that the best blows of all are those struck by his own sword Durendal. Immediately after praying to Gabriel, he tries to destroy his sword to escape reproach, rather than to keep his sword from being used against his fellow Christians. When the Arab approaches to take his sword and says: "Charles' nephew has been vanquished," Roland is offended and indignantly strikes him dead with his horn and then taunts him and boastfully declares that anyone who heard of this incident would consider the Arab a fool for having dared to touch him. He next tells his sword that it has won many victories and conquered many lands and that it has belonged to a brave warrior. Thereupon he again enumerates the many lands he has conquered, in which case he recalls even more than he did earlier in the song. Roland then faces the enemy so that Charlemagne and his men will *say* that he has died as a conqueror, and only then does he confess his sins, of which pride is certainly not one. His dying thoughts are of the lands he has conquered, of France, of his kinsmen, of Charlemagne who has nourished him, and then, almost as an afterthought, of his soul. He makes no mention whatever of any remorse or sense of guilt, nor does he think of the men who died because of his pride.

In view of Roland's acts and thoughts, he can hardly be called an exemplary Christian. And it is hard to agree with Renoir

and others that Oliver's tongue-lashing had any salutary effect
on him. He may have been chastised, but not chastened. It is
even debatable whether Turold really understood remorse as dis-
tinct from regret; for he does not seem to have had any words
with which to distinguish the two sentiments. He uses the word
repentir only in a secular sense, as when Charlemagne says that
the Arabs will pay dearly if they do not renounce their plan of
attacking, and when Baligant offers peace provided Charlemagne
will give up his present policy toward him.[30] Turold uses no word
meaning "penitence". As we have seen, Turpin's reference to
penitence refers to the penance of killing pagans.

When Roland uses the word *doel* to express the emotion evoked
by the sight of his dead and dying men, Renoir assumes that his
emotion is grief,[31] and this is no doubt partially true, since Roland surely regrets the death of his men. Turold sometimes uses
the word *doel* to express the sorrow felt at the death of a loved
one; but, as we have seen, he also uses it to express a desire to
avenge rather than a desire to mourn. The latter generally seems
to be the case when the word *doel* is used by or of Roland. When
Aelroth slanders Charlemagne, Roland feels *doel* and immediately
wreaks vengeance, and he likewise feels *doel* when he sees his
friend Sansun slain by Valdabrun, whom he straightway kills.
When Grandonie kills six of his friends and discourages the
Franks, Roland feels such *doel* that he almost bursts and immediately curses and kills his offender.

Upon learning that his vassal Gualter has been defeated and
has lost all his men, Roland has *doel* and is very angry; and just
before his death he strikes ten blows with *doel* and rancor. In all
these cases *doel* seems to refer to an acute vexation caused by

[30] Si Arrabiz de venir ne se repentent (3011); Si pren cunseill que vers mei
te repentes (3590).
[31] "Then Roland concludes his encomium of the dead with a deeply moving
expression of his own grief" (Renoir, p. 573). Bédier translates *doel* here and
elsewhere as "douleur."

insult or injury or by a sense of failure or frustration. This is no doubt what the word *doel* means in *Laisse CXL;* for the very next strophe tells how Roland kills Faldrun de Pui and twenty-four other Saracens and says that no other man was ever so anxious to avenge himself. As we have seen, Turold's use of the words *doel, dolent, dolur, ire, irur,* and *rancune* shows that he did not distinguish clearly between anger and sorrow, and this suggests that he and his public did not categorize their emotional spectrum into the same primary colors as we do. In fact he did not have to "convert grief to anger," since the two were one.

If the word *doel* in *Laisse CXL* is translated as "chagrin", then there is no inconsistency in Roland's character or in the motivation of the song. Turold never presents Roland as crushed by feelings of guilt, whereas he constantly refers to his dependence upon other people's opinions. As Le Gentil (p. 123) so aptly expresses his condition, he is "a prisoner of the admiration of which he is the object." [32] Instead of an excusable weakness, as the Stoic philosophers had maintained, solicitude for other people's opinions was a laudable virtue for twelfth-century knights, a virtue more admirable than fear of hell and damnation. [33]

As previously noted, Turold repeatedly states that Roland fears public censure more than death. In assigning Roland to lead the rear guard, Charlemagne gives him a staff as symbol of command, and Roland boasts that people will never reprove him for letting it drop, as Ganelon had previously done. When Charlemagne offers his army for the mission, Roland declines lest he bring reproach upon his family. He extols loyalty to one's leader, but then he reveals that such virtue is performed not for its own sake but to avoid being lampooned in scurrilous songs; and this

[32] "prisonnier de l'admiration dont il est l'objet" (Le Gentil, p. 123).
[33] When vassals had to choose between feudal loyalty and excommunication, they usually placed their worldly honor above their immortal soul. An excellent literary example of a choice between soul and honor can be seen in Rüdiger's dilemma in the *Lay of the Nibelungs.*

same fear later impels him to fight to the finish. He refuses to summon aid because he desires to protect his reputation in France, to save his kinsmen from reproach, and to keep people from *saying* that he did so through fear of the pagans. In every case in which Roland's motivation is clarified, his deeds are sanctioned by fear of shame and blame.

Roland has previously expressed the hope that France will not be disgraced through him because he would rather die than be reproached, and he echoes this sentiment in *Laisse CXL* in saying that he will die of *doel* if nothing else kills him first. This *doel* is chiefly the chagrin he feels upon realizing that he will lose the fame he has struggled so long to win. This explanation will seem blasphemous to those critics who see Roland as a penitent sinner, but it will accord with Ruth Benedict's observation (p. 222) that "in a culture where shame is a major sanction, people are chagrined about acts which we expect people to feel guilty about." As we have seen, shame was Roland's chief, and almost sole, sanction. It is to escape such chagrin that Roland wishes to resume the battle and strike the enemy: death in battle will not save him from the ignominy of defeat, but at least it will save him from a life of shame. Renoir himself comments on the bitter humiliation Roland endures at being unable to defend his men,[34] yet he seems to attribute his distress to sense of guilt rather than to loss of honor.

When Roland's *doel* is understood as chagrin, not only does all inconsistency disappear in plot and character, but Roland's tragedy becomes even more intense. For the Christian, a tragedy

---

[34] "Thus, in acknowledging his obvious inability to do anything for the sake of his men, Roland is in effect acknowledging his utter failure as Charlemagne's most trusted captain. From one point of view, his turning them over to God's care, as he does in the last line of the section, is similar to a compulsory and humiliating relinquishing of his command. As for the extent of that humiliation, it may be gathered by contrasting Roland's position to that of his dead warriors: unlike their commander, their very death dramatically proclaims that *they* have kept their part of the feudal contract" (p. 574).

based on guilt and sin is always mitigated by the possibility of forgiveness. As Cardinal Newman states (p. 249), a sinful man can free himself of sin by one act of contrition; and this fact probably explains why there has never been a great Christian tragedy, even though hagiographies offer an abundance of potentially tragic situations. On the other hand, there is no surcease of the chagrin caused by loss of honor; for, as Cardinal Newman continues, it is impossible to restore the honor of a man once it has been sullied. Ruth Benedict continues her previous statement with the conclusion that "chagrin can be very intense and it cannot be relieved, as guilt can be, by confession and atonement."

Renoir denies that Roland "sinks into vulgar despair" (p. 575); yet, vulgar or not, despair is just what Roland experiences at realizing that he will lose his honor because of his defeat and his inability to protect his men. Naimes, Charlemagne's wisest counselor, knows that Roland is despairing as soon as he hears his horn.[35] To comprehend Roland's despondency, we should recall the mental anguish of Japanese prisoners of war in World War II, for whom defeat meant dishonor, and for whom dishonor meant severance of all social ties and consequent collapse of personal integrity. Stoic philosophers, Christian martyrs, and modern "inner-directed" men have inner resources which enable them to disregard social reprobation, provided their conscience is clear and their inner honor is still intact; but "other-directed" men lose the very source of their moral fiber when they lose the approbation of their peers. As we have seen, the major motivating force of all Roland's actions is his desire to win fame and avoid shame. Like Norfolk in Shakespeare's *Richard II*, his honor is his life, both grow in one. Take honor from him, and his life is done.

But how can we deny an obsession with sin and repentance in

[35] Asez oez que Rollant se dementet! (v. 1795). Roland's despair can be gaged by comparing his dejected speech in *Laisse* 128 with the *paroles haltes* (1097) which he uttered while fortune still smiled his way.

this scene so redolent of Christian martyrdom? How can we be-little the importance of humility and forgiveness when Roland's soul is taken up to heaven? This is easy, if we only remember how superficial Christianity was in northwestern Europe in the twelfth century. A solution to this apparent enigma may be furnished by a theory of André Burger, who suggests that Turold based his battle of Roncevaux on a *passio Rotolandi*.[36] Even if Burger is not entirely convincing in his efforts to reconstruct the hexam-eters of the original Latin poem, it is tempting to think that Turold faintly recollected some holy legend, of which he bor-rowed the trappings, even if not the ethos.

All literary matter was grist for Turold's mill, be it holy or profane. Being the inspired genius that he was, he stamped his personality on his work and was in no way hampered by the moral intent of his sources. This can be seen in the previously men-tioned scene in which Charlemagne reaches Roncevaux and seeks the bodies of his friends. "Where are you, fair Nephew?", he cries, "Where is the archbishop? Where is Count Oliver? . . ." Here Turold is no doubt influenced by the rhetorical tradition of *ubi sunt,* which was conventionally used to argue the meaningless-ness of worldly endeavor. But Turold has not composed a *memento mori.* He is not implying that the heroes died in vain. Quite to the contrary, their emperor's grief is the highest honor they could achieve, an honor well worth living and dying for, an honor that will live as long as the *Chanson de Roland* is sung or read. Turold has used a clerical theme, but he has imbued it with a heroic ethos. In letting Marsilie turn to the wall to die, Turold is prob-ably making use of some faint subconscious recollection about King Hezekiah, who did likewise.[37] But the Hebrew king turned

[36] "La légende de Roncevaux avant la *Chanson de Roland,*" *Romania,* 70, 1948–49, pp. 433–73.

[37] vers sa pareit se turnet (3644); Qui convertit faciem suam ad parietem et oravit Dominum dicens . . . (*Liber IV Regum* 20, 2; King James *II Kings* 20, 2). It is debatable whether turning to the wall to die is a *topos* or an *einfache Form.* In either case, the custom still appears, for example in Albert Camus' *La Peste* (Librairie Gallimard, 1947, p. 237) when tears

to the wall to pray to God, whereas the maimed and defeated king of Saragossa turned to the wall to hide his shame and sorrow. Here again the form is old, but the moral content is new.

Roland's courage, pride, and loyalty to friend and liege were qualities just as dear to the pagan Franks and Northmen as to their Christian descendants. Nowhere does he concern himself with Christian dogma or Christian ethics until a few minutes before his death, and only after it is too late to count on self-help. Even then he does not ask divine aid for his safety but only for his salvation. Unlike Charlemagne's, his campaign is in no way a holy war; and he appeals to his men's greed for glory and wealth but not to their religious duty. There is no evidence that he looks upon his men's massacre as a martyrdom. It is ironic that he first uses the word martyrdom to describe the death of the pagans; and, when he finally uses the word in connection with his own men, he is concerned with their immortal fame rather than with their eternal salvation, since he calls shame upon any who do not sell their lives dearly so that they will not bring disgrace upon France.

Roland's pride and death suggest the proverb that "pride goeth before destruction, and an haughty spirit before a fall." [38] But, even though Roland has "an haughty spirit" even *after* his fall, this does not prevent him from rising again, at least it does not keep his soul from rising to heaven. Disapproval of pride is not a peculiarly Christian attitude. Roland's plight suggests the words of the Greek poet Theognis, who said to Kyrnos a half millennium before Christ: "Pride (*hybris*) is the first evil which a god sends to a man whom he wishes to destroy." [39]

---

prevent Rieux from seeing Tarrou "se tourner brusquement contre le mur, et expirer . . .". A few pages earlier Grand had likewise turned to the wall, apparently to die, but had recovered ("Celui-ci avait le dos tourné et sa face touchait presque au mur," p. 217).

[38] Contritionem praecedit superbia, et ante ruinam exaltatur spiritus (*Proverbs* 16, 18).

[39] Théognis, *Poèmes Élégiaques*, ed. J. Carrière, Paris, 1948, I, 151–152.

Believing Roland to be truly Christian, Renoir states that Turold "specifically tells us that Roland recalls Charlemagne so that the dead French may receive Christian burial" (p. 578). He does not document this statement, perhaps because he could not find a single verse with which to do so. To the contrary, Roland clearly states that he is calling Charlemagne to avenge his fallen men,[40] and he never mentions Christian burial in connection with blowing his horn. Even Archbishop Turpin stresses vengeance and only casually mentions burial.[41] When Roland gathers the bodies of his peers, he is following Germanic rather than Christian tradition. Christ might even have let the dead bury their dead: it was Germanic custom that required a leader to recover the bodies of his men or else suffer shame.[42] Charlemagne's efforts to preserve his men's mortal remains is primarily pagan in origin.

Having freed ourselves from all a priori assumptions, let us judge Roland's humiliation as Turold actually depicts it. To appreciate his humiliation, we must first comprehend the magnitude of the pride that preceded it. We first hear Roland boast of his past victories (196–213), and we next see him volunteer for the mission to Saragossa, only to be disqualified by Oliver because of his violent temper (256). When Ganelon threatens him for having nominated him for the mission, Roland laughs and says that every-

[40] Li emperere nos devreit ben venger (v. 1149); Mult grant venjance en prendrat l'emperere (v. 1459). Renoir also makes the categorical statement that "there is not the least suggestion in the poem . . . of an invasion of France" (p. 574), although there are at least two. Esturganz and Estramariz promise to deliver France to Marsilie (Tere Majur vos metrum en present, v. 952), and Margariz promises him that the Saracens will sleep in the city of Saint Denis (Gesir porrum el burc de seint Denise, v. 973).

[41] Venget li reis, si nus purrat venger (1744); Carles repairet, ki ben nus vengerat (2145). When he tells how Charlemagne will take their bodies to the minsters, he thinks it is to protect them from swine, wolves, and dogs (Enfuerunt nos en aitres de musters; n'en mangerunt ne lu ne porc ne chen, vv. 1750–51).

[42] Tacitus remarked that the Germanic warriors recovered the bodies of their dead even in dubious battle (corpora suorum etiam in dubiis proeliis referunt, Germania, #6).

one knows that he is not afraid of threats (293). Arriving in Saragossa, Ganelon tells Marsilie how Roland has promised to deliver all kingdoms to Charlemagne, and he predicts that Roland's pride will bring him to shame (389). He also warns the Saracen king that Roland will be a haughty partner when Charlemagne divides Spain between them (474); and he declares that Charlemagne will be safe only as long as Roland lives (557). When Ganelon nominates Roland for the rear guard, Roland thanks him for the opportunity and boasts that he will not let Charlemagne lose a single beast of burden (756); and he further boasts that he will not drop the staff that Charlemagne gives him (763).

Roland's reputation, i.e., his image in other people's eyes, is enhanced when each of the twelve Saracen leaders promises to defeat him; and Roland reveals his overweening self-assurance by swearing that all the pagans will die.[43] As long as the battle goes well for the Franks, Roland remains in high spirits; but his spirit begins to falter when he sees the battle turning out badly. As he has often attested, he is not afraid of dying, but only of being dishonored by defeat, especially after he has staked his honor upon victory. At last he decides that help from Charlemagne will be less shameful than defeat, but then Oliver spitefully reverses himself and deters him from summoning help by repeating all the arguments Roland previously used when Oliver urged him to do so.[44] Reminded of the shame he and his kinsmen will suffer, Roland refrains from blowing until Turpin convinces him that he can do so without jeopardizing his good name.[45] Once it is too late for help, it is no longer shameful to blow the horn. On the other hand, by blowing his horn Roland assures himself that Charlemagne will avenge his death and thus partially diminish the disgrace of defeat, or at least deprive the victors of the pleas-

[43] vv. 1058, 1069, 1081.
[44] vv. 1705–10, 1715–21.
[45] vv. 1742–51.

ure of their victory. It will also guarantee honorable burial for the dead.

After his famous lament for his men, Roland fights with a courage born of desperation; and Turold frankly says that he and his sixty remaining followers defend themselves like men who expect no quarter.[46] Seeing Marsilie kill several of his men, Roland curses him and boasts that he will pay for his deed and will learn the name of Roland's sword; and he fulfills his threat by cutting off Marsilie's right hand and killing his son. Thereupon most of the surviving pagans flee with their injured king, but Marsilie's uncle Marganice attacks with vastly superior numbers and gives Oliver a fatal blow from behind. Blinded by blood, Oliver strikes Roland by mistake; yet, although he is unhurt and despite their long friendship, punctilious Roland does not forgive him until he is sure that Oliver did not strike him on purpose.[47] By asking Oliver if he has struck him on purpose, Roland clearly shows that he is still more concerned about his personal reputation than about his guilt at having caused the debacle and the death of his friends.

After Oliver's death, Roland, Gualter, and Turpin fight so fiercely that the Saracens stand back and throw their spears from a distance, thereby killing Gualter and mortally wounding Turpin. Roland continues to fight until the pagans realize that, because of his great ferocity, he can never be defeated by any mortal man; and thereupon they flee and leave him in control of the field.[48] Thus Roland is able to vindicate his honor by conquering, as he swore he would, and by recovering the bodies of his fallen comrades. No doubt Roland deeply mourns his dead friends, as

---

[46] Home ki ço set que ja n'avrat prisun en tel bataill fait grant defension: pur ço sunt Francs si fiers cume leuns (1886–1888).

[47] Sire cumpain, faites le vos de gred? Ja est ço Rollant, ki tant vos soelt amer! Par nule guise ne m'aviez desfiet! (vv. 2000–2).

[48] Li quens Rollant est de tant fiertet ja n'ert vencut pur nul hume carnel. Lançuns a lui, puis sil laissums ester (vv. 2152–53).

he attests in his laments,[49] yet this neither lessens his concern for his own posthumous fame nor suggests any remorse. As we have seen, Roland tries to destroy his sword to avoid reproach, he tells his sword of his great victories, and he advances toward the enemy to prove he died victorious. As long as his comrades live, he can play to a living audience, but after they are dead and he has no witnesses to report his exploits, he must carefully set his stage so that Charlemagne will know how well and successfully he has fought. Carrying his horn and sword as proof of his victory, he seeks out a hill on which stand four large blocks of marble, as if these were a fitting monument to commemorate his heroic death.

Turold makes it amply clear that Roland has vindicated himself and has repaired his injured honor. Upon returning to Roncevaux after pursuing and destroying Roland's enemies, Charlemagne knows right where to find his body, since he remembers Roland's boast that he would lie in front of his men; and thus Roland succeeds in proclaiming to posterity that he has died as a conqueror. The whole tragedy of Roland's death can be explained in heroic terms, without reference to Christianity and without any loss of tragic intensity. An overconfident leader risks defeat and jeopardizes his followers in a foolhardy attempt to enhance his worldly fame. Realizing that his temerity has cost him his honor, he is overwhelmed by chagrin at the thought of disgrace. But, despite despair, he challenges fate and fights against superhuman odds with a strength born of desperation, until he finally vindicates his good name. Like Byrhtnoth at Maldon and like the Burgundians at Etzel's court, Roland struggles manfully against fate and relies entirely on his own efforts rather than call on human or divine aid. And, unlike Byrhtnoth and the Burgundians, he succeeds in his task even though he dies in the effort.

Nor does Roland have any more need of penitence, in its sense

---

[49] Especially in *laisses* 163–167.

of contrition, than the rest of his men. His soul is taken to heaven largely because he excels in *penitence,* in Turpin's sense of the word, in which it means penance done by killing pagans. Let us try to imagine Roland's reaction if Turpin had set him some less glorious penance. Let us suppose that, to cleanse him of his sin of pride, Turpin had demanded some voluntary humiliation, such as playing the coward before his men. What would Roland have done if his penance had been to drop his sword and shield and flee to the rear, with every expectation of being chained and loaded on a pack horse for transport to Aachen and some undignified punishment? Surely his Christian faith was not strong enough to accept a penance in conflict with his martial ethos. It is a poor proof of Christianity to do in God's name what you would gladly do without ever having heard of God.

Like Germanic heroes taken to Valhalla and like Mohammedan warriors taken to paradise, the Franks achieve salvation more on their own merits and through good works than through faith. There is little evidence that Turpin's, or Turold's, idea of martyrdom differed materially from the Mohammedan's belief in Shahid. David Wright (p. 16) has written that "the consolation of Beowulf is not a Christian consolation but an heroic one . . ." This is also true to a large extent of Roland, who is consoled by knowing that Charlemagne and his men will say that he has won the field and recovered the bodies of his companions and that he has advanced further than any of his men and has died as a conqueror. Roland frequently expresses deep longing for a spotless reputation, but he never expresses any deep longing for eternal life. Such a preference was by no means rare in medieval heroic literature.

Renoir's three-fold division of *Laisse CXL* is based on his interpretation of Roland's moral motivation. He states: "In the first section, Roland perceives the extent of the tragedy before him; in the second, he realizes his own responsibility and his utter helplessness; in the third, he turns to desperate action" (p. 573). This three-fold division is entirely arbitrary: the *laisse* could just as well be divided into two, four, five, or even six sections. The most obvious division is between the narrative introduction (1–3) and the soliloquy (4–18). The soliloquy, in turn, can be further subdivided into three addresses to the dead barons (4–6, 7–9, 10–12, the last of which includes an aside to France), one to the dead and dying barons (13–15),[50] and one to Oliver and, perhaps, to the surviving barons as well (16–18).[51] Thus we have:

Narrative Introduction

1. Rollant regardet es munz e es lariz;
2. De cels de France i veit tanz morz gesir,
3. E il les pluret cum chevaler gentill:

Seeing the dead, Roland weeps and then declaims:

Address to the dead barons

4. "Seignors barons, de vos ait Deus mercit!
5. Tutes vos anmes otreit il pareïs!
6. En saintes flurs il les facet gesir!

"May God have mercy on your souls!

7. Meillors vassals de vos unkes ne vi;
8. Si lungement tuz tens m'avez servit,
9. A oes Carlon si granz païs cunquis!

You have served me and Charlemagne well.

10. Li empereres tant mare vos nurrit!
11. Tere de France, mult estes dulz païs,
12. Oi desertet a tant robustl exill.

What a pity that you were in Charlemagne's service, for now France is bereft of you.

---

[50] Until reading Owen (pp. 395–96), I had assumed that vv. 1863–65 were addressed to the surviving barons and that Roland was relinquishing command of the rear guard, as maintained by Renoir (p. 575). Despite the present tense of *vei* in v. 1863, I now agree with Owen that Roland is commending only the dead barons to God and trusts himself to defend those still living.

[51] Roland's exhortation in vv. 1866–68 should logically include the sixty surviving barons, who are still an organized force. In addressing Oliver, his second-in-command, he is addressing the remnant of the rear guard also. Although the vocatives are singular, the pronoun *vos* can be both singular and plural at the same time: "Oliver, my brother, I shall not fail you (and the rest of our men) . . . Sir companion, let us all strike the enemy."

Address to the dead and dying barons

13. Barons franceis, pur mei vos vei murir:	Although I see you dying for
14. Je ne vos pois tenser ne guarantir;	me, I cannot protect you, so
15. Aït vos Deus, ki unkes ne mentit!	may God help you.

Address to Oliver (and the surviving barons?)

16. Oliver, frere, vos ne dei jo faillir.	I will not fail you. I shall die
17. De doel murra, s'altre ne m'i ocit.	of chagrin if nothing else kills
18. Sire cumpainz, alum i referir!"	me first, so let us strike the
	enemy."

This method divides the *laisse* into an introduction, a benediction, a eulogy, a lament, an apology-benediction, and an exhortation; and it will be noted that each of these comprises precisely three verses, which combine to express a single thought or two closely related thoughts. Such a division into triads is more in keeping with Turold's usual tripartite constructions than are the irregular divisions suggested by Renoir in order to feature Roland's remorse.[52] But, whether we dissect Turold's *laisse* into three or into six parts, the division serves only to satisfy our own curiosity; for Turold intended it to be what it is, a single and indivisible unit, a unit as well integrated in thought and feeling as it is in assonance.

[52] See Woods, pp. 1247–62.

CONCLUSION

In conclusion we see that the SR portrays the inward thoughts of twelfth-century France, at least of the ruling classes of twelfth-century France, and that its ethos was acceptable to the ruling classes of the neighboring Christian countries as well. Regardless of any earlier literary tradition, the SR preserved in the Oxford manuscript depicts the moral physiognomy of the age in which it was composed, rather than that of the historical period it treats. A comparison of the SR with several early translations helps clarify some of its obscurities by showing how they were understood by men living soon after its composition.

In studying the value-words used by Turold (the name most justifiably ascribed to the poet), one must remember that their meanings often differed sharply, sometimes even diametrically, from those of their modern French derivatives and were usually closer to those of their Latin or Old High German sources. In order to remain uninfluenced by later semantic developments, this study has endeavored to deduce the meanings of the Old French terms directly from their context and then to test the meanings so deduced by relating them to their sources and to the general culture of their time. The most important terms for a study of an ethos are those which deal with right and wrong, good and bad, and honor and shame. Turold's treatment of these concepts shows that the society he depicts is a "shame culture", notwithstanding a strong admixture, or superimposition, of Christian "guilt culture". Good is what society admires, bad is what it censures. A

191

purpose of the SR was to inspire courage and loyalty by showing that they win honor and to deter cowardice and perfidy by showing that they incur shame. In addition, courage and loyalty in the Lord's service earn eternal life in heaven.

Although its style and means of expression were strongly influenced by classical Latin literature and Christian liturgy, the SR presents and preaches an ethos basically similar to that of the heathen Germanic tribesmen. This similarity can be explained by the social predominance of the Frankish invaders and their descendants, who furnished most of the medieval aristocracy and set a social pattern scarcely affected by their acceptance of the outward forms of Christianity. The Franks' warlike ethos was later reinforced by struggle against the Scandinavian invaders and still later by assimilation with the Northmen who settled in Normandy. Friction with Mohammedans in Spain may have helped strengthen their warlike attitudes, which were theologically justified by passages in the Old Testament.

Despite much reference to Christianity, the SR shows little understanding of Christian charity and forgiveness; and good works, mostly in the form of military service and pious endowments, are bartered in return for salvation. The Christian faith can demand great physical sacrifice from its adherents, provided it does not try to modify their traditional values, which remain martial and heroic. It can ask them to risk their lives, but not their honor; and therefore it cannot demand love in place of hate or forgiveness in place of vengeance. A man of honor must avenge all injuries to himself, his reputation, his friends, his kinsmen, and especially his sister's son. Despite many confessions, the warriors of the SR show little understanding of sin or guilt. They never question the existence of pagan deities, but merely believe their own God more powerful and more helpful. For them, love seldom means Christian charity. Sometimes it means personal affection, but at other times it merely means truce or alliance.

The chief well-spring of morality lies less in the tenets or teachings of Christ than in solicitude for public opinion, in concern for the admiration of men living and still unborn. Hope of salvation is also a strong incentive, but this incentive is usually subordinated to considerations of public repute. Religious duty is primarily a loyalty to the Church as a political entity and to Christendom as the broadest expression of the in-group, as the totality of all men fighting against a common enemy. Such a loyalty would be inculcated less by Christian ethics than by outward forms and ceremonies, splendor of buildings, elegance of costumes, wealth of church treasures, power of relics, and emotional appeal of music, to say nothing of the belief that the hierarchy held the keys to heaven.

However great their loyalty to Christendom, that is to say, to Charlemagne's universal empire, the Franks in the SR are more devoted to France proper; and it is safe to assume that their patriotism derived from Latin literature and from the Gallo-Roman occupants of Gaul.

The ethos of the SR is consistent throughout and does not indicate that any one episode was written by a different poet. However, because the Baligant episode changes the battle of Roncevaux into an apocalyptic struggle between Cross and Crescent, it could have been a later and tendentious addition, perhaps by the same author.

Even more conspicuous than the lack of Christian ethics in the SR is its lack of Stoic values, with which all Western codes of honor and decency are now imbued. The song shows little appreciation of tolerance, modesty, self-control, introspection, virtue for its own sake, or independence of other people's opinions. Oliver preaches moderation, but foolhardy Roland is the hero of the song. There is little comprehension of fair play, sportsmanship, defeat with honor, or chivalry toward the underdog, even though public fancy has subsequently ascribed these virtues to an ill-defined "age of chivalry".

This study does not mean to pass judgment on the heroes of the

SR—rather it argues that they must be judged by a set of standards markedly unlike those we profess today. To understand their actions and motives, and thereby to appreciate the great literary value of the song, we must free ourselves of all the ideas and values so slowly and painfully acquired by our more recent ancestors. By refusing to attribute our highest ideals and aspirations to the warriors of the *SR*, this study may offend certain critics who consider the song typically and essentially French. But to attribute modern French ideals to the rowdy Frankish barons of the twelfth century is to disparage the contributions of later men like Montaigne, Pascal, and Voltaire, who made French civilization what it later became. It is to be noted that, quite unintentionally, this study always referred to the warriors of the *SR* as Franks and never as Frenchmen.

Even if the noble Christian knights of the *SR* would rate as brutal and bigoted barbarians if judged by modern standards, this in no way diminishes the literary excellence of the song. A work of art should be judged by its aesthetic rather than by its moral standards. Although built for human sacrifice, an Aztec temple may be aesthetically more pleasing than many Christian churches; and a poem by Baudelaire may be more enjoyable than one by Edgar Guest. By remembering that the basic values of the *SR* were more heroic than Christian, a reader will avoid being misled by the Christian and Stoic values subsequently acquired by so many of its terms. If we read Turold's words with the meanings he intended, we find the action of his epic well-motivated and his characters well-drawn. Even Ganelon acts logically, given the values and standards of his day. Being surpassed, slighted, and ridiculed by his stepson, he has lost his honor and impugned that of his kindred and has nothing more to lose but his life.

Goethe once wrote of a little boy who caught a dragon-fly and dissected it to see why it was so pretty. But, once dismembered, it was no longer pretty. Fortunately, the *SR* is not like a dragon-fly. It is more like a skilfully fitted time-piece. By observing the precision-made watch being disassembled, we can enhance the pleasure we get in seeing it after it is reassembled. And this has been the case during the research for this study. An analysis of the *SR* and a scrutiny of its parts has revealed Turold's masterful workmanship and literary genius, and a score of readings have uncovered beauties formerly missed. Charles A. Knudson advocates that all studies of the *Roland* "should lead us toward the poem and not away from it," and it is hoped that this study has led in the right direction.

Works Abbreviated in Text and Notes

ADOLF, HELEN: *Visio Pacis, Holy City and Grail,* Pennsylvania State University Press, 1960.

AEBISCHER, PAUL: "Défense et illustration de l'épisode de Baligant", *Mélanges . . . Ernest Hoepffner,* Paris, 1949, pp. 173–82.

————: *Rolandiana Borealis,* Lausanne, 1954.

Aeneid: Virgil, ed. H. R. FAIRCLOUGH, Cambridge, 1956, *Loeb.*

Aiol, ed. J. NORMAND & G. RAYNAUD, Paris, 1877.

Aliscans, ed. E. WIENBECK, W. HARTNACKE, R. RASCH, Halle, 1903.

Alpharts Tod, in *Deutsches Heldenbuch,* II, ed. ERNST MARTIN, Berlin, 1866.

Armer Heinrich: Der Arme Heinrich von Hartmann von Aue, ed. H. PAUL, Tübingen, 1953.

BATTAGLIA, SALVATORE: "Il 'compagnonaggio' di Orlando e Olivieri", *Filologia Romanza,* 5, 1958, pp. 113–42.

Battle of Maldon, ed. E. V. GORDON, London, 1937.

BECKER, PHILIP A.: "Streifzüge durch die altfranzösische Heldendichtung", *Zeitschrift für französische Sprache und Literatur,* 6, 1938, pp. 1–22, 129–56.

BÉDIER: *La Chanson de Roland,* publiée d'après le manuscrit d'Oxford et traduite par Joseph Bédier, Paris, 1922.

————, *Commentaires: La Chanson de Roland,* commentée par Joseph Bédier, Paris, 1927.

————, *Légendes:* Joseph Bédier, *Les légendes épiques,* Paris, 1908–1913.

BENEDICT, RUTH: *Patterns of Culture, Mentor Books,* New York, 1936.

————, *The Chrysanthemum and the Sword,* Cambridge, 1946.

BERTONI, GIULIO: *La Chanson de Roland,* Firenze, 1935.

BESZARD, L.: "Les larmes dans l'épopée, particulièrement dans l'épopée française jusqu'à la fin du XIIe siècle", *Zeitschrift für romanische Philologie,* 27, 1903, pp. 385–413, 513–49, 641–74.

BOISSONNADE, PROSPER: *Du nouveau sur la Chanson de Roland,* Paris, 1923.

BRAUNE, WILHELM: *Althochdeutsches Lesebuch,* Halle, 1949.

Brennu-Njálssaga, ed. F. JÓNSSON, Halle, 1908.

BRÜCH, JOSEF: *Der Einfluss der germanischen Sprachen auf das Vulgärlatein,* Heidelberg, 1913.

Brut: Le Roman de Brut, ed. IVOR ARNOLD, Paris, 1938.

BURGER, ANDRÉ: "La légende de Roncevaux avant la Chanson de Roland", *Romania,* 70, 1948–1949, pp. 433–73. For unfavorable review by Jean Rychner, see *Romania,* 72, 1951, pp. 239–46.

Carmen de Bello Saxonico Lamberts von Hersfeld, ed. A. PANNENBORG, Göttingen, 1892.

Carmen de prodicione Guenonis, ed. GASTON PARIS, *Romania,* IX, 1882, pp. 465–518.

CHADWICK, NORA K.: *Poetry and Letters in Early Christian Gaul,* London, 1955.

La Chançun de Willame, ed. E. S. TYLER, New York, 1919.

Les chansons de croisade, ed. J. BÉDIER, Paris, 1909.

CHIRI, GIUSEPPE: *L'Epica latina medioevale e la Chanson de Roland,* Genova, 1936.

CLARKE, M. L.: *The Roman Mind,* Cambridge, Mass., 1956.

Cligés: Les Romans de Chrétien de Troyes, ed. A. MICHA, Paris, 1957.

Le Couronnement de Louis, ed. E. LANGLOIS, Paris, 1888.

CROSLAND, JESSIE: *The Old French Epic,* Oxford, 1951.

CURTIUS: Ernst Robert Curtius, "Über die altfranzösische Epik", *Zeitschrift für romanische Philologie,* 64, 1944, pp. 232–320.

————, *Carmen:* Ernst Robert Curtius, "Das Carmen de prodicione Guenonis", *Zeitschrift für französische Philologie,* 62, 1942, pp. 492–509.

————, *Eur. Lit.:* Ernst Robert Curtius, *Europäische Literatur und lateinisches Mittelalter,* Bern, 1954.

De Ira, in *Seneca Moral Essays,* ed. JOHN BASORE, New York, 1928, *Loeb.*

DELBOUILLE, MAURICE: *Sur la genèse de la Chanson de Roland,* Brussels, 1954.

DESSAU, ADALBERT: "L'idée de la trahison", in *Cahiers de la civilisation médiévale,* 3, 1960, pp. 23–26.

Deutsche Rechtsaltertümer von Jacob Grimm, ed. A. HEUSLER, 1899, reprint Darmstadt, 1955.

Dictionnaire d'ancien Français, ed. R. GRANDSAIGNES D'HAUTERIVE, Paris, Larousse, 1947.

DILL, SAMUEL: *Roman Society in Gaul in the Merovingian Age,* London, 1926.

Die Disciplina Clericalis des Petrus Alfonsi, ed. A. HILKA, Heidelberg, 1911.

DOUGHERTY, DAVID: "The Present Status of Bédier's Theories", *Symposium,* 14, 1960, pp. 289–99.

EINARSSON, STEFÁN: *A History of Icelandic Literature,* New York, 1957.

Eneas, ed. J. J. SALVERDA DE GRAVE, Paris, 1929.

ERDMANN, CARL: *Die Entstehung des Kreuzzugsgedanken,* Stuttgart, 1935.

Exempla aus Handschriften des Mittelalters, ed. J. KLAPPER, Heidelberg, 1911.

FARAL, EDMOND: *La Chanson de Roland,* Paris, 1934.

FARNSWORTH, W. O.: *Uncle and Nephew in the Old French Chansons de Geste,* New York, 1913.

FAWTIER, ROBERT: *La Chanson de Roland,* Paris, 1933.

Fierabras, ed. A. KROEBER and G. SERVOIS, Paris, 1860.

FISON, LORIMER: *Tales of Old Fiji,* London, 1907.

FREYTAG, GUSTAV: *Bilder aus der deutschen Vergangenheit,* Leipzig, 1876.

FUCHS, A.: "Du climat moral dans la Chanson de Roland", *Mélanges . . . Ernest Hoepffner,* Paris, 1949, pp. 191–93.

The Gallic War, ed. H. J. EDWARDS, *Loeb,* London, 1917.

GANSHOF, F. L.: *Was ist das Lehnswesen,* Darmstadt, 1961.

GEDDES, J.: *La Chanson de Roland,* New York, 1906.

GENUSS, HELMUT: *Lehnbildungen und Lehnbedeutungen im Altenglischen,* Berlin, 1955.

Germanentum: Andreas Heusler, *Germanentum,* Heidelberg, n.d.

Germania: Cornelii Taciti de Origine et Situ Germanorum, ed. J. G. C. ANDERSON, Oxford, 1938.

Germanische Altertumskunde, ed. HERMANN SCHNEIDER, München, 1951.

Gesta Danorum: Saxonis Grammatici Gesta Danorum, ed. A. HOLDER, Strassburg, 1886.

Gesta Romanorum, ed. W. DICK, Erlangen, 1890.

Girart de Viënne, ed. F. YEANDLE, New York, 1930.

GORDON, E. V.: *The Battle of Maldon,* London, 1937.

Gospel Harmony: Otfrids Evangelienbuch, ed. O. ERDMANN, Halle, 1934.

GOUGENHEIM, G.: "De 'chevalier' à 'cavalier'," *Mélanges . . . Ernest Hoepffner,* Paris, 1949, pp. 117–26.

GREENE, THOMAS: "The Norms of the Epic", *Comparative Literature,* 13, 1961, pp. 193–207.

Gregorius von Hartmann von Aue, ed. H. PAUL, Tübingen, 1953.

GRÖNBECH, WILHELM: *Kultur und Religion der Germanen*, Darmstadt, 1954.

GUMMERE, F. B.: "The Sister's Son", in *An English Miscellany Presented to Dr. Furnivall*, Oxford, 1901, pp. 132–49.

HALL, ROBERT A., JR.: "Ganelon and Roland", *Modern Language Quarterly*, 6, 1945, pp. 263–70.

————: "Linguistic Strata in the Chanson de Roland", *Romance Philology*, 8, 1959, pp. 156–61.

————: "On Individual Authorship in the Roland", *Symposium*, 1960, pp. 297–302.

HEISIG, KARL: "Die Geschichtsmetaphysik des Rolandsliedes und ihre Vorgeschichte", *Zeitschrift für französische Philologie*, 55, 1935, pp. 1–87.

Heliand und Genesis, ed. O. BEHAGEL, Halle, 1948.

Historiarum libri decem, ed. R. BUCHNER, Darmstadt, 1959.

HOLLYMAN, K. J.: *Le développement du vocabulaire féodal en France pendant le haut moyen âge*, Paris, 1957.

HOLMES, URBAN T.: "The post-Bédier Theories on the Origins of the Chansons de Geste", *Speculum*, 30, 1955, pp. 72–81.

HOPPE, RUTH: *Die romanische Geste im Rolandslied*, Diss. Königsberg (Albertus Universität), 1937.

HORRENT, JULES: *La Chanson de Roland dans la littérature française et espagnole au moyen âge*, Paris, 1951.

Iwein: Hartmann von Aue Erec Iwein, ed. H. NAUMANN & H. STEINGER, Leipzig, 1933.

JACKSON, W. T. H.: *The Literature of the Middle Ages*, New York, 1960.

JENKINS, T. A.: *La Chanson de Roland*, Boston, 1924.

JOINVILLE, JEAN DE: *Histoire de Saint Louis*, ed. N. DE WAILLY, Paris, 1874.

JOLLES, ANDRÉ: *Einfache Formen*, Halle, 1930.

JONES, GEORGE F.: "The Ethos of the Waltharius", *Festschrift for John G. Kunstmann*, Chapel Hill, 1959, pp. 1–20.

————: "Grim to your Foes and Kind to your Friends", *Studia Neophilologica*, 34, 1962, pp. 91–103.

————: *Honor in German Literature*, Chapel Hill, 1959.

————: "Lov'd I not honour more", *Comparative Literature*, 9, 1959, pp. 131–45.

————: "Rüdiger's Dilemma", *Studies in Philology*, 57, 1960, pp. 7–21.

JUNKER, ALBERT: "Stand der Forschung zum Rolandslied", *Germanisch-romanische Monatsschrift*, Neue Folge, 6, 1956, pp. 97–144.

Karlamagnús saga, ed. BJARNI VILHJÁLMSSON, Vol. III, Reykjavik, 1950, pp. 771–851.

KETTNER, ROBERT P.: *Der Ehrbegriff in den altfranzösischen Artusromanen,* Diss. Leipzig, 1890.

KLOSE, FRIEDRICH: *Die Bedeutung von Honos und Honestus,* Diss. Breslau, 1933.

KNUDSON, CHARLES A.: "The Problem of the Chanson de Roland", *Romance Philology,* 4, 1950, pp. 1–15.

KS, see *Karlamagnús saga.*

LE GENTIL, P.: *La Chanson de Roland,* Paris, 1955 (*Connaissance des Lettres,* 43).

LEJEUNE, RITA: "Le péché de Charlemagne et la *Chanson de Roland*", in *Homenaje a Dámaso Alonso,* Madrid, 1961, pp. 339–70.

————: *Recherches sur le thème: Les chansons de geste et l'histoire,* Liége, 1948.

LIVINGSTON, ARTHUR: "The Carmen de Prodicione Guenonis", *Romanic Review,* 2, 1911, pp. 61–79.

LOMMATZSCH, E.: "Darstellung von Trauer und Schmerz in der altfranzösischen Literatur", *Zeitschrift für romanische Philologie,* 43, 1923, pp. 20–67.

Lusiads: Luis Vaz de Camõens, *The Lusiads,* trans. W. C. ATKINSON, *Penguin Books,* 1952.

MCNAMEE, MAURICE: *Honor and the Epic Hero,* New York, 1960.

MENENDEZ PIDAL, RAMÓN: *La Chanson de Roland y el neotradicionalismo,* Madrid, 1959.

MITTEIS, HEINRICH: *Der Staat des hohen Mittelalters,* Weimar, 1953.

MONTAIGNE: *Oeuvres complètes de Michel de Montaigne,* ed. A. ARMAINGAUD, Paris, 1925.

Das Moralium Dogma Philosophorum des Guillaume de Conches, ed. JOHN HOLMBERG, Uppsala, 1929.

MORTIER, RAOUL: *La Chanson de Roland,* Paris, 1940.

NEWMAN: John Henry, Cardinal Newman: *Certain Difficulties Felt by Anglicans,* London, 1897, Vol. I, Lecture VIII.

Das Nibelungenlied, ed. K. BARTSCH and H. DE BOOR, Leipzig, 1949.

NL, see *Nibelungenlied*

Nota emilianense: cited in Dámaso Alonso, *La primitiva épica francesca a la luz de una nota emilianense,* Madrid, 1954.

O'HAGAN, JOHN: *Song of Roland,* London, 1880.

Orderici Vitalis, Historiae ecclesiasticae libri XIII, ed. H. LE PRÉVOST, III, 1845.

OTTO MORENA: *Das Geschichtswerk des Otto Morena,* ed. F. GÜTERBOCK, Berlin, 1930.

OWEN, D.: "The Secular Inspiration of the *Chanson de Roland*", *Speculum*, 37, 1962, pp. 390–400.

PAINTER, SIDNEY: *French Chivalry*, Baltimore, 1940.

———: *William Marshal*, Baltimore, 1933.

Parzival: Wolfram von Eschenbach, ed. K. LACHMANN and E. HARTL, Berlin, 1952.

PAUPHILET, ALBERT: "Sur la Chanson de Roland", *Romania*, 59, 1933, pp. 161–98.

Perceval: Le Roman de Perceval, ed. WM. ROACH, Paris, 1956.

The Pseudo-Turpin, ed. H. M. SMYSER, Cambridge, 1937.

Raoul de Cambrai, ed. P. MEYER and A. LONGNON, Paris, 1882.

Renaus de Montalban, ed. H. MICHELANT, Stuttgart, 1862.

RENOIR, ALAIN: "Roland's Lament", *Speculum*, 35, 1960, pp. 572–83.

RL, see *Rolandslied*.

Roelantslied, see Van Mierlo.

Rolandslied: Das Alexanderlied des Pfaffen Lamprecht—Das Rolandslied des Pfaffen Konrad, ed. F. MAURER, Leipzig, 1940.

ROSENFELD, HANS-FRIEDRICH: "Humanistische Strömungen", in *Deutsche Wortgeschichte*, ed. F. MAURER and F. STROH, Berlin, 1959, I, pp. 329–438.

RUGGIERI, RUGGERO: *Il Processo di Gano nella Chanson de Roland*, Firenze, 1936.

Ruodlieb, ed. E. W. ZEYDEL, Chapel Hill, 1959.

RYDER, FRANK G.: *The Song of the Nibelungs*, Detroit, 1962.

Sachsenspiegel, ed. K. A. ECKHARDT, Göttingen, 1955.

SAYERS, DOROTHY: *La Chanson de Roland*, Baltimore, 1957.

SCHUTZ, A. H.: "Roland v. 337", *Modern Language Notes*, 62, 1947, pp. 456–61.

SETTEGAST, FRANZ: "Der Ehrbegriff in dem altfranzösischen Rolandslied", *Zeitschrift für romanische Philologie*, 9, 1885, pp. 204–22.

SICILIANO, ITALO: *Les origines des chansons de geste*, Paris, 1951.

SINCLAIR: *The Conquest of Peru*, trans. JOSEPH H. SINCLAIR, New York, 1929.

Song of Roland: The English Charlemagne Romances, II, ed. S. J. HERR-TAGE, London, 1880, pp. 107–36.

STEVENS, C. E.: *Sidonius Apollinaris and his Age*, London, 1933.

STOWELL, W. A.: *Old French Titles of Respect in Direct Address*, Baltimore, 1908.

———: "Personal Relationships in Medieval France", *PMLA*, 28, 1913, pp. 388–416.

STRICKER: *Karl der Grosse von dem Stricker*, ed. K. BARTSCH, Quedlinburg & Leipzig, 1857.

TAVERNIER, WILHELM: "Beiträge zur Rolandsforschung, IV" (*Wal-*

tharius, Carmen de prodicione Guenonis und *Rolandsepos*), *Zeitschrift für französische Sprache und Literatur*, 42, 1914, pp. 41–81.

TEISSIER, MAURICE: *La Chanson de Roland, traduite en français moderne*, Paris, 1944.

THÉOGNIS, *Poèmes Elégiaques*, ed. J. CARRIÈRE, Paris, 1948.

Thesaurus Linguae Latinae, Leipzig, 1910.

VAN MIERLO, J.: "Het Roelantsleid", *Kon. Vlaamsche Academie voor Taal- en Letterkunde, Verslagen en Mededeelingen*, 1935, pp. 31–166.

VENDRYÈS, J.: "Sur les plus anciens emprunts germaniques en Latin", *Études Germaniques*, 3, 1948, pp. 131–37.

Vita Karoli: Einhardi Vita Karoli Imperatoris, ed. A. HOLDER, Tübingen, 1882.

VOLLMER, VERA: *Die Begriffe von Triuwe und Staete in der höfischen Minnedichtung*, Diss. Tübingen, 1914.

VRIES, JAN DE: *Die geistige Welt der Germanen*, Halle, 1945.

WALPOLE, RONALD N.: "The *Nota Emilianense*", *Romance Philology*, X, 1956, pp. 1–18.

Waltharius, ed. KARL STRECKER, Berlin, 1947.

WALTHER: *Die Gedichte Walthers von der Vogelweide*, ed. CARL VON KRAUS, Berlin, 1950.

WAPNEWSKI, PETER: "Rüdigers Schild. Zur 37. Aventiure des Nibelungenliedes", *Euphorion*, 54, 1960, pp. 380–410.

WERNSINCK, A. J.: "The oriental doctrine of the martyrs", *Mededeelingen der Koninglijke Akademie van Wetenschappen, Afdeeling Letterkunde, Deel* 53, Serie A, Amsterdam, 1922.

WHITEHEAD, A. N.: *Science and the Modern World*, New York, 1947.

WHITEHEAD, F.: "*Ofermod et desmesure*", *Cahiers de civilisation médiévale*, III, 1960, pp. 115–17.

WILMOTTE, MAURICE: "*L'Épopée française*, Paris, 1939.

WOODS, W. S.: "The Symbolic Structure of the Chanson de Roland", *PMLA*, 65, 1950, 1247–62.

WRIGHT, DAVID: *Beowulf, Penguin Classics*, 1957.

VERSE INDEX

WORD AND NAME INDEX